Village in the Rhone Valley/Switzerland

The Little & Ives
ILLUSTRATED
Ready Reference
ENCYCLOPEDIA
FOR HOME AND SCHOOL USE

Volume Eighteen

•

EDITOR-IN-CHIEF

Franklin Dunham, Mus.D., Litt.D., L.H.D.
U.S. Office of Education, Washington, D.C.

•

J. J. LITTLE & IVES CO., INC.
NEW YORK
1962 Edition

EDITORIAL STAFF

Executive Editor
ROBERT W. MURPHEY

Editorial Director
GILMAN PARK, JR.

Copy Editor
GLEN A. HILKEN

Volume Editors
PETER GLASSGOLD   BARBARA HACKNEY   MARY McGRAW

Editorial Assistants
NANCY FAYE DAVENPORT   JUDY SLESINGER   NANCY TYSON PARK
MICHEL WEINER   JAMES HANEY   BETSY STEVENS   MARK DOYLE
BETSY THORNTON   KRISTEN OCHERHAUSER   GEORGE MILLARD

Production Supervisor
ARNOLD SYLVESTER

Art Director
FRANK MACERO, JR.

Assistant Art Director
CONSTANCE SALAMONE

Designers
STUART MILLER   GIL DE PAOLIS

Production Assistants
CARL MACERO   HENRY SALA   RUDY S. MARCELLO

DESIGNED & PRODUCED BY COLOR OFFSET CO., INC., BROOKLYN, N. Y.

Type set by Harry Sweetman Typesetting Corp.

© Copyright 1962 by J. J. Little & Ives Co., Inc., New York

No part of the text or illustrations in this work may be used without formal permission from J. J. Little & Ives Co., Inc. *All rights reserved* under Pan-American Copyright Convention and the International Copyright Convention

Printed in the United States of America

Switzerland, federated republic of central Europe bordering France (W), Germany (N), Austria and Liechtenstein (E), Italy (S); area 15,941 sq. mi. pop. 5,240,000; capital Berne; largest city Zurich; other leading towns Basel, Geneva, Lausanne, St. Gallen, Winterthur, Lucerne, Biel, La Chaux-de-Fonds. Politically Switzerland consists of 22 autonomous cantons, of which 3 are split into half-cantons. German is the prevailing language in 16 of these cantons (almost ¾ of the people). French in the 5 cantons of SW (Geneva, Vaud, Valais, Neuchâtel, Fribourg), and Italian in the S canton of Ticino. Romansch, the fourth official language since 1937, is spoken

The flag of *Switzerland*

in the Grisons. Mountainous, noted for great scenic beauty, attracting summer and winter visitors from all over the world, Switzerland has such renowned resorts as St. Moritz, Davos, Arosa, Zermatt, Interlaken, Flims, Montreux, Lugano, and Lucerne. The majestic Alps cover more than half of Switzerland's territory, and many snowcapped peaks (Matterhorn, Weisshorn, Jungfrau, Bernina, etc.) dominate the skyline. Highest point is the Dufourspitze (15,203 ft.) of the Monte Rosa massif. A particular attraction are the many beautiful lakes, *e.g.* Maggiore, and the lakes of Geneva, Constance,

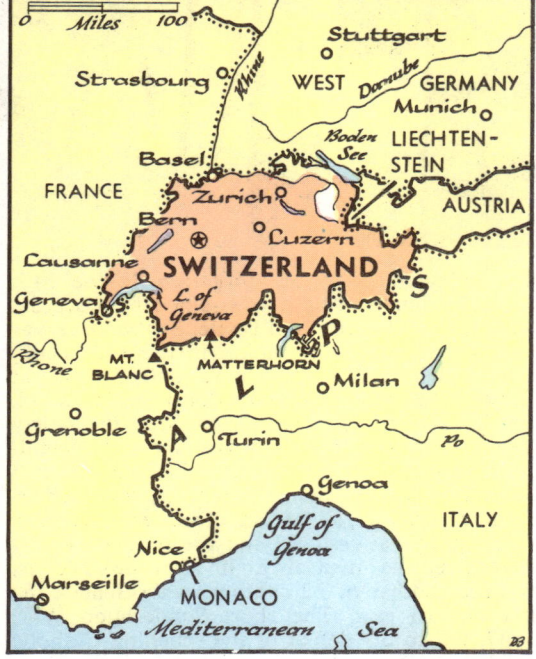

Zurich, Lucerne, and Thun. Both the Rhine and the Rhone have their source in the Swiss Alps. The largest river entirely in Switzerland is the Aare. The Alps are easily crossed by a number

Pan American Airways
This tiny *Swiss* village lies in the Rhone valley between the Bernine and Pennine Alps.

of passes, some of great historic and strategic importance, among them the Great St. Bernard, Splügen, Bernina, Maloja, Susten; underneath the Simplon and St. Gotthard are long tunnels for international railroads. Much lower, though related to the Alps, are the Jura Mts., which stretch along the Franco-Swiss boundary. Between the Alps and the Jura lie the so-called Midlands or Swiss Plateau, where the great majority of the people live. Despite the difficulty of the terrain, almost ¼ of the people are farmers. Agricultural crops include cereals, potatoes, sugar beets, vegetables, and tobacco. Several cantons yield fine wines. However, condensed milk, chocolate, butter, and cheese are of far greater importance for foreign trade and are held in high repute. Many industries have achieved a high degree of excellence, notably the manufacturing of watches, clocks, precision instruments, Diesel engines, armaments, chemicals, pharmaceuticals, chocolate, beer, and textile goods. The hotel industry plays a leading part in the country's economy. Apart from some salt, asphalt, iron, manganese, and low-quality coal, Swiss mineral resources are scant; this is somewhat compensated for, however, by considerable hydroelectric resources. Switzerland has also long been a favorite meeting place of international conferences. Geneva, once the seat of the League of Nations, is headquarters of the Red Cross, the International Bureau of Labor, and several subagencies of the United Nations. The International Postal Union convenes at Berne. Politically stable, the nation enjoys one of the highest living standards among the countries of Europe. Its educational level is as high. There are 7 universities and a federal institute of technology. The Swiss Confederation

Left: an impressive example of the chalet, *Switzerland's* most distinctive form of architecture.

Pan American Airways

Below: *Switzerland* is famous for its fine skiing areas, like this one near the Breithorn, in the Alps.

Trans World Airlines

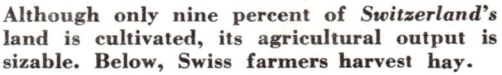

Although only nine percent of *Switzerland's* land is cultivated, its agricultural output is sizable. Below, Swiss farmers harvest hay.

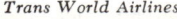

Trans World Airlines

has as its highest executive branch a seven-member federal council elected by parliament for a 4-year term. The country's first magistrates are the president of the confederation and the vice president of the federal council, holding 1-year nonsuccessive terms. Parliament, the legislative and judicial body, consists of the council of states (44 members—2 from each canton—with manner of election and term of office varying by canton), and the national council (196 members directly elected for 4 years on a proportional basis). Suffrage is limited to males, and veto of laws through popular referendum is common.

Inhabited by lake dwellers in prehistoric times, the region was peopled by the Celtic Helvetians when subdued by Julius Caesar, 58 B.C. Alemanni and Burgundians settled here later. As a nation Switzerland originated, 1291, when the Forest Cantons of Uri, Schwyz, and Unterwalden formed a league against Austria, whom they defeated, 1315, at Morgarten. In the 14th cent. the Confederation was joined by Lucerne, Zurich, Zug, Glarus, and Berne. Switzerland was a center of the Reformation in the 15th cent., with Calvin active at Geneva and Zwingli at Zurich. Renaissance culture flourished at Basel. The Treaty of Westphalia, 1648, after the Thirty Years' War confirmed Switzerland's independence from the Holy Roman Empire. French occupation set up the Helvetic Republic, 1798-1803. Upon the fall of Napoleon, Switzerland's sovereignty was restored and the foreign powers guaranteed its neutrality. It then attained its present number of 22 cantons, with Geneva the last one to join. The short Sonderbund War, 1847, led to the defeat of the rebelling Catholic cantons, and a year later a new constitution was adopted (replaced 1874). Switzerland maintained strict neutrality in World Wars I and II and thereafter. It has a well-equipped militia and air force, and military service is compulsory.

sword, weapon for use in personal combat consisting of a steel blade set in a hilt, or handle, protected by a metal case, or cross-guard. A sword is used for cutting or thrusting, or for both. The origin of the sword is unknown, but it has been found among the prehistoric relics of man, and is mentioned in the earliest records. With the exception of the club and spear, it is probably the most ancient of man's weapons. Ancient swords were usually short, with a broad, pointed blade, but in medieval types the sword was long and often cross-hilted. Two-handled swords of considerable length were also used by the knights of that period. In the Middle Ages, the best blades were made at Toledo, Spain, and by the Arabs in Damascus. The advent of firearms rendered the sword obsolete as a weapon, and it is now used chiefly as a badge of office. It is usually carried enclosed in a scabbard, and belted or hung at the side. Special types of swords include the rapier, the épée and the saber, which today are used primarily for the sport of fencing (*q.v.*).

swordfish, marine bony fish (family Xiphiidae) of which there is but one species (*Xiphias gladius*), found in the Atlantic, Pacific, and Mediterranean waters. Highly valued as a food fish, it is caught in large numbers. Adults sometimes weigh 800 lb. The fish receives it name from its upper jaw, which is lengthened into a long weapon resembling a sword; it uses this to hack and transfix its prey, consisting chiefly of mackerel. It has no teeth. The swordfish is 3 to 14 ft. long, the sword being about a third of the total length. It swims rapidly.

Sybaris, ancient city, S Italy, founded *c.*720 B.C. by Achaean Greeks. Controlling the neck of land between the Gulf of Tarentum and the Tyrrhenian Sea, it became a trading and farming center, so prosperous that the luxury of its people gave rise to the word sybarite, meaning "voluptuary." In a war with neighboring Croton, Sybaris was destroyed, 510 B.C.

sycamore, common U.S. name for the genus (*Platanus*) of plane trees, including about six species, three native to the U.S. Sycamores are large, flaky-barked, attractive trees used commonly for plantings in city parks and along streets. In Europe the name sycamore is applied to a handsome maple (*Acer pseudoplatanus*), a few of which are planted in the U.S. The sycamore fig (*Ficus sycomorus*) is the sycamore of the Bible.

Sydney, capital of New South Wales, SE Australia, on Port Jackson inlet; metropolitan pop. 2,054,800. The city, noted for its beautiful harbor, has large exports of grain, meat, and wool, and its varied industries include texile milling and automobile production. Among its educational institutions is the Univ. of Sydney, 1852. The city had its beginnings in the establishment, 1788, of a penal settlement near here.

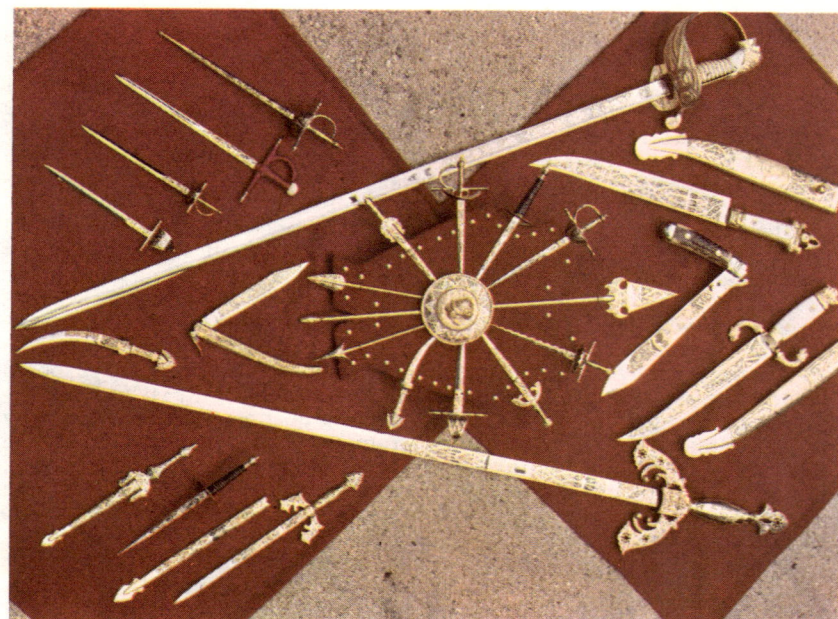

Since the Middle Ages, Toledo, Spain, has been the world's leading manufacturer of *swords*, a position once held by the city of Damascus. These are examples of several types of swords, daggers, and similar weapons produced in Toledo.

Graphic House

Otis Elevator

Day and night views of *Sydney*, Australia, and its excellent harbor.

Sydney, city, NE Cape Breton Island, Nova Scotia; pop. 32,162. Founded 1783 by United Empire Loyalists, it was capital of Cape Breton province, 1784-1820. It is the center for a coal-mining and agricultural area, and has important steel mills.

syllogism, argument of deductive reasoning expressed in logical form. It should contain three, and not more than three, propositions, the first two being the premises and the last the conclusion. It contains also three terms: the major, the minor, and the middle. An example:
All birds are winged creatures,
Swallows are birds:
Therefore swallows are winged creatures.
In this *swallows* is the minor term, *winged creatures* is the major term, and *birds* is the middle term. The propositions of a syllogism may be either universal or particular, affirmative or negative. "All men are liars" is a universal affirmative. "No horses are men" is a universal negative. "Some men are fools" is a particular affirmative. The theory of the syllogism was formulated by Aristotle; little was added in later times. The modern view of syllogisms is that they are tautological, *i.e.* the conclusion is implicit in the first, major premise, and no knowledge is gained.

symbiosis, in biology, a mutually beneficial parasitism between two (or more) living organisms. In symbiotic relationships each type of organism performs a service vital to the other. Two well-known examples are the pea-crabs, which live within the shells of various molluscs, and the bacteria and other micro-organisms which live in the stomachs of many animals while assisting in the digestion of their food. Lichen, an intermixture of algae and fungi found on many barren spots where no other life could subsist, are symbiotic; the algae, through photosynthesis, provide necessary quantities of organic material for the fungi; who, in turn, supply inorganic salts and water.

symbolic logic—see *logic*.

symbolists, literary school which began in France toward the end of the 19th cent. First manifested in poetry, it was greatly influenced by the works of Baudelaire and attempted to break away from realism or naturalism by the imaginative use of allusion and allegory, and from the prevalent rigidity of verse by the use of novel prosody or free verse. Its technique was to suggest the original image or idea by a secondary image, and its style was adopted to its content. Early symbolists included Verlaine, Rimbaud, and Mallarmé. As the movement develope, it spread into music, particularly through Debussy, and into the theater, Maeterlinck being one of its chief exponents there. It also preluded development of the decadent and imagist schools, and its influence pervaded modern poetry, music, and art.

Symonds, John Addington, 1840-93, English writer. His great work, *The Renaissance in Italy* (7 vols., 1875-86), is still considered authoritative. He also wrote, always in impeccable and imaginative style, travel books; biographies of Shelley, Ben Jonson, and Michelangelo; and studies of the Greek poets. His translation of Cellini's autobiography is a classic.

Symons, Arthur, 1865-1945, British poet and critic, b. Wales. He was associated with the *Saturday Review* and edited the *Savoy*, 1896-1908. Among his verse collections are *Days and Nights* (1889) and *The Fool of the World, and Other Poems* (1906). He also translated Baudelaire and Pierre Louÿs, and was an advocate of the symbolists in England, explaining their role in *The Symbolist Movement in Literature* (1899).

sympathy, in psychiatry—see *empathy*.

symphonic poem, a 19th cent. term first used by Liszt, to identify a musical work of program music type, but of about the length and seriousness of a symphony. There is usually little emphasis on formal structure, and the effect is less that of abstract relationihips than of the evocation of mood and emotion. It is a musical genre characteristic of romanticism, usually descriptive or interpretive of something non-musical, such as a literary work. "Tone poem" is sometimes used as a rough synonym, and "symphonic study," a term used by Elgar, is also a close equivalent, but is applied to highly formal and abstract compositions derived from elements of a symphony, such as Schumann's *Symphonic Studies*, variations (*q.v.*) for piano. Liszt, Richard Strauss, and Debussy were among the romantic composers who produced many symphonic poems.

symphony, musical composition for full orchestra. Since the mid-18th cent. it has usually been in sonata (*q.v.*) form. Earlier compositions for several instruments were also known as symphonies, in the literal sense of the word (Gr. *syn*, "with" or "together"; *phone*, "sound"); thus Bach called some of his three-part keyboard compositions symphonies, and Haydn so designated certain string quartets. The true symphony developed from the Italian overture under the influence of parallel development of the sonata, and is recognized in its mature form in the compositions of Haydn, who wrote over 100 symphonies. The form was further developed by Mozart, and realized its highest embodiment in the great Beethoven works. Thereafter the form, which has been paralleled in its growth by that of the symphony orchestra, was accepted as the ultimate for instrumental composition and used by most major 19th-cent. composers, each adapting it to his temperament. The German musicians Schubert, Mendelssohn, and Shumann composed symphonies in the romantic style, while Brahms tended to revert to classical form, and Bruckner used it to express Wagnerian effects. In France, Berlioz introduced a theatrical element; Franck's D minor symphony abandoned the traditional four movements. Of the Russian composers, Tchaikovsky wrote symphonies in the 19th cent.; while Shostakovich and Prokofiv continued the tradition. Other recent symphony composers include Sibelius, Hindemith, Vaughan Williams, Bloch, and Copland. Related to the symphony is the single-movement symphonic poem (*q.v.*), a term first used by Liszt.

synagogue, Jewish place of worship. It probably originated during the Babylonian captivity, 6th cent. B.C., when the Jews would not worship in the Temple at Jerusalem (which had been razed, 586 B.C.). The word (Gr. for assembly) is also used for the community of worshipers. In each such community the building served, and often

SYNTHETIC

FSTC

Like many other forms of religious architecture, the *synagogue* of today often has a modern design which nevertheless retains the dignity befitting a house of God. The synagogue above, with brick and ceramic façade, is the Temple Emanu-El in Lynbrook, New York. Below, a synagogue choir, led by a cantor, participates in a Jewish religious service.

still serves, as a center of learning and communal activity as well as devotion. It has no images; at one end is the Ark, containing the Torah, with a reader's place nearby. The oldest existing synagogue in the U.S. is at Newport, R.I. (completed 1763), now a national monument.

syncopation—see *rhythm*.

syndicalism, movement aimed at overthrowing the existing order of society by paralyzing the economy through industrial slowdowns, sabotage, and the general strike, the object being to destroy the state and reorganize society. Syndicalists, like anarchists, believe that all forms of the state are oppressive. They aim to make the trade union the fundamental unit of government and production. The works of Proudhon (*q.v.*) and Sorel have influenced syndicalists, who flourished principally in France, Spain, and Italy. In the U.S. the most prominent syndicalist organization was the Industrial Workers of the World. See *guild socialism*.

Synge, John Millington, 1871-1909, Irish dramatist. He studied music in Germany and was working in Paris when he met Yeats, who persuaded him to return to Ireland. He wrote two short plays, the second of which, *Riders to the Sea* (1904), is still performed. He then joined Lady Gregory and Yeats on the directorial staff of the Abbey Theatre (*q.v.*). His most famous play, *The Playboy of the Western World* (1907), was first performed at the Abbey Theatre (*q.v.*).

Synoptic Gospels—see *Gospel*.

synthetic fabrics, cloth woven from man-made fibers, such as rayon, nylon (*q.v.*), Orlon, and Dacron. Not until 1890 did man attempt to produce artificial textile fibers, an innovation which would enable him to determine the nature of his product and relieve him of such disadvantages of natural-fiber production as distant sources of raw materials and possible supply shortages. As early as 1664 an English scientist, Robert Hooke, suggested the possibility of producing synthetic fibers, and in 1842 an English silk weaver, Louis Schwabe, created a machine which featured nozzles with fine holes through which a liquid glass was forced to make filaments. The discovery of nitrocellulose (a nitrated solution derived from wood pulp), by a Swiss chemist, advanced the development of rayon and by 1891 the first rayon-producing factory was opened in Besançon, France, by Count Hilaire de Charbonnet, the "father of the rayon industry." The nitrocellulose process was followed by the cuprammonium, viscose process, and acetate processes, each using different solvents and chemical reactions. In 1902 Arthur D. Little, of Boston, Mass., and his two partners, William K. Walker and Harry S. Mork, were granted the first U.S. patent for spinning man-made fibers which led to the first successful production of acetate rayon. All man-made fibers are produced in the form of filament yarn (continuous strands similar to silk) or staple fiber (short fibers spun into yarn, as are cotton and wool) and are of four general types: cellulosic fibers, true synthetic fibers, protein fibers, and inorganic fibers. Rayon and acetates were the earliest synthetic fabrics. They still exceed all others in poundage, world production being about 3.5 billion pounds a year, a third of which is of American manufacture. Rayon is used for clothing, underwear, linings, and, as a blend, in blankets, carpets, and fusing. True synthetic fibers are made of coal, water, air, petroleum, and limestone which combine to form longchain molecules. Nylon, a generic term given the first true synthetic fabric by its developers, E. I. Du Pont de Nemours & Co., revolutionized the textile industry with its introduction in 1939. Its discovery was a fortunate laboratory accident which occurred in the late 1920s when a du Pont chemist, experimenting with molten polymer, found it could be stretched into strong, silken strands. Within a few years nylon replaced silk in that fiber's most important product: women's hosiery. The strong, resilient qualities of nylon also made it useful as

SYPHILIS

brush bristles, rope, tire cord, parachute shrouds, and carpeting. As a filament yarn, it is popular as a fabric for ladies' clothing, especially lingerie of tricot knit. Other true synthetic fibers, all developed in the 1940s and '50s, include: Orlon and Acrilan, resistant to high temperatures and acid conditions, used for awnings, sailcoth, automobile tops, suiting; Dynel, simulated wool, used for blankets, socks, pile fabrics and as a blend for clothing; Dacron, called Terylene in England, developed as an answer to the unstable wool market, used in apparel; Saran, principally used as screening, and for upholstery, racquet strings, shoes and handbags; Vinyon, best when used in filter fabrics, such as nets, curtains, industrial clothing, and as a blending agent with other fibers. Those synthetic fabrics used for clothing have been developed to resist wrinkles, to dry quickly, hold a crease, and be laundered with little or no ironing. Protein fibers, generally made with a milk casein base, have a chemical composition similar to wool. So far, they are the least commercially important among synthetic fibers. Inorganic fibers of glass, being fireproof, are used chiefly for draperies and insulation. Most synthetic fibers are woven into fabrics on the cotton system, but the conversion of mill machinery to accommodate the new man-made fibers involved great expense on the part of the textile industry; it foresaw, however, their potential, and also invested heavily in research. In 1957 the U.S. produced 1.8 billion pounds of synthetic fibers, more than a third of the world production. Most of the U.S. production was accounted for by rayon and acetates, but it is predicted that the true synthetic fabrics, such as nylon, Dacron, etc., will equal the cellulosics in production by 1975.

syphilis, venereal disease (named for the legendary shepherd Syphilus) caused by a corkscrew-shaped microorganism, *Spirocheta pallida*. It first appeared in Europe after the Middle Ages; an early outbreak was reported during the siege of Naples, 1495, by Charles VIII of France. Syphilis is most frequently caused by sexual intercourse, but can be acquired congenitally (*i.e.* the fetus can be infected by the mother) and from kissing. The spirochete causing it is very delicate, dying easily on exposure to air; hence transmission from towels, toilet seats, and eating and drinking utensils rarely occurs. The primary stage of syphilis, or chancre, generally appears at the point of contact (usually the genitals or lips) 2 or 3 weeks after exposure; it often has a central ulcerated area. But this stage may be absent or hidden (particularly in the female). Usually several weeks after the chancre, a rash or sores in the mouth or genitals appear; this is the secondary stage, during which the patient remains highly infectious. When the rash subsides, the disease may become dormant and finally die away, or may go on eventually to tertiary syphilis, involving nervous system, heart, and blood vessels, or, more rarely, other organs. General paresis, a type of insanity, and tabes dorsalis (locomotor ataxia), a disturbance in coordination, are due to syphilis. The Wassermann test and its modern modifications help in diagnosis. Penicillin has virtually replaced all other therapy, though heat treatment is useful in some nervous-system cases. Prior to penicillin, Salvarsan, invented by Paul Ehrlich, and neo-Salvarsan provided the best means of therapy, particurly when supplemented with bismuth.

Syracuse, co. seat of Onondaga co., central New York; pop. 216,038. It has foundries and machine shops, and makes cans, typewriters, silverware, automobile bodies and parts, air-conditioning machinery, farm machinery, and chinaware. Syracuse Univ. and the Museum of Fine Arts are here. A big railroad center, it is a port of entry and is on the N.Y. State Barge Canal, whose predecessor, the Erie Canal, helped the city develop. It was settled in 1805.

Syracuse, ancient city, SE Sicily, founded by Corinthian Greeks, c.734 B.C. In 485 B.C. Gelon, tyrant of neighboring Gela, captured the city and made it his home; after his defeat of the Carthaginians, 480 B.C., Syracuse became and remained the leading Greek city and cultural center of the West. It was a democracy during the 5th cent. B.C., but supported Sparta in the Peloponnesian War, decisively defeating Athens, 413 B.C. Renewed Carthaginian invasions resulted in the rise of Dionysius, who repelled them and ruled Syracuse and most of Sicily and Greek Italy, 405-367 B.C. During his reign Syracuse was at the height of its power, but his son Dionysius and brother Dion were unpopular; the Syracusans chose a Corinthian general, Timoleon, to restore their democracy, 344 B.C. The tyranny was revived by Agathocles, 317 B.C., and ended after the rule of the pro-Roman Hieron II, 270-215 B.C. After a brief war, during which the new military weapons devised by Archimedes failed to save the Syracusans, the Romans seized the city, 212 B.C. Thereafter it remained administrative center of the Roman province of Sicily (*q.v.*). The modern city of Siracusa, on part of the ancient site, pop. 57,138, is a major Italian port.

Syr Darya River, c.1500 mi. long, in Uzbek, Tadzhik, and Kazakh Republics, U.S.S.R. It is nonnavigable, but important for irrigation.

Syria, republic, SW Asia, bounded W by Mediterranean Sea, Israel, and Lebanon, E by Iraq, N by Turkey, and S by Jordan; area 71,227 sq. mi.; pop. 4,656,688; capital Damascus, other centers

The aerial view at left is of the region near Damascus in *Syria*.

Graphic House

At right is Al Shouhada Square at the heart of Damascus.

Aleppo, Homs, Hama, and Latakia. Roughly in the central area is the Syrian Desert, while in the north is the region of the Euphrates River Valley (forming part of the Fertile Crescent) and in the south the plain of Hauran. Among the mountain ranges are the Anti-Lebanon Mts. (with Mt. Hermon, 9232 ft.) and the Jebel Druse. Internal communications are not well developed, but several international airlines go through Damascus. The chief occupations are stock raising and agriculture, with grains, olives, fruits, cotton, and tobacco the main crops. There is an oil industry, but the country's mineral resources have not been exploited. Silk textiles and metalware are produced in the major cities. The people are mostly Arabic-speaking Sunni Moslems.

The flag of *Syria*

In ancient times Syria, located between the cultures of Mesopotamia and Egypt, was a melting pot of peoples. Occupied during the 2nd millennium B.C. by Amorites, it was soon settled also by Hurri, Hittites, and, after 14th cent. B.C., largely by Aramaeans and Phoenicians. Its prosperous trading cities were at times independent, at other times dominated by Egypt, the Hurri, or the Hittites. Its subjection by Egypt, c.1471 B.C., was followed by successive conquests by Babylonians, Assyrians, Persians, and Macedonians. After its subjugation by Alexander the Great, Syria came under rule of the Seleucids and subsequently, 64 B.C., under Roman rule. The Arabs gained control of the region, 7th cent. A.D., when Damascus became a great Moslem center, but the earlier Christian religion was far from overthrown. During the early Crusades the country was under the rule first of the Seljuk Turks and later of Saladin. The period after Saladin's reign was chaotic until the Ottoman Turks established their rule, 1516. The country was briefly occupied by Napoleon's forces, 1799, and by the Egyptians, early 19th cent., but the Turks did not lose Syria permanently until 1917. The Turkish massacres of native Christians spurred a nationalist movement supported by Moslems and Christians alike. After World War I the nationalist cause was frustrated by the establishment, 1920, of a French mandate over the Levant States, which comprised Syria and Lebanon. A series of revolts ultimately led to creation of the republic of Lebanon, 1926, and the republic of Syria, 1930. The French mandate did not end, however, until 1941, when both Lebanon and Syria were proclaimed independent; complete independence was granted, 1944. In World War II Syria's support of the Vichy government led the British and Free French forces to invade and occupy the country, 1941. Becoming a member of the Arab League, 1945, Syria took part in the war on Israel, 1948. After several military *coups d'état* a new, 1950, constitution was framed; it strengthened the power of the unicameral legislature, popularly elected every 4 years.

In 1958, the government, fearful of Communist subversion, acceded to Egyptian pressure to join in a union under the name United Arab Republic. Egyptian officials took over much of the government and instituted many economic reforms. But in 1961, Syrian nationalists seized power, broke the union with Egypt and set up a new government. Elections were promised for 1962.

Syrian language—see *Arabic languages*.

syringa, common name for an attractive garden shrub of the genus *Philadelphus,* sometimes called the mock orange. It has large, fragrant white or cream-colored flowers. Several species are native to the eastern U.S.; additional ones are from Europe and Asia. The scientific name of the lilac genus is *Syringa*.

Szczecin—see *Stettin*.

Szechwan, province, S central China; area 219,691 sq. mi.; pop. 72,160,000; capital Chengtu. In 1955, most of Sikang province was annexed. This largest and most populous of Chinese provinces has a fertile central plain which makes possible enormous rice crops. The region is entirely surrounded by mountains. Transportation is almost exclusively by junks on the Yangtze and other rivers. Szechwan's chief commercial products are rice, sugar cane, silk, tung oil, tea, tobacco, hides, and salt. Gold, iron, coal, copper, and petroleum sources are exploited. After Japan's attack on China, 1937, Chungking, in the E section, served as Nationalist capital and many industrial enterprises were moved from E China. Road and railroad construction have been increased under the Communist regime.

Szeged, city and river port, S Hungary, on Tisza River near Yugoslav border, c.100 mi. SSE of Budapest; pop. 99,061. It is the trading and processing center of a fertile agricultural lowland, and has a university and other educational institutions. The older section of the city was destroyed by flood, 1879.

Szold, Henrietta, 1860-1945, U.S. Zionist leader, b. Baltimore. She was editor for the Jewish Publication Society, 1892-1916. Her chief work was the organization, 1912, of Hadassah, a U.S. women's organization for the Zionist cause, engaged in philanthropic and educational activities. She served as its president until 1926, and from 1920 directed its relief and medical work from Palestine.

T, the twentieth letter and sixteenth consonant of the English alphabet. In the Phoenician alphabet the corresponding sign was the twenty-second and last; all letters that follow *t* in Greek and Latin, and also in the English scheme, are the result of successive additions made to the system borrowed from the Phoenician. The value of *t* has been practically the same through the whole history of its use; it denotes the so-called breathed mute (or check) produced by a quick and strong emission of the breath after the end of the tongue has been placed against the roof of the mouth near the roots of the upper teeth. By Grimm's Law (see *Germanic languages; Grimm, Jakob*), *t* in English corresponds to *d* in Latin, Greek, and Sanskrit, and to *ss* or *z* in German.

tabasco—see *pepper*.

table, an article of furniture (*q.v.*) consisting of a flat top (the table proper), of wood, stone, or other solid material, resting on legs or on a pillar, with or without connecting framework. The term is generally applied to any piece of furniture with a flat top on which meals are served, articles of use or ornament are placed, or some occupation is carried on: as a dining table, writing table, work table, kitchen table; a billiard table; a surgeon's operating table. The table developed from the raised altars built by primitive man for sacrificial purposes. Eventually such platforms were modified for personal use. Tables of the Third Kingdom of Egypt, a period of exquisite furniture design, were square, round, or oblong, and supported by three delicately carved legs or a single pedestal. The Greeks used small tables of low construction to be set beside a couch. The table became more common during the Roman Empire and included massive rectangular pieces made of marble and supported by carved end slabs. Tables of the Elizabethan Age were supported on bulbous legs and included the draw table, forerunner of the extension dining table. Designers who created distinctive types of tables included Adam, Chippendale,

The *table* above, with mosaic top and sculpted legs, was made in 17th-cent. Florence. At left is a "shovelboard" table, *c.*1660, England.

Many *tables* today have distinctive shapes and bright colors in accordance with the modern trends of interior design. The use of plastic, Fiberglas, and similar materials makes possible the construction of such tables as these.

Hepplewhite, Sheraton, and Phyfe (*qq.v.*).

tableland—see *plateau*.

Table Mountain, W Cape Province, Union of South Africa. It is *c*.3600 ft. high and overlooks Table Bay, which was discovered by the Portuguese, 1503.

table tennis—see *Ping-pong*.

tableware, those utensils used for dining, including mainly knives, forks, spoons, and incidental table pieces, such as saltcellars. The first cutlery was primitive man's sharp-edged shell or flint. The Neolithic caveman had knives of chipped flint. Later copper and bronze replaced flint and were in turn replaced by steel. Knives and spoons, the latter also being of shell origin, were the earliest eating implements manufactured. In the later Middle Ages each person probably possessed a personal knife and spoon which he brought to table with him. Knives had sharp steel blades; spoons had fig-shaped bowls and thin hexagonal handles with a device or figure at the end—the apostles being a common relief. Forks were not in use until their introduction in Italy in the 15th cent. In Elizabethan England, they were ridiculed as a foreign affectation. Spoons, however, were used extensively by the Elizabethans, and were often employed as ceremonial devices, a custom dating from ancient times. The British Coronation spoon, used in anointing England's monarchs, dates from the 12th cent. During the 17th cent. spoons with oval bowls and plain flat handles appeared; after the Restoration (1660) the handles were often ornamented. Table forks began to be popular, first with three, then four times, their handles matching those of contemporary spoons. Tableware developed very much in the 18th cent., with a growing number of specialized pieces and increasingly distinctive designs. Until mid-20th cent., table silver was largely in imitation of these patterns. Recently, modern Scandinavian designers have greatly influenced tableware styles. The Danes in particular have produced beautifully simple designs not only for silver, but also for stainless steel; thus the more inexpensive metal has won new respect and has come into wide popularity for everyday table-settings. The finest knife blades today are forged from high-carbon steel. Solingen, Germany and Sheffield, England have been centers of cutlery manufacture since the Middle Ages and continue to produce consistently fine tableware. See *chinaware*; *glass*.

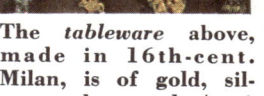

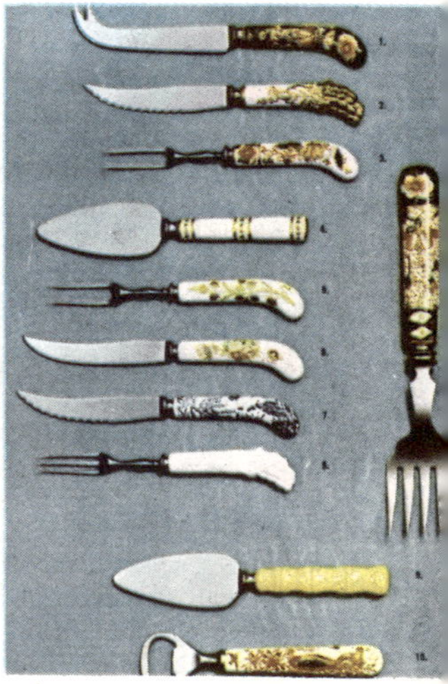

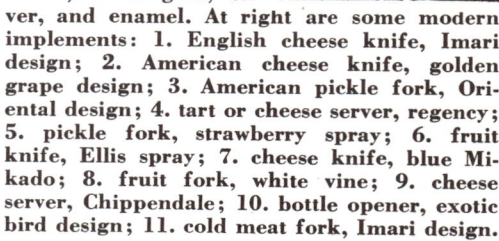

The *tableware* above, made in 16th-cent. Milan, is of gold, silver, and enamel. At right are some modern implements: **1.** English cheese knife, Imari design; **2.** American cheese knife, golden grape design; **3.** American pickle fork, Oriental design; **4.** tart or cheese server, regency; **5.** pickle fork, strawberry spray; **6.** fruit knife, Ellis spray; **7.** cheese knife, blue Mikado; **8.** fruit fork, white vine; **9.** cheese server, Chippendale; **10.** bottle opener, exotic bird design; **11.** cold meat fork, Imari design.

taboo or **tabu,** term of Polynesian origin applied to objects, persons, or places subject to a religious restriction, usually forbidding use or touching. The prohibition is generally imposed by a priest or chief, or constitutes part of the accepted tradition. The object is believed either unclean or sacred; if the latter, violation is believed to bring evil on the violator and possibly make him taboo. Imposition of taboos is widespread among primitive peoples, notably the Polynesians, among whom typical objects of taboo are the persons of priests and chiefs, pregnant women, and the dead and certain foods; an object might be taboo only to specific groups, as women, or on specific occasions. Objects religiously restricted and so identifiable as taboo may be found in all cultures, including the most advanced. A familiar example among historic peoples is the category of objects forbidden as not *kosher* (*q.v.*) among the Jews.

tabor—see *tambourine*.

TABRIZ

Tabriz, capital of Azerbaijan province, NW Iran; 1950 est. pop. 289,996. The ancient Tauris, now 2nd-largest city in Iran, it has long been an important commercial center with a large trade in rugs and dried fruits. There is a university. The city has often suffered from invaders (including Tamerlane) and earthquakes, but has always risen from its ruins. In 1946 it was the center of a revolution inspired by the Communist-led Tudeh Party, which set up a short-lived regime. The city was occupied by Russian forces in World Wars I and II.

tabu—see *taboo*.

tachycardia, rapid and sometimes irregular heartbeat. The heart responds normally with a tachycardia to such conditions as fever, emotional excitement, and physical exercise. However, in these situations, the heartbeat returns to normal when the causitive stimulus is removed. There are many individuals who develop tachycardia without any apparent or discoverable cause. In these patients, the tachycardia may persist for prolonged periods and require such medication as digitalis or quinidine (*qq.v.*). There is, finally, that group of patients whose tachycardia is due to heart disease. The tachycardia in these cases is frequently dangerous, even life-threatening, and therefore usually demands immediate treatment.

Tacitus, Cornelius, b. A.D. *c.*55, Roman historian. He held public office under the emperors Titus and Domitian, and governed the province of Asia under Trajan; little more is known of his life. His *Germania* is a major source for early history of Germanic peoples. His great works, known as the *Annals* and *Histories,* originally covered Roman history from Tiberius through Domitian; lost for centuries, large portions were rediscovered in the 15th-16th cent. they have full portrayals of important personalities, in succinct, dramatic style.

Tacna-Arica Controversy, dispute arising between Chile at Peru at the end of the War of the Pacific, won by Chile, 1883. The Treaty of Ancón provided that these two provinces should be held by Chile and that a plebiscite should then determine their sovereignty. Dispute occurred over the procedure for the plebiscite, and settlement efforts, 1925-6, with the U.S. as arbitrator failed. Finally, 1929, the region was divided, Tacna going to Peru and Arica remaining with Chile, a free port being built there for Peru.

Tacoma, city, co. seat of Pierce co., NW Washington, on Commencement Bay of Puget Sound; pop. 147,979. Lying in view of Mt. Rainier (which local citizens long preferred to call Mt. Tacoma), this 3rd-largest city in the state has a fine port which handles Oriental and coastwise trade and is a railroad terminus. Industries includes lumber and flour mills, smelters, railroad shops, and electrochemical plants. Settled 1852, the city grew with lumbering. Fort Lewis is near Tacoma.

tactics, the employment of military forces in combat; the disposition and movement of such forces in relation to each other and to the enemy so that at the critical time in the battle, maximum firepower and shock action can be applied against the enemy's most vulnerable point. As distinguished from strategy (*q.v.*), which comprehends the movement of forces and their logistic support when not in the presence of the enemy, tactics encompasses the maneuvers of military units when in contact with the enemy. The purpose of strategy is to ensure wherever possible the favorable outcome of tactical engagements: the aim of tactics is to develop or complete the strategic concept. In modern war, weapons, movement, and terrain are the elements from which tactics are constructed and which govern the outcome of battles. Examples of tactical maneuvers are: the concentric attack used by the Greeks at Marathon (490 B.C.); the oblique order employed by Epaminondas at Leuctra (371 B.C.); the famous double envelopment at Cannae (216 B.C.); Cyrus' use of the eccentric attack in the Battle of Thymbra (545 B.C.); and the flank attack which met with overwhelming success at Leuthen (1757). During World War I, the outstanding tactical development was trench warfare and the "continuous front," a trench system stretching from the North Sea to Switzerland. World War II brought such tactical innovations as: *"blitzkreig"* or "lightning war"; urban

Invention of the airplane brought an entirely new dimension to warfare *tactics*. These ruins in central London show the effects of the German "blitz" used during World War II.

The siege was a basic military *tactic* used against stone fortresses in the Middle Ages. Here, Duras, France, is besieged.

Use of the phalanx was a *tactic* introduced by Spartans and developed highly by the Macedonians. It was a tight formation of shielded soldiers bearing long spears. Alexander the Great used it in units corresponding to modern divisions, brigades, and regiments. But its weaknesses — lack of maneuverability and a vulnerable right flank (shields were carried on the left)—were demonstrated when Rome defeated Macedonia.

areas converted into "hedgehog" defense systems; the tank-airplane team; vertical envelopment with airborne forces; amphibious warfare (*q.v.*); and the use of resistance movements (*q.v.*) in tactical support of regular armies. During that war, air tactics were developed for long-range bombardment, close ground support, and air defense. Naval tactics, which have been relatively unchanged for centuries, have included coastal raids; attacks on the enemy's overseas trade and against his naval lines of communication; blockade; and defense of coasts and critical focal areas. The 20th cent. has seen the introduction of the submarine (*q.v.*) and the aircraft carrier, both of which have radically altered the tactics of naval warfare. In recent years, increasing attention has been paid to tactical atomic warfare. Soviet and U.S. military studies have recognized the tactical implications of nuclear weapons as requiring greatly increased dispersion of troop formations, maximum mobility to permit rapid concentration of forces to achieve the decision on the battlefield, and highly efficient reconnaissance. See *airborne operations; war.*

Tadema—see *Alma Tadema, Lawrence.*

tadpole, larva of a frog or toad. The tadpole lives in the water, which it leaves when the tail vanishes, the legs appear, and the lungs develop.

Tadzhik Soviet Socialist Republic or **Tadzhikistan** (sometimes spelled Tajik and Tajikistan), constituent republic of the U.S.S.R., in central Asia; area c.55,600 sq. mi.; pop. 1,982,000; capital Dushanbe. It is bounded S by Afghanistan, W by the Uzbek Soviet Socialist Republic, N by the Kirghiz and Uzbek Soviet Socialist Republics, and E by China. Most of the Pamir Mt. Range lies within the area. Stalin Peak (24,585 ft.) is the highest in the U.S.S.R., and Lenin Peak (23,377 ft.) next highest. Mineral resources are great, including lead, zinc, silver, petroleum, coal, antimony, bismuth, salt, and arsenic. It is also a grazing and irrigated agricultural area, with cotton, silk, rice, and wheat as the chief crops. Dushanbe (called Stalinabad until 1961; pop. c.130,000) was built 1929 on a Tadzhik village site. It has cotton and silk mills, tanneries, tobacco factories, and distilleries, and is a railroad center. The other chief city, Leninabad (formerly Khodzhent; pop. c.60,000), is a cotton and silk center on an ancient site once captured by Alexander the Great. Tadzhikistan was acquired by Russia, 1895, becoming part of the Uzbek Soviet Socialist Republic, 1924, and a constituent republic, 1929.

Taegu, city, South Korea, c.50 mi. N of Pusan; pop. 488,690. It is a textile-milling and trading center. An important military target during the Korean conflict, it was a principal point of retreat of the U.N. forces in the 1951 Chinese Communist offensive.

Taejon, capital S Chungchong province, S Korea; pop. 173,143. A transportation and industrial center, it was largely built during the Japanese occupation (1910-45) of Korea. It is at the junction of several railroads and an important rice-milling center. Badly damaged during the Korean conflict (1950-53), it is rapidly being rebuilt.

Taft, Lorado, 1860-1936, U.S. sculptor, b. Elmwood, Ill. Working in Chicago, he wielded great influence on development of sculpture in the Midwest. Besides portraiture, he executed many large public works and lectured and wrote on sculpture theory.

Taft, Robert Alphonso, 1889-1953, U.S. Senator, b. Cincinnati, son of Pres. W. H. Taft. A Republican member of the Ohio house of representatives, 1921-6, and its speaker in 1926, he served in the state senate, 1931-2, and from 1939 in the U.S. Senate, where he championed Republican isolationism before World War II. In 1947 he was co-author of the Taft-Hartley Act for the regulation of organized labor. Repeatedly an unsuccessful candidate for the Republican Presidential nomination, from 1936, he rose to Republican leadership in the Senate and won much conservative support for Pres. Dwight D. Eisenhower's administration, 1953.

Taft, William Howard, 1857-1930, 27th U.S. President (1909-13), b. Cincinnati. A graduate of Yale, 1878, he practiced law, becoming U.S. solicitor general, 1890-2, and a U.S. circuit court judge, 1892-1900. He was first U.S. civil governor of the Philippines, 1901-4. Pres. Theodore Roosevelt made him Secretary of War, 1904-8, and incidentally provisional governor of Cuba, 1906. Groomed by Roosevelt to succeed him as Republican President, Taft was elected, 1908, over W. J. Bryan. In his administration, anti-trust cases were pressed; the Dept. of Labor was cre-

ated, 1911; the postal-savings, 1910, and parcel-post, 1912, systems were established; and the 16th and 17th Amendments to the Constitution providing for income taxes and direct election of U.S. Senators were passed. However, the Payne-Aldrich high protective tariff, 1909, dismissal of Gifford Pinchot as head of the U.S. Forest Service, and "dollar diplomacy" in Latin America turned Roosevelt and other progressives against Taft. When in 1912 the Republican nomination again went to Taft, Roosevelt bolted and ran as Progressive Party (*q.v.*) candidate, splitting the Republican vote and enabling Woodrow Wilson, the Democrat, to win. Taft was professor of law at Yale, 1913-21, and Chief Justice of the U.S. Supreme Court, 1921-30.

Taft-Hartley Labor Act or **Labor Management Relations Act,** U.S. labor law passed by Congress, 1947, to supersede the National Labor Relations Act of 1935. Principally concerned with the settling of labor disputes, it granted greater power to the National Labor Relations Board, provided for a 60-day "cooling off" period before a strike could take effect, and made the closed shop illegal. The union shop was made allowable under certain conditions. Petitioning unions must certify that their officers do not belong to the Communist Party and must provide full financial data. Strikes of government employees are outlawed. The act was bitterly opposed by organized labor. The act also provided for a government injunction, directing striking workers to return to their jobs for 80 days, if a fact-finding board reported that a strike, deemed a threat to national safety, appeared deadlocked. After this period, if no solution had been reached, the strike could continue. Issues here have been what constitutes a threat to national safety, and who has the burden of proof, the government and courts, or the workers and unions. The first major federal labor legislation to follow the Taft-Hartley Act was the labor bill of 1959. It was essentially designed to limit union abuses of authority, and to limit union freedom in regard to the allocation of union funds. It was bitterly opposed and criticized by the unions. It included: measures against secondary boycotts of businesses dealing with other business having labor troubles; measures against picketing aimed at forcing employees to join a union, or forcing employers to recognize a union; measures restricting the authority of union officials, and a "bill of rights" for union members in relation to their unions; and measures requiring ramified reports of union financial affairs. The Bureau of Labor-Management Reports was created to handle the increased volume of work stemming from the increased government participation in labor affairs, as legislated in this bill. See *fair employment; National Labor Relations Board; open and closed shop; strike.*

Taganrog, city, S European Russia, on Gulf of Taganrog, an arm of the Sea of Azov; pop. 201,000. It ships grain and coal, is a heavy-machinery manufacturing and metallurgical center, and has fish canning and processing plants. Peter the Great established a fort here, 1698. Gen. Denikin's counterrevolutionary forces had their headquarters here, 1918, and the Germans occupied it, 1941, and again, 1942-3.

Taglioni, Maria, 1804-84, Italian ballet dancer. She was trained by her father, Filippo Taglioni (1777-1871), a famous choreographer. A leading proponent of romantic ballet, she was most popular in *La Sylphide,* first presented in 1832. Her dancing is legendary for its grace.

Tagore, Sir Rabindranath, 1861-1941, Indian author, b. Calcutta. Educated in India, he traveled extensively and was for a time an active nationalist. In 1901 he founded, at Santiniketan, Bengal, a school which gradually developed into

a kind of international university, called Visva-Bharati. Deeply influenced by the Sanskrit scriptures, he produced more than 200 books, including volumes of poetry, essays, novels, dramas, and sermons. He was also a composer. His works, in their variety of style, appealed to all classes in India, and his own English translations increased his reputation in the West. In 1913 he received the Nobel Prize in Literature; in 1915 he was knighted.

Pan American Airways

The scene at left is just outside of Papeete, the capital of *Tahiti*. Right, fishing nets are hung on the island of Moorea, Cook's Bay, twelve miles northwest of Tahiti itself.

Tahiti, most important of the Society Islands, S Pacific Ocean; area 388 sq. mi.; pop. 36,326; chief town Papeete, which is capital of French Polynesia. The mountainous island rises to 7618

Tahitians celebrate several festivals during the summer, the largest being the anniversary of the fall of Paris' Bastille; these gayly dressed natives are taking part in the month-long July celebration introduced by French colonials.

ft. Along the coast the soil is fertile, and agriculture (sugar cane, vanilla, copra) is the main occupation of the Polynesian natives. Phosphates are exported. The beauty of Tahiti, depicted in the paintings of Gauguin, who lived here for a time, has drawn many artists and writers. It was discovered by the British, 1767, and visited by the *Bounty* (*q.v.*), 1788, but the French took complete possession, 1880. In World War II the Tahitians joined the Free French movement. By 1960, a strong movement for formation of an independent Tahitian republic (as part of the French Community) had developed on the island.

Tahitian languages—see *Polynesian languages.*

Tahoe Lake, in California and Nevada, 20 mi. long, at the base of the Sierra Nevada. It is drained by the Truckee River.

taiga, region, Soviet Russia, S of the arctic lowlands. It is largely covered with conifers and has a bleak climate. Chief products are timber and livestock.

Taihoku—see *Taipeh.*

Taimyr Peninsula, NW Siberia, between Yenisei and Khatanga Rivers. Cape Chelyuskin is the northernmost point of Asia. The **Taimyr River** rises in its center and flows E and N *c.*400 mi. through **Taimyra Lake** (*c.*2700 sq. mi.) into Taimyr Bay, on the Arctic Ocean. The **Taimyr National District** of the U.S.S.R. takes in the Taimyr Peninsula; it is *c.*287,000 sq. mi.; pop. 36,200; capital Dudinka. The district has gold, nickel, copper, platinum, and coal mines. Nomadic tribes here live by fishing, hunting, and raising reindeer.

Taine, Hippolyte Adolphe, 1828-93, French historian and critic. Professor of aesthetics and history of art (from 1864) at the École des Beaux Arts, he wrote the important *Histoire de la littérature anglaire* (1864) and *Les Origines de la France contemporaine* (1876-93). His deterministic philosophy, his view of man as molded by his environment, and his conception of history as resulting from the social structures of nations profoundly influenced the naturalistic school of writing.

Taipeh or **Taipei** (Jap.: *Taihoku*), capital of Formosa, and since 1949 capital of the Nationalist Government of China; pop. 809,169. Keelung and Tansui (*q.v.*) are its ports. The present city was originally three towns which were rebuilt before World War II by the Japanese. Varied industries include steel manufacturing and tea and camphor processing. Coal is mined nearby. After the complete Communist conquest of the

TAIPING

Chinese mainland, 1949, Chiang Kai-shek set up his Nationalist headquarters at Taipeh. The city has been capital of Formosa since 1895.

The City Hall of *Taipeh*, capital of Formosa, is decorated for a celebration with a huge picture of Nationalist leader Chiang Kai-shek.

Taiping Rebellion, 1850-65, in Chinese history, an uprising against the Ch'ing dynasty. Its leader was Hung Hsiu-ch'üan (1812-64), who declared himself chosen by God as the Heavenly Prince to found a dynasty called Taiping (Great Peace). His doctrines, which involved political reform as well as elements of Christianity, had broad enough appeal to attract large numbers of people. Overrunning Nanking, which they made their capital, 1853, the rebels threatened to overthrow the imperial government entirely. The latter therefore accepted the offer to help from the Western Powers, who were interested in retaining their rights under the Manchus. Under Frederick Ward, an American, and later a British soldier, Charles George Gordon, Nanking was recaptured, 1864, and the rebel movement was destroyed.

Taisho—see *Yoshihito*.

Taiwan—see *Formosa*.

Taiyuan, capital, Shansi province, China; pop. 1,020,000. It is a trading center for the area which produces wheat, cotton, beans, and tobacco. Since 1949 the Communists have intensified the industrialization of the city. They increased the output of the already existing iron and steel plant and constructed a heavy machine-building plant. Taiyuan is the meeting point of railroads from Mongolia, Shantung province, and W China. An old city, it was visited by Marco Polo in the 13th cent.

Taj Mahal, mausoleum at Agra, Uttar Pradesh,

Taj Mahal

India. Built, 1632-50, by the Mogul emperor Shah Jehan for his wife Mumtaz Mahal and for himself, this marble structure, regarded as one of the most beautifully graceful structures in the world, is the best example of late Indian Moslem architecture. It is set in a large, formally designed garden and is reflected in a long, oblong pool. The tomb chamber is a room in the center of the building.

Takoradi-Sekondi, twin cities of Ghana, W Africa, that together form the chief port of Ghana; pop. 120,793. Sekondi was the major port of the Gold Coast until the 1920s when more modern harbor facilities were constructed at nearby Takoradi. Sekondi was the site of Dutch and English forts in the 17th cent. A railroad connects the two cities and goes inland to Kumasi. Cacao is the chief export passing through the harbor.

talc, soft mineral of greasy texture, a hydrated magnesium silicate, occurring in silvery-white or greenish masses which readily split into thin flexible but inelastic plates. Steatite or soapstone and potstone are varieties of talc. Talc is used in manufacture of toilet powders, soap, paper, rubber, and lubricants.

Talien—see *Dairen*.

Tallahassee, capital of Florida, co. seat of Leon co., NW Florida; pop. 48,714. It is a processing and shipping point for farm produce and timber. Settled by Spanish missionaries, in 1825 it became capital of Florida Territory. The ordinance of secession was adopted here, 1861, and the city repulsed Union troops in the Civil War. It is noted for its state capitol, Florida State Univ., and Florida Agricultural and Mechanical College.

Talleyrand or **Talleyrand-Périgord, Charles Maurice de,** 1754-1838, French statesman. Of noble family, he entered the church and, despite free-thinking and radical tendencies, was made a bishop, 1789, shortly before he represented the clergy in the meeting of the States-General which preluded the French Revolution. Influential in the National Assembly, 1789-91, as an associate of Mirabeau, he was excommunicated soon after resigning his bishopric, 1791. While in London, 1792, attempting to secure British neutrality in the French Revolutionary Wars, he increasingly doubted the growing radicalism and violence of the Revolution, which destroyed his diplomatic efforts in Great Britain. Following British entrance into the war, Feb. 1793, he departed for the U.S. Returning to France, 1797, after establishment of the Directory, he became foreign minister but had to resign, 1799, because of his part in the XYZ Affair (*q.v.*) and Napoleon's failure to win Egypt. Being close to Napoleon, however, he was rewarded for his role in Napoleon's *coup d'état*, 1799, by reappointment as foreign minister. A peacemaker, he was readmitted to the church, 1802, for his work in negotiating the Concordat, 1801, with the pope, and for his assistance to Napoleon was made prince of Benevento, 1806. However, having long disapproved of Napoleon's extreme ambitions, and having hoped to preserve the European state system which Napoleon had destroyed, Talleyrand resigned his post after the defeats of Prussia and Russia, 1807, remaining only a member of the imperial council. Finally, after

Napoleon's defeats in Russia, Spain, and Germany, 1812-14, he persuaded the victorious allies that only by restoration of the Bourbons in France could European peace be secured. As Louis XVIII's foreign minister he then negotiated for France the first Treaty of Paris, 1814, which gave France the frontiers of 1792, considerably enlarged from those of 1789, before the outbreak of the French Revolutionary Wars. As Bourbon representative at the Congress of Vienna, 1814-15, he used international suspicions to restore the international position of France. He opposed Napoleon during the Hundred Days, 1815, but following electoral victories of the ultra-royalists, Sept. 1815, was dismissed as foreign minister along with other persons who had served Napoleon. His memoirs were written in retirement. After the July Revolution, 1830, he became ambassador in London, helping importantly in negotiations on establishment of Belgian independence, 1830, and of the Quadruple Alliance, 1834, of Great Britain, France, Spain, and Portugal. Talleyrand was largely responsible for the resurgence of France as a power after her defeats in the final Napoleonic wars.

Tallien, Jean Lambert, 1767-1820, French revolutionist. Editor, 1791, of a Jacobin-sponsored Paris placard newspaper, he participated in the storming of the Tuileries, 1792, and was made secretary of the Paris Commune. Elected to the National Convention, Sept. 1792, and the Committee of General Security, Jan. 1793, he was ruthless toward anti-revolutionists, but after falling in love with a prisoner, Thérèse, comtesse de Fontenay, later his wife, he became more moderate. In self-protection he led in the overthrow of Robespierre, July 27, 1794. Elected to the Committee of Public Safety, he was powerful until the establishment of the Directory, 1795. Eventually disowned by both radical and moderates, and divorced by his wife, Thérèse, he died in poverty.

Tallin (Ger.: *Reval*), capital and Baltic seaport of the Estonian Soviet Socialist Republic, W Soviet Union, on S coast of Gulf of Finland opposite Helsinki, *c.*220 mi. WSW of Leningrad; pop. 280,000. A handsome city with fine medieval and modern buildings, Tallin is a manufacturing and shipbuilding center. Nearby are phosphorite deposits. The city is crowned by a hill with an imposing cathedral, below which is a medieval, walled section. Founded by the Danes, 13th cent., the city became a member of the Hanseatic League, and in the 16th cent. passed to Sweden, which ceded it, 1721, to Russia. After World War I it was made capital of the new republic of Estonia, annexed 1940 by the Soviet Union. The Germans occupied it in World War II.

tallow, fat rendered by heating beef or, occasionally, mutton. It is a solid, melting between 40° and 50°C. Its chief use is in soapmaking, where it is used admixed with other fats or oils because soap produced by tallow alone is very hard. It is used also in certain greases and in candles.

Tallow is the basic material used for making candles. Here, in the Old Sturbridge Village Museum, Massachusetts, the centuries-old process is demonstrated for visitors.

Talmadge, Eugene, 1884-1946, U.S. politician, b. Forsyth, Ga. Governor of Georgia, 1933-7, 1941-3, he denounced Pres. Roosevelt's New Deal and insured local support of proclaiming white supremacy. In 1942 Ellis G. Arnall defeated him for governor, but in 1946 Talmadge was re-elected. Following his death shortly thereafter, his son **Herman Eugene Talmadge,** 1913- , won the office in a special election, Nov. 1948. In 1950, he was re-elected governor and, 1956, elected U.S. Senator.

TALMUD

Talmud, books of Jewish law and lore, supplementing the Torah. They consist of two parts, the Mishnah and the Gemara. The former, written in Hebrew, A.D. 2nd-3rd cent., contains sections on agriculture, worship, feasts, liturgy, rites, domestic relations, and litigation. The Gemara has two versions, the shorter one of the Palestinian Jews and the longer, more authoritative version of the Babylonian community; it is a commentary on the Mishnah. Both versions, in Aramaic dialects, were composed before the end of the 5th cent.

Talon, Jean Baptiste, *c.*1625-94, first administrator of New France, b. France. As intendant, 1665-8 and 1670-2, he promoted shipbuilding, lumbering, trade, and agriculture. Much new land was opened to an increasing tide of immigration.

talus, an accumulation of rock rubble at the base of a weathered cliff or the slope established by this material. Talus slopes are generally quite steep, since the angle of repose of debris is high. If cementation of a talus occurs before chemical weathering (see *weathering*) has changed it to soil, a breccia (*q.v.*) is formed.

tamarack—see *larch*.

tamarind, ornamental leguminous tree (*Tamarindus indica*) grown throughout the tropics for the sugary pulp which surrounds the seeds. The pods and bark are used medicinally, while the leaves yield a yellow coloring matter. The tree is planted also for shade.

tamarisk, evergreen tree or shrub (*Tamarix gallica*) which has feathery branches with minute leaves and tiny white or pale pink flowers. This graceful Old World species has been planted widely as an ornamental, but in SW states of the U.S. it has become a serious pest, dominating many thousands of acres of moist, fertile rangeland.

tambourine, a musical instrument of the percussion family, consisting of a ring or hoop of wood or metal over which is stretched a single head of parchment; in addition, the hoop carries several pairs of loose corrugated metal discs which jingle when the instrument is struck. Of oriental origin, the tambourine is much used by the peasants of Spain and Italy. It is played by means of striking it with the hand, fist, or elbow, by shaking, or by drawing the fingers along the drum head and jingling the discs manually. The tambourine is a standard percussion instrument (*q.v.*) in the modern symphony orchestra. Two well-known variations are the tabor, a small drum beaten with a stick, and used as accompaniment to a pipe or fife, and the timbrel or tabret, much the same as the tambourine.

Tamerlane or **Timur,** 1336?-1405, Mongol conqueror, b. near Samarkand; the name is from Timur Leng ("Timur the Lame"). A descendant of Genghis Khan, he succeeded his father as chief of the Turkish tribe of the Berlas. Conquering the rival tribes of Turkestan, he established his capital at Samarkand, 1370. By 1392 he had conquered Persia and a considerable part of Russia; in 1398 he began his invasion of India and, after destroying Delhi, advanced as far south as the Ganges. His next campaign involved a successful war with the Ottoman Turks in Asia Minor. He died during an invasion of China. Remembered for his cruelty, Tamerlane is said to have built pyramids with the skulls of thousands mercilessly slaughtered in captive cities. He was also a patron of the arts and sciences.

Tamil language—see *Dravidian languages*.

Tammany Hall, New York City political organization. In the post-Revolutionary period several so-called Tammany societies—fraternal groups named for a Delaware Indian chief, Tamanend or Tammany, noted for his wisdom and love of liberty—formed in Eastern cities. The New York Tammany Society, or Columbian Order, was incorporated, 1789, by William Mooney. It affected Indian titles and rituals, and met in a hall called the Wigwam. Exploited politically first by Aaron Burr, 1800, in support of Jeffersonian Democrats against the Federalists, it gradually developed into the chief organization of the Democratic Party in New York City, often championing the underprivileged. In the 1840s and '50s, with the great increase in immigration from Europe, Tammany district leaders helped the foreign-born and, in return, secured their votes. But with power came corruption. Through the notorious William M. Tweed (*q.v.*)

This Thomas Nast cartoon, captioned "The *Tammany* Tiger is Loose—What are you going to do about it?" was published in *Harper's* during the 1871 election campaign in New York City. Earlier, Tammany Boss Tweed, in the face of mass denunciations, had sneered, "What are you going to do about it?" The answer: Tammany lost the election and Tweed was indicted for grand larceny.

and his cronies Tammany defrauded the city of millions. Its power broken by Samuel Tilden in 1872, Tammany Hall revived in the early 1880s under "Honest John" Kelly, who was succeeded by Richard Croker and Charles F. Murphy, its leader from 1902. Murphy eventually succeeded in making his Tammany protégé, Alfred E. Smith, governor of New York. After the death of Murphy, 1924, Tammany bosses lacked the power of their predecessors. Scandals during the Tammany mayoralty of James J. Walker resulted in reform city administrations, 1933-45, under Fiorello H. La Guardia. Tammany Hall lost patronage and power, but continued as a local political force during some subsequent mayoralties. It received a damaging blow in 1961, when reform forces led by Mayor Robert F. Wagner defeated major Tammany Hall candidates in the Democratic primary election.

Tammuz—see *Adonis*.

Tampa, city, co. seat of Hillsborough co., W Florida, on Tampa Bay; pop. 274,970. The 2nd largest city in Florida, Tampa is a resort, and from the beautiful harbor are shipped chiefly canned grapefruit, phosphate rock, and the cigars made in Tampa's Ybor City district; there are also diversified industries. Fort Brooke, built 1823 by U.S. forces, was the nucleus of Tampa.

Tampere, city on Lake Näse, Häme co., SW Finland; pop. 121,422. It is the 2nd largest city in Finland.

Tampico, city, Tamaulipas state, NE Mexico; pop. 134,204. Founded c.1554, it is an important port on the Gulf of Mexico. It expanded rapidly after the discovery of oil, c.1900, much of the population being foreign until the expropriation of foreign-owned lands by the Mexican government. Oil is refined here. The city was captured, 1846, by U.S. troops in the Mexican War, and by the French in 1862.

Tamsui—see *Tansui*.

tanager, any bird of the American family Thraupidae, found chiefly in the tropics. Tanagers are brilliantly colored; the male scarlet tanager, one of the two species found in eastern U.S., is the most vivid birds of that region. Though a com-

The scarlet *tanager*

mon summer resident there, it is partial to leafy forest trees and is seldom seen by those who do not know its song.

Tanaka, Giichi, Baron, 1863-1929, Japanese general and government official. As prime minister, 1927-9, he advocated military intervention in Chinese affairs. He is said to have prepared the **Tanaka Memorial,** a document published 1927, which outlined Japan's dreams of conquest. Although thought by many to have been a forgery, the memorial nevertheless expressed the sentiment of many Japanese.

Tananarive or **Antananarivo,** capital of the Malagasy Republic (Madagascar), in the central part of the island; pop. 210,000. There is a university. Much meat canning is done here, and there are other industries.

Tancred, c.1078-1112, Norman crusader. Departing with his uncle Bohemund I on the First Crusade, 1096-9, he played a brilliant role in the siege of Antioch, 1098, and capture of Bethlehem and Jerusalem, 1099. He was later prince of Galilee and governor of Edessa.

Taney, Roger Brooke, 1777-1864, U.S. jurist, b. Calvert co., Md. A Federalist in the Maryland legislature from 1816, he supported the Presidential campaign of Democratic Andrew Jackson, 1824, and was Attorney General in Jackson's cabinet, 1831-3. Jackson then appointed him Secretary of the Treasury, but the Senate, opposing Jackson's plan to remove federal funds from the Bank of the U.S., refused to confirm the appointment. Jackson then appointed Taney to the Supreme Court. The Senate again refused confirmation, but in Mar. 1836 a new Senate confirmed his nomination as Chief Justice of the Supreme Court, to which post he was nominated on the death of John Marshall, and in which he served until his death. He came from a slaveowning family and on the Court stood firm for states' rights and the Fugitive Slave Law, denying the right of free-soil states to refuse to surrender slaves, and he was author of the opinion in the famous Dred Scott Case (*q.v.*). Taney also ruled against Lincoln's suspension of the writ of habeas corpus during the Civil War.

T'ang, dynasty of China (618-907), founded by Li Yüan; capital, Changyan (*q.v.*). The T'ang emperors controlled large areas in the north,

This pottery horse made during the *T'ang* Dynasty is decorated with rare blue glaze and touches of red paint on the saddle.

TANGANYIKA

including Manchuria and Korea, and regions westward as far as the Caspian Sea. Known as the golden age of Chinese culture, the T'ang period is celebrated especially for the perfection of its poetry, sculpture, and painting. Printing from movable blocks was invented, commerce flourished, and China became a world culture and trade center. Confucianism became the state religion. Decline began in the mid-8th. cent., and collapse, 907, began a period of strife that was ended by emergence of the Sung dynasty.

Tanganyika, an independent republic and member of the British Commonwealth, until Dec. 1961; a British United Nations trust territory, E Africa, on Indian Ocean; area 362,688 sq. mi., of which

The flag of *Tanganyika*

19,982 sq. mi. are water; pop. 9,238,000; capital Dar-es-Salaam. Partly surrounded by Lakes Victoria, Tanganyika, and Nyasa, Tanganyika rises to Mt. Kilimanjaro (19,565 ft.), highest peak of

Above is Dar-es-Salaam ("Haven of Peace"), the capital of *Tanganyika* and a major seaport. Within the area of the Rufiji basin is the Little Ruaha River, below, which flows past Iringia into the Great Ruaha River.

British Information Services

British Information Services

Tribal chieftains and their followers gather to celebrate the opening of a new bridge across *Tanganyika's* Wami River. It will replace a ferry system and eliminate the danger of attacks from crocodiles.

Africa. Agriculture is the dominant occupation, chief exports being sisal (of which Tanganyika produces half the world's supply), peanuts, rice, cotton, and coffee. Gold and diamonds are found, and timber, hides, and skins produced. The region was controlled by Arabs, then by the Portuguese, 16th-17th cent. In 1885 the colony of German East Africa was established. After heavy fighting in World War I, the German colony was divided into Ruanda-Urundi and Tanganyika. Britain administered the latter from 1920 under a League of Nations mandate and from 1946 under a U.N. trusteeship. The native population is composed of more than 100 tribes; Bantus are predominant. German law had decreed freedom for every native born after 1905, but a mild serfdom was in effect. Legislation in 1926 aimed at the abolition of slavery. First territorial elections were held in 1958. Through a customs union (1927), Tanganyika, Kenya, and

Uganda are virtually a single trade unit. There are close economic ties with Nyasaland and Katanga province, the Congo.

Tanganyika, Lake, 12,700 sq. mi., E Africa, forming the Tanganyika-Congo border. 2nd largest lake of Africa, it is up to 4700 ft. deep. It was discovered, 1858, by John Speke and Sir Richard Burton. The famous meeting between Stanley and Livingstone took place here, near Kigoma, 1871. Chief ports are Kigoma, Tanganyika, and Albertville, Congo, connected by steamer service.

tangent—see *circle*.

tangerine—see *orange*.

Tangier, seaport, former chief city of the Tangier international zone, Morocco, on Strait of Gibraltar; area *c*.145 sq. mi.; pop. 141,926. The city was the most important of the region until the 9th cent. It changed hands several times, 15th-17th cent., and in 1925 became an international zone. The Spanish controlled it, 1940-5, then international control was restored until the establishment of the sovereign kingdom of Morocco, 1956. The city is a trading center, with businesses clustered at the waterfront.

tank, armored, turreted, heavily gunned vehicle for offensive warfare. Manufactured in secrecy, they were first introduced by the British during the battle of the Somme (Sept. 1916). However, it was not until the attack at Cambria (Nov. 1917) that they achieved their first important success. In that battle 378 tanks were deployed on a seven-mile front, followed closely by six infantry divisions. They were designed especially for attack against machine guns, barbed wire, and trenches, which could be surmounted by a caterpillar-tracked vehicle. Tanks of World War II were more commonly fitted with wheels inside the caterpillar treads for more speed in open-country warfare. They were used somewhat like cavalry by Nazi Germany in the rapid over-running of Europe, 1939-42, and great tank battles later took place between the Allies and Germans following the invasions of North Africa and Europe. Modern tanks, 25 to 80 tons in weight, have 1-5 inches of armor, carry guns up to 90-, 105- and 120-mm caliber and travel at *c*.40 m.p.h. Effective on open ground against light defenses, they are vulnerable to such counterweapons as aircraft, the tank destroyer, flame-throwers, recoilless anti-tank weapons, and the infantryman's bazooka. See *armor*.

Tanks being manufactured in England, 1941

Tannenberg, village, NE Poland, *c*.75 mi. S of Königsberg (now called Kaliningrad), formerly in East Prussia, Germany. Here in 1410 the Teutonic Knights were defeated by the Poles and Lithuanians, and in Aug. 1914 the Russians were beaten by the Germans under Hindenburg in one of the decisive battles of World War I.

tanning, process by which leather is made from skins of animals. Its purpose is to make the hides more pliable and decay-resistant. In vegetable tanning the process depends upon the action of tannic acid upon the skin, and the tannins used are from oak, hemlock, willow, sumac, divi-divi, etc. Chromium salts are used in making chrome leather, a highly resistant material, while alum is the tanning agent in another process. Oil tanning is used in making chamois leather to give the required soft, supple character.

Tannu Tuva—see *Tuva Autonomous Region*.

Tansui, one of the ports of Taipeh (*q.v.*), on the N Coast of Formosa; pop. 10,000. It was the site of several combats between the Chinese and the French, 1884. It is important because of its trade with Hong Kong.

Tanta, city, N Egypt, in Nile Delta; pop. 175,400. A communications center for the delta region, it has annual Moslem festivals with many visitors.

tantalum, element no. 73 (sym. *Ta.*; at. wt. 180.88; m.p. 2850°C; sp. gr. 16.6), a lustrous, white

The Italian medium-weight *tank* at left was relied upon heavily by the Axis forces during the North African campaign in World War II. At right is the Mark IV, a famous British weapon, one of those which initiated the era of warfare based on mechanized, armored vehicles.

TANTALUS

metal discovered by Ekeberg, 1802, in rare Scandinavian ores. It offers great resistance to corrosion and is easily worked. It is used in surgery as the only metal on which flesh will grow, and for electrodes of high-vacuum tubes.

Tantalus, in Greek legend, a son of Zeus who was often disrespectful of the gods. Once he boiled his own son, Pelops, and served him to the gods to test their knowledge. As punishment for his misdeeds, Tantalus was made perpetually thirsty and hungry, then set in a cool lake, the waters of which receded whenever he stooped to drink, while above him fruit-laden branches forever eluded his grasp. He was thus the first to be *tantalized.*

Taoism, religion of China. Its doctrine is based on the *Tao-teh-king,* attributed to the 6th-cent. B.C. philosopher Lao-tze (*q.v.*) but probably written 3rd cent. This work, anticipating some of the pantheism of Spinoza, advocated a nonstriving, quietistic approach to life, with acceptance of the natural order. Release from the bondage of

The enameled statuette at right, is of Kuan-ti, *Taoist* god of war. At left is a 16th-cent. portrayal of the god Lan Ts'ain-ho, one of the Eight Immortals.

human life was to be found by substitution of mystic contemplation for desire and worldly ambition. By A.D. 5th cent. Taoism was a full-fledged polytheistic religion with acquired Buddhist elements; it soon established itself as chief rival to Confucianism. Taoism is still the major religious tradition of China.

Taormina, resort town, NE Sicily, on Mediterranean Sea near the foot of Etna volcano, *c.*25 mi. SW of Messina; pop. 6521. On its coastal escarpment it occupies a site famed for beauty and ancient ruins. The mild climate attracts winter visitors. Taormina dates from ancient Greek times.

Taos, village, co. seat of Taos co., N New Mexico, at base of Sangre de Cristo Mts.; pop. 2163. Settled by the Spanish, early 17th cent., it was the center of the Pueblo revolt of 1680. It has been an art center since the 1880s, attracting D. H. Lawrence and other notable writers and painters. Nearby are an Indian village, San Gerónimo de Taos, and the old Indian farming center, Ranchos de Taos.

tapa—see *bark cloth.*

Tapajós River, *c.*500 mi. long, rising in N Brazil. Created by the junction of the Juruena and São Manuel Rivers, it flows NE to the Amazon.

Along it rubber plantations have been set up.

tape recording—see *sound recording.*

tapestry, heavy hand-woven textile, especially any type of heavy machine-made fabrics used as wall hangings, carpets, or furniture covering. True tapestries are reversible, both sides having the

The weaving of tapestries reached a peak of craftsmanship in the 1500s. Above is a silken tapestry entitled "Pastorale," woven in France. Below is a detail of a tapestry depicting the French king Louis XIV at Dunkirk.

same kind of surface. The wool or linen warp threads provide a strong backing for the soft weft threads of silk, wool, or metal which form the pattern. The so-called Bayeux (*q.v.*) tapestry is actually a work of embroidery. Among the

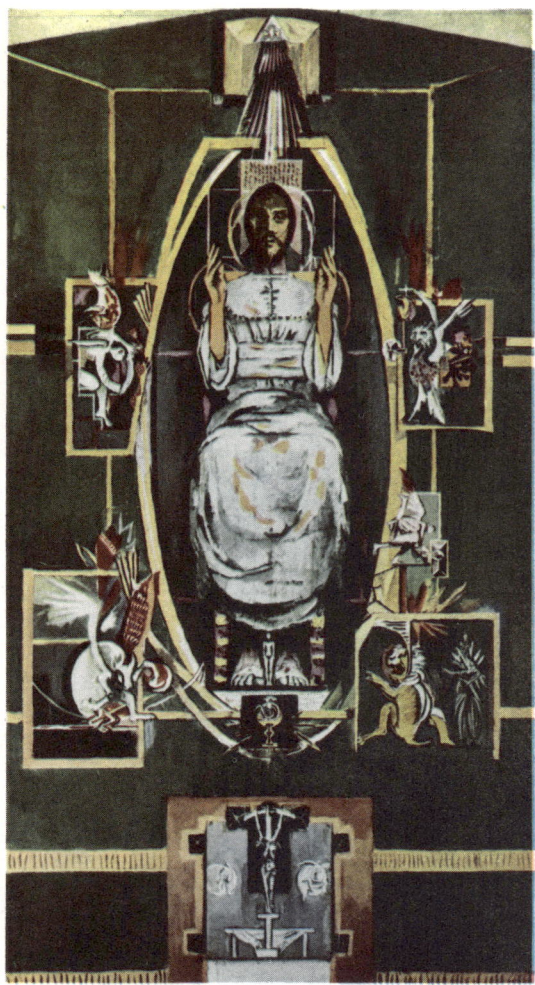

This is the design for the largest *tapestry* in the world. Measuring 75 feet high and 38 feet wide, it was designed by Graham Sutherland and will hang behind the High Altar of the Coventry Cathedral, England. Byzantine in style and subject, it is entitled "Christ in Glory" (see *New Testament*).

The 20th-cent. French *tapestry* above is called "The Salamander" because of the tiny reptile at bottom center. The modernistic design below was designed by Pablo Picasso in the 1930s. It is titled "Confidence."

Hunt of The Unicorn now in the Cloisters in New York City. The Philadelphia Museum of Art houses a Gobelin tapestry valued at $50,000, depicting U.S. troops departing for World War I; it was a gift of the French government. Many contemporary artists, including Miró and Picasso, have designed tapestries. The art has seen a revival in France since World War II, spearheaded by Lurçat.

earliest tapestries, some of which are extant, are those made by the ancient Egyptians and the Chinese. In the early 14th cent., Arras in France became known as a great wool-weaving center but was soon rivaled by Brussels. In the early 17th cent. the Gobelin (*q.v.*) family of Paris began producing fine tapestries, and with the further rise of the industry at Beauvais and Aubusson, France became the dominant producer of the highly prized textile. Many of the more famous European tapestries were woven as copies of cartoons or paintings done by well-known artists. Raphael's cartoons were the basis for the Acts of the Apostles, the famous set of the Renaissance period; François Boucher executed paintings for use by the Gobelin weavers. In England tapestry manufacture began in the 16th cent. Among the most famous tapestries is the 16th-cent. set of six, called *The Lady and The Unicorn*, in the Cluny Museum in Paris. Another set of exquisite workmanship is *The*

tapeworm, any of a number of parasitic flatworms (class Cestoda) inhabiting the intestines of humans. Attaching themselves to the mucous membrane, they absorb nutriment through the skin. The embryos are found in contaminated soil, where they are eaten by some animals. In pigs, the embryo bores through the intestinal wall and is carried to the bloodstream to the muscles, where it forms a cyst. When the meat is inadequately cooked, the tapeworm is transmitted to the human and matures in the intestine, reaching 6 to 9 ft. in length.

tapioca, starchy food derived from the root of the manioc or cassava bush (*Manihot esculenta*), native to tropical America and a staple food source for many millions of people in various tropic lands. The roots, poisonous before processing, are harvested by hand, crushed, and boiled. Starch separates from the mash and rises to the top, forming small clumps which are dried to form tapioca.

tapir, ungulate mammal (genus *Tapirus*) of the order Perissodactyla, found in Central and South America, Sumatra, and Malaya. On the front feet there are four digits, on the hind feet, three.

A shy, nocturnal animal, inhabiting forest regions near water, it is vegetarian in diet. The body, like a pig's, has short legs and short tail; the snout is prolonged into a proboscis. The skin is dark brown or black. The Malayan species has a band of white about its middle and reaches a shoulder height of 3½ ft.

tar, dark brown or black viscid liquid with a peculiar aromatic odor, obtained when wood, coal (see *coal tar*), or similar substances are subjected to destructive distillation. It is variable in composition. By distillation coal tar yields numerous substances of great importance in industry, as benzene, toluene, xylene, a naphthalene, anthracene, and phenol. Tar is used also as a protective coating for wood and iron, and for road making.

Taranto, city and naval base, Apulia region, S Italy, on Gulf of Taranto, an embayment of the Mediterranean between Italy's "toe" and "heel," c.45 mi. SSE of Bari; pop. 180,500. Here are important shipyards and a naval arsenal. Fishing is the leading industry. Taranto, ancient Tarentum, was founded by the Greeks and was one of the richest cities on the Mediterranean until partly destroyed by the Romans, 3rd cent. B.C. Here the Italian fleet was bottled up through much of World War II. The city was heavily bombed by the British, 1940.

tarantula, any of various large spiders of the tropics and warm temperate regions. The American kinds belong to the family Aviculariidae. The bite of most species is no worse than that of a bee; a few are dangerously poisonous.

Tarawa, atoll, central Pacific Ocean, one of the Gilbert Islands; area 8.7 sq. mi.; pop. 3848. On it is the capital and business center of the British colony of the Gilbert and Ellice Islands. Occupied early in World War II by Japanese, it was regained by U.S. Marines after a heavy 4-day battle, Nov. 1943.

Tarbell, Ida Minerva, 1857-1944, U.S. journalist, b. Pennsylvania. One of the "muckrakers" who in *McClure's Magazine* exposed abuses in industry, finance, and politics, she collected some of these pieces in her *History of the Standard Oil Company* (1904). She wrote a *Life of Abraham Lincoln* (1900) and biographies of Elbert H. Gary (1925) and Owen D. Young (1932).

Tardieu, André, 1876-1945, French statesman and writer. Elected to the chamber of deputies, 1914, he became close to Clemenceau, supporting him during the Paris Peace Conference, 1919, and later opposing revisions of the Versailles Treaty which increased the power of Germany. A conservative and nationalist, he was a member of several cabinets and premier twice, 1929-30, 1932.

tare—see *vetch*.

tariff, duty or tax imposed on shipments of goods. In the U.S., as in Great Britain, there is tariff only on imports, none on exports. It is collected by the federal government through custom houses and agents. If the tariff is imposed to raise revenue, it is usually small. If it is a protective tariff, imposed to aid home industries by raising the price of foreign goods to a level more favorable to domestic competition, it may be very high. Tariffs have often caused—and have been a means of waging—bitter trade wars.

Protective tariffs have been a source of frequent controversy in the U.S. This 1905 cartoon satirized the conservative opposition to President Theodore Roosevelt's attempts to reduce tariff barriers and to promote free trade among the nations of the world.

Customs duties have been known at least since ancient Greece. Tariffs imposed on colonial goods were one of the causes of the American Revolution. After the war Alexander Hamilton advocated a protective tariff to assist new industries in the U.S., and Congress passed a tariff as early as 1789. As home industries developed, there was further agitation for protection. The result was the high tariff of 1828, dubbed the "Tariff of Abominations" because it was so hated; it was a cause of the nullification (*q.v.*) movement. In 1832 these high rates were abandoned. Subsequent history of the tariff in the U.S. was one of high rates under national administrations interested more in business expansion than in immediate advantages of low prices on imported goods. After the Civil War the Republicans became identified as the high-tariff party, and after World War I Republican protectionism reached its peak in the Fordney-McCumber Act of 1922 and the Hawley-Smoot Tariff of 1930—the latter so severe as to cause strong retaliation by some foreign countries. In 1931 Great Britain, abandoning its long-established policy, imposed high protective duties. With the growth of intense nationalism, many other countries enacted protective tariffs. The World Economic Conference of 1933 in London failed to reduce tariff barriers. In 1934 the F. D. Roosevelt administration in the U.S. initiated tariff-reciprocity agreements with several foreign countries. The U.S. Tariff Commission, established 1916, is the principal government agency concerned with proposing and executing tariff legislation in the U.S. Its powers were enlarged by the F. D. Roosevelt and Truman administrations. After World War II, the General Agreement on Tariffs and Trade (GATT) was worked out, consisting of a series of bilateral agreements covering more than 50,000 commodities. Gradually developed from 1947, GATT came to cover about 80% of total world trade, providing substantial reductions in tariffs. While the U.S. Congress failed to ratify U.S. membership in GATT, presidential powers permitted the U.S. to adhere to it in principle. Further tariff reductions came about from 1958-59, with the development of the European Economic Union (Common Market) and the European Free Trade Association. Member countries embarked on a program of gradual abolition of tariffs on trade between them, over a ten-year period. Britain's move in 1961 to join the Common Market presaged eventual inclusion of most of Western Europe, and perhaps other countries as well, in a common free-trade area. Similar free-trade areas were opened in Central and South America in 1960.

Tarim River, *c.*1250 mi. long. Sinkiang province, W China. Formed by the union of two streams it flows to the marshy region of Lop Nor.

Tarkington, Booth (Newton Booth Tarkington), 1869-1946, U.S. author, b. Indianapolis. He achieved success with *The Gentleman from Indiana* (1899) and many other popular mellow novels of Midwestern life, including *The Magnificent Ambersons* (1918; Pulitzer Prize, 1919) and *Alice Adams* (1921; Pulitzer Prize, 1922). His entertaining stories of boys and girls include *Penrod* (1914), *Seventeen* (1916), and *Gentle Julia* (1922). Many of his novels were drama-

This illustration is from Booth *Tarkington*'s most widely read novel, *Penrod*, published in 1914, which recounts humorously the adventures of a young boy in midwestern U.S.

tized either by himself or by others.

Tarleton, Sir Banastre, 1754-1833, British soldier. He enlisted in the British army on the outbreak of the American Revolution and, after serving under Cornwallis, Clinton, and Howe in the North, was placed in command of the British Legion (a mixed force of cavalry and infantry) in the South. His stealthy, bloody raids (1780-1) earned him the special hatred of the colonials, who, under Morgan, finally routed him at Cowpens, Jan. 1781. Returning to England (1782), he was elected to Parliament where he served from 1790-1806 and from 1807-12.

taro, Asiatic tropical herb (*Colocasia esculenta*) cultivated extensively in warm regions for its edible starchy tubers. One indication of its popularity is the fact that there are *c.*1000 horticultural varieties. The plant is also called dasheen, and in Hawaii, the famous poi is made from it. Taro belongs in the same genus as the ornamental elephant's-ear.

Tarpeia, in Roman legend, daughter of the commander of the citadel atop the Capitoline Hill in the reign of Romulus. The Sabine soldiers attacking the hill promised her golden bracelets for opening the gate, but instead crushed her beneath their shields. The Tarpeian rock on the Capitoline, from which the Romans threw criminals to their death, was named after her.

tarpon, marine fish (*Tarpon atlanticus*) related to the herrings but forming a family of its own (Megalopidae). Abundant in Gulf Coast waters, it often weighs 200 lb. The body is elongated and covered with large silvery scales. It affords good sport to anglers; within its range, natives prize it as food.

Tarquin, name of two kings of ancient Rome, whose reigns are known only through legend. Lucius Tarquinius Priscus, fifth king of Rome,

TARRAGONA

was of Etruscan origin; during his reign, 616-579 B.C., the temple of the Capitoline Triad was begun. His son, Lucius Tarquinius Superbus (Tarquin the Proud), killed his predecessor, Servius Tullius, to become seventh king of Rome. When his son Sextus seduced the matron Lucretia, who killed herself after revealing the event to her husband, Tarquin and his sons were driven from Rome, and a republic was established. The tale, the theme of Shakespeare's *Rape of Lucrece,* probably reflects a historic Roman revolt against Etruscan domination.

Tarragona, Mediterranean seaport, Catalonia, NE Spain, capital of Tarragona province, c.50 mi. SW of Barcelona; pop. 36,807. Renowned for wines, it produces flour, silk, and tobacco. Chartreuse liquor is now made here and Tarragon vinegar was first made in this province. Landmarks are a cathedral, an archiepiscopal palace, and a Roman aqueduct. The ancient city of Tarraco was the capital of the extensive Roman province of Tarraconensis. Later it passed to the Visigoths and Moors. It was reconquered, 1089. During the Peninsular War it was sacked by the French, 1811.

Tar River, rising in N North Carolina and flowing SE into an estuary known as the Pamlico River. Together they are c.215 mi. long.

Tarrytown, residential village, SE New York, on Hudson River; pop. 11,109. Settled by the Dutch, 17th cent., it was the home of Washington Irving, who wrote of the neighborhood. Adjacent Irvington is named for him. Maj. André, the British spy, was captured here 1780. A bridge over the Hudson was built here in the 1950s and it is a major junction point on the New York and New England thruway systems. Marymount College for women is here.

Tarsus, town, S Turkey, on Tarsus River (called the Cydnus in ancient times); pop. 24,400. Now a trade center for an agricultural and mining region, it was important in ancient times as capital of Cilicia. The ruins of the ancient Tarsus cover a large area. Saint Paul was born here.

tartan—see *plaid.*

Tartars—see *Tatars.*

Tartarus, in Greek mythology, the realm where the shades of the wicked spent eternity. It was usually identified as a separate walled portion of the underworld, but sometimes was used as a synonym for Hades, and by Homer was described as far below Hades.

Tashkent, capital of the Uzbek Soviet Socialist Republic, Soviet central Asia; pop. 911,000. An oasis city, it produces irrigated crops of cotton, silk, fruit, and vegetables. There are factories, with cotton textile industries and food processing. A university, museums, libraries, theaters, and technical schools are here. Founded and ruled by Arabs, 7th-12th cent., Tashkent was taken by Genghis Khan, 13th cent., and Tamerlane, 14th cent. The Russians captured it, 1865. It became capital of the Uzbek Soviet Socialist Republic, 1930, succeeding Samarkand.

Tasman, Abel Janszoon, 1603-59, Dutch navigator. On the most important of his expeditions for the Dutch East India Co., in 1642-3, he discovered Tasmania (named after him) and New Zealand, and by sailing around Australia proved it a separate continent.

Tasmania, island S of Australia, between Indian Ocean and Tasman Sea; area 26,215 sq. mi.; pop. 342,315; capital Hobart; other cities Launceston, Burnie, and Stanley. Together with many smaller nearby islands, Tasmania constitutes a state of the Commonwealth of Australia.

The Derwent River in *Tasmania,* flows southeast from New Norfolk to the Tasmanian Sea.

The island is mountainous but generally fertile and is known for scenic beauty. Its varied mineral resources include copper, zinc, coal, and gold. Fruit growing, stock raising, and dairying are economically important. The island was named Van Diemen's Land by Tasman, who discovered it 1642. Visited by Capt. James Cook, 1777, it was annexed by the British, 1803, and made a prison island which was attached to New South Wales. It became a separate colony, 1825, and was federated, 1901, as one of the states of the Commonwealth of Australia. The aboriginal Tasmanians are now entirely extinct.

Tasman Sea, part of the S Pacific Ocean bounded E by New Zealand and W by Tasmania and SE Australia. It is c.1200 mi. wide.

Tassigny, Jean Joseph Marie Gabriel de Lattre de, 1889-1952, French general. In World War II he held the Germans in his sector until Pétain asked for an armistice. Escaping, he joined General de Gaulle in North Africa, became commander of all French forces there, and, upon the Allied invasion of France, was put in command of the French 1st Army and the U.S. 36th Division. He assumed the French command in Indo-China against Communist forces in 1951.

Tasso, Torquato, 1544-95, Italian poet, b. Sorrento. Son of a poet and courtier, he grew up in a cultured environment. He served the Este family at Ferrara, but frequent lapses into insanity caused him to wander over Italy from court to court. His work includes the beautiful pastoral play *Aminta* and his immortal epic *Jerusalem Delivered,* which deals with the First Crusade. Tasso was summoned to Rome to be crowned poet laureate, but died before the ceremony could take place.

taste, that one of the five senses which distinguishes flavors. It is closely associated with the sense of smell. The papillae, or taste buds, on the tongue and soft palate are chemically affected by the stimuli (*i.e.* flavors of food), so that nervous impulses are transmitted to the brain and there identified as taste sensations. The basic tastes are classified as sour, sweet, bitter, and salty.

Tatar Autonomous Soviet Socialist Republic, E central European Russia, in Volga and Kama River valleys; area *c.*26,000 sq. mi.; pop. 2,847,000; capital Kazan. In this rich grain-producing region, with large forests, about half the people are of Turko-Tatar origin. Bulgars occupied it from the 5th cent.; then the Mongols took it, 1236. It was a Tatar khanate when Ivan the Terrible seized it, 1552. It was created a Soviet autonomous republic, 1920.

Tatars or **Tartars,** originally a people inhabiting E central Asia and speaking a Turkic language. They became assimilated and identified with the Mongols after the conquests of the Mongol leader Genghis Khan, 13th cent., so that great Mongol invasions themselves were often called Tatar invasions. The Tatar empire of the Golden

One of the most colorful of all *Tatar* leaders was Tamarlane, who claimed to be a direct descendant of Genghis Khan. In this Moslem painting, a conquered Sultan appears before Tamerlane, thought of as a cruel conqueror.

Horde (*q.v.*), flourishing 13th-15th cent., encompassed most of Russia. Meanwhile Islam was embraced as the popular religion. With the decline of the empire, the area split into several khanates which eventually came under Russian and Turkish control. Crimea, the last Tatar state, was joined to Russia, 1783. Today many Tatars live in the Tatar Autonomous Soviet Socialist Republic, but the majority are dispersed over other parts of Russia.

Tate, Allen—see *regionalism*.
Tate Gallery, London, opened 1897 as the National Gallery of British Art. Its nucleus was a collection of then modern British paintings given by Sir Henry Tate. The collection includes many fine works by Turner, Sargent, and other British and American artists, and is especially well known for its gallery of modern European art.
tattooing, practice of indelibly coloring the skin by inserting pigment beneath the surface. It is found among primitive light-skinned peoples, especially

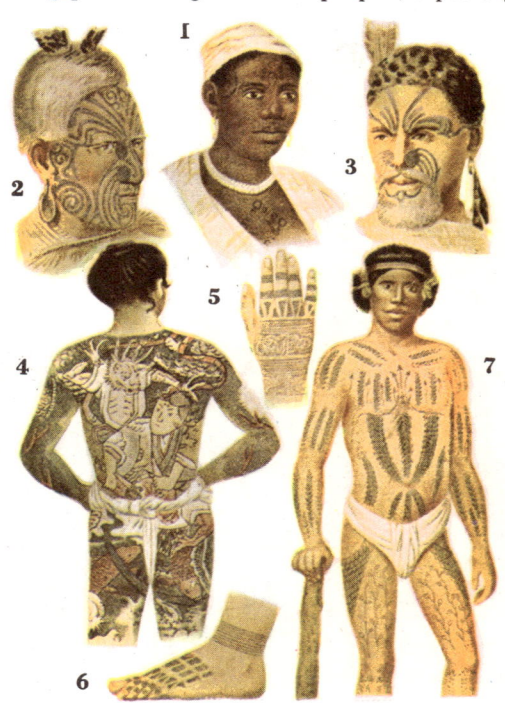

These *tattoos* are on: 1. a Sudanese Negro woman; 2 & 3. Maoris of New Zealand; 4. a Caroline Islander; 5. & 6. hand and foot of a Dyak of Borneo; 7. a Japanese.

in Oceania, where the coloring is usually produced by charcoal pricked into the flesh. The Maori were noted for the quality of their tattooed designs. Tattooing has been adopted by individuals, especially sailors, of more advanced cultures, modern pigments being introduced by an electric needle. Primarily ornamental, tattooing also carries prestige.
Taunton, municipal borough and co. town of Somersetshire, SW England, on Tone River; pop. 35,178. It is the center for a flourishing agricultural area and produces woolen and leather goods. The Saturday market dates from before the Norman Conquest. Its ancient castle, dismantled at the Restoration, is now a museum.
Taunus, mountain range, Hesse state, Western Germany, in a bend of the Rhine and along the lower Main N of Frankfurt. It is *c.*55 mi. long and rises in places to *c.*2880 ft. (Grosser Feldberg). It is celebrated for its ruined castles, vineyards, and spas, among them Bad Homburg and Wiesbaden.
Taurus, the Bull; second sign of the zodiac (*q.v.*) which the sun enters about Apr. 20th, containing two well-known clusters, the Pleiades and the Hyades. See *constellation; ecliptic*.
Taurus Mts., range, S Turkey, paralleling Mediterranean coast and rising to 12,251 ft. at Ala Dag. In a spur of the Taurus proper is Erciyas Dag (the ancient Mt. Argaeus), 12,848 ft.,

highest peak of Asia Minor. Transecting the range north of Tarsus is the famous pass of the Cilician Gates, used for centuries by traders and invading armies. The Taurus range is continued in the northeast by the Anti-Taurus.

Taussig, Frank William, 1859-1940, U.S. economist, b. St. Louis. Long a teacher at Harvard, he was an adherent of the Classical School of economics as expounded in his *Principles of Economics* (1911). He was also chairman of the U.S. Tariff Commission, 1917-9.

taxation, practice of raising money from a people to maintain the state. Payment is compulsory, and the amount paid by a taxpayer is not usually proportionate to the services he receives from the government. Taxes are generally levied according to ability to pay, irrespective of benefits obtained. The execution of this policy is difficult, since an absolute criterion for ability is wanting.

The ancient Romans also *taxed* subject nations heavily, as suggested by this illustration for the Biblical passage: "And it came to pass . . . that there went out a decree from Caesar Augustus that all the world should be taxed."

Taxation is one of the oldest of governmental institutions. These panels found in the ancient Persian city of Persepolis portray tax-bearers from nations subject to the rule of the Persian emperor Darius in the 5th cent. B.C.

A direct tax is one imposed immediately on the individual, *e.g.* income tax. Indirect taxes are those imposed on commodities or services (*e.g.* liquor tax or amusement tax), the tax being paid originally by the producer, who then adds it to the price of his product and thus reimburses himself from the public. It is an accepted axiom of liberal politics that if a person is taxed he should also be represented in the legislature. Violation of this principle hastened the outbreak of the American Revolution. Today in the U.S. taxes range all the way from the federal to the municipal level. In private enterprise economies, businesses are usually taxed, as well as individuals. Since the rate on business income is usually less onerous than that on personal income, individuals in high brackets find it profitable in many instances to incorporate themselves. Taxes on capital gains are more modest generally than those on income, with the result that financial strategists often advise clients to seek the former and shun the latter. Distinctions, as in the U.S., between long-term (over six months) and short-term (under six months) capital gains, with tax rates favoring the former, also may determine financial strategies. Certain categories of investments, such as municipal bonds, are tax exempt. Medical and other deductible expenses may be so staggered fiscally that the individual maximizes tax advantages. Business expense accounts, a flexible concept in practice, are not taxable. Non-profit organizations are not taxed, or only lightly. These various considerations have lead in modern times to the proliferation of tax experts and advisers, tax manuals, costly cases leading to multitudes of tax decisions, and elaborate machinery for tax assessment, enforcement, and legislation. See *excess profits tax; excise; income tax; Internal Revenue, Bureau of; land tax; poll tax; sales tax; single tax; tariff.*

Taxco, city, Guerrero state, SW Mexico; pop. 10,025. It became important, 18th cent., as a silver-mining center. The unspoiled Spanish colonial architecture of the city and its famous silversmiths attract many tourists and artists, particularly Americans. The Mexican government maintains the town virtually as a museum, rigidly controlling all improvements and construction to prevent alteration of the town's colonial character.

taxidermy, preparation and preservation of the skins of animals. The process was introduced in the 16th cent. to answer the demands of sportsmen. Formerly the skin was stripped with fine knives or scissors and stuffed with tightly packed tow, being made to stand in the desired posture by the judicious use of wire. Today modeling has generally replaced stuffing; a copy of the body is prepared in full anatomical detail and the skin placed around it; or the skin is fitted over a wire or wooden framework.

taxonomy—see *scientific name.*

Taylor, Bayard, 1825-78, U.S. author, b. Kennett Square, Pa. He roved the world as a correspondent for the New York *Tribune,* writing many romantic travel books, including *Views Afoot* (1846). Among his books of poetry are *Ximena* (1844) and *Poems of the Orient* (1854), including the "Bedouin Song." He also made a highly regarded translation of *Faust* (1870-1).

Taylor, Deems (Joseph Deems Taylor), 1885- , U.S. composer and music commentator. Besides songs and other pieces he composed the operas *The King's Henchman* (1927; libretto by Edna St. Vincent Millay), *Peter Ibbetson* (1931) and *The Dragon* (1954). He wrote *Of Men and Music* (1937), *Music To My Ears* (1949), *The One-Track Mind* (1953), and *Some Enchanted Evenings* (1953). He became well known as a radio commentator.

Taylor, Elizabeth (Rosemond), 1932- , U.S. actress, b. London, Eng. Her American parents lived in England where her father had business interests. Just before the outbreak of World War II, her father sent his wife and children to Pasadena, Calif., and later joined them there. Her unusually good singing voice secured her a one-year motion picture contract in 1940, but she made no film appearances. She was later engaged for other films, such as *Lassie Come Home, White Cliffs of Dover,* and *Jane Eyre,* but attracted little attention until her starring role in *National Velvet* (1945). Thereafter she appeared in a series of pictures, making a fairly smooth transition from juvenile to adult roles, including *A Date with Judy* and *Little Women.* Her first major adult role was in *A Place in the Sun* (1951), which established her as one of the best boxoffice attractions in the film industry. She was awarded an Oscar for her performance in *Butterfield 8* (1960).

Taylor, Jeremy, 1613-67, English clergyman. He was chaplain to Charles I and, under Charles II, bishop of Down and Connor. He was noted for his eloquence, and his writings, especially *Holy Living* (1650) and *Holy Dying* (1651), are valued devotional literature.

Taylor, John, 1753-1824, U.S. politician, b. Virginia. U.S. Senator (1792-4, 1803, 1822-4) from Virginia, and a strong supporter of Jefferson, he wrote *An Inquiry into the Principles and Policy of the Government of the United States,* containing one of the first expositions of the doctrine of state sovereignty.

Taylor, Tom, 1817-80, English dramatist. He wrote or adapted more than 100 plays, notably *Our American Cousin* (1858), which was the offering at Ford's Theatre in Washington on the night of Lincoln's attendance and assassination.

Taylor, Zachary, 1784-1850, 12th U.S. President (1849-50), b. Montebello, Va. He joined the army at 24, serving in the War of 1812 and the Black Hawk and Seminole Wars. Ordered to

Texas, 1845, to command the army on the Mexican border, he invaded disputed territory and precipitated war with Mexico. He then won victories at Palo Alto, Resaca de la Palma, and Matamoras. Becoming major general commanding the Army of the Rio Grande, and ignoring Pres. Polk's orders to fight only defensively, he

These entertainers are performing during a fiesta on a rooftop patio in *Taxco,* Mexico. In the background is the town's famed San Sebastian church; elaborately ornamented, it was constructed in the early 1700s and is typical of the Spanish colonial architecture which was wide-spread in Latin America in that period.

Pan American Airways

TAY

advanced to storm Monterrey, Sept. 24, 1946, and at Buena Vista, Feb. 22-3, 1847, defeated Mexican Gen. Santa Anna, ending the war in Northern Mexico, "Old Rough and Ready," as Taylor was called, now the hero of the day, was elected President on the Whig ticket, 1848. Although a Southern planter, he opposed the South in the slavery controversy and argued for admission of California as a free state. His death came after 16 months in office, and Vice Pres. Millard Fillmore succeeded him.

Tay River, 118 mi. long, largest river of Scotland, rising on Ben Lui in Argyllshire and flowing through Perthshire (where it is known as Dochart River) to its estuary, the **Firth of Tay.** The firth, *c.*25 mi. long, opens into the North Sea. Dundee, site of the 2-mi. Tay Bridge, is on its N bank. The river is famous for its salmon.

Tchad—see *Chad, Republic of.*

Tchaikovsky, Peter Ilyich, 1840-93, Russian composer. He composed his first large work in 1865, in 1866 began teaching at the Moscow conservatory, and in 1866 finished the first of his six symphonies. In 1876 he was provided with an annual

A scene from *Tchaikovsky's* "Swan Lake," performed by the Sadler's Wells Ballet in London. First performed in 1876, "Swan Lake" has been an international favorite.

income by a wealthy widow, Mme von Meck, with the stipulation that they should not meet. During the 14 years of this patronage, Tchaikovsky produced many of his major works. He first appeared as conductor in 1887, the next year toured Europe, and in 1891 visited the U.S., inaugurating Carnegie Hall. He wrote his "Pathetique" Symphony in 1893, surviving its performance by only a few days. Though he was not one of "the Five" who furthered Russian naionalist music, his work is Russian in mood and he utilizes some folk-song elements. He was a master melodist and used brilliant orchestral colors. His works include, besides the symphonies, several operas, including *Eugen Onegin* and *Pique Dame;* the orchestral *Romeo and Juliet* overture and *Francesca da Rimini;* the ballets *Swan Lake, Sleeping Beauty,* and *Nutcracker;* a violin and three piano concertos; three string quartets; piano pieces; and songs.

Tchitcherin, George Vasilievitch—see *Chicherin.*

tea, dried terminal leaves of a shrub or small tree, *Thea sinensis,* grown in China for centuries, but known in Europe only since 1645, when the Dutch introduced it. The young leaves are picked,

The *tea*-picker above works in a mountain district of Java, world famous for its quality tea leaves. Only the young leaves at the top of the plant are used. Below are tea-tasters in Mincing Lane, center of London's large wholesale tea trade. These experts rely on smell as well as taste in testing for precise blends.

spread on trays to wither, then passed through rolling machines. The three main varieties are green tea (heated immediately after rolling), black tea (heated after fermentation or oxidation), and oolong (heated after being partially oxidized). Gunpowder tea from China is green,

TECHNOLOGY

and other green tea is widely grown in Japan. Pekoe and orange pekoe from India and Ceylon are black. Oolong comes principally from Formosa.

teachers' college, in the U.S. an institution for training teachers for primary and secondary schools. The first state normal school was opened in Massachusetts, 1839. The earliest normal schools, requiring 2 years of study, were designed primarily for elementary-school teachers, but the growing need for training for the secondary level led to expansion of normal schools into teachers' colleges (requiring 4 years of study) which could provide for both levels of teaching. Today, however, teachers' colleges are less influential than in previous years. Only 24% of elementary and 17% of high school teachers come from teachers colleges, the rest coming from liberal arts colleges. Most teachers' colleges are state-controlled institutions. Educators who have profoundly influenced the development of teacher training in the U.S. have included John Dewey, Horace Mann, and Henry Barnard. Teachers College, 1889, Columbia Univ., is a leading institution.

teaching machines, a name popularly given to various devices developed in the later 1950s and thereafter purporting to replace teachers in programmed instruction of individual students in various subjects, usually such skills as language or mathematics. Most such machines have in common the principles of repetition of subject matter so long as the student fails to understand a point, thus permitting the student to proceed at his own pace. Educators, while applauding the over-all purpose of these machines, criticized many of them for being essentially commercial "gimmicks," making undue claims and often being unnecessarily mechanized. Serious educators found that many of the principles could be adapted and refined without the use of unnecessary gadgetry and to far better results. At the same time they worked on far more complicated machinery that would be useful in education but would be applicable to whole classes rather than to individuals. Developments in this direction seemed to imply the widespread use of electronic devices of many types in future education.

teak, large-leaved Asiatic timber tree (*Tectona grandis*) which attains an immense height and bears panicles of small white flowers. The wood is used in shipbuilding, furniture, and houses. It is perhaps the most valuable of all tropical woods.

teal, name applied to various small wild ducks of importance to sportsmen. The North American species are the widespread blue-winged and green-winged teals and the western cinnamon teal.

Teapot Dome, oil reservation, central Wyoming, set aside 1915 for the U.S. Navy by Pres. Woodrow Wilson along with other oil property at Elk Hills, Calif. In Pres. Harding's administration, Albert B. Fall, Secretary of the Interior, had these reservations transferred from the Navy Dept. to his jurisdiction, 1921, then secretly leased Teapot Dome to Harry F. Sinclair, and Elk Hills to Edward L. Doheny, 1922. A Senate investigation, begun 1923 under Sen. Thomas J. Walsh, disclosed that Sinclair and Doheny had given large bribes, called "loans," to Fall. Fall was convicted, 1929, of bribery, sentenced to a year in jail, and fined $100,000. Doheny and Sinclair were acquitted of bribery, but Sinclair was sentenced to nine months and fined $1000 for contempt of court. In 1927 the reservations were returned to the government.

This cartoon from the N.Y. *World* describes the predicament of the Republican Party resulting from the *Teapot Dome* scandal, which bared corruption in Pres. Harding's administration in the 1920s.

tear gas, any of various gases, also called lachrymators, which irritate the eyes and are easily distributed, and hence are used in warfare or in quelling civil disorders. Tear gas causes profuse, involuntary weeping, temporarily blinding the victim. Types used in civil disorders are generally considered harmless, but bad after-effects have occasionally been reported. The gas may be disseminated directly from cylinders or from bursting shells fired from mortars, specially designed pistols, or other devices.

Teasdale, Sara, 1884-1933, U.S. poet, b. St. Louis. Her *Helen of Troy and Other Poems* (1911) was followed by *Flame and Shadow* (1920) and *Dark of the Moon* (1926), among other volumes.

technetium, chemical element no. 43 (sym. *Tc*; at. wt. 92-102, 104, 105, 107), radioactive, artificially produced in nuclear fission.

Technocracy, socio-economic theory originated in the U.S. by Howard Scott and others during the depression period, 1930-3. Its proponents, the so-called Technocrats, demanded reorganization of industry by a control board of specialists, including qualified scientists and engineers. They argued that distribution of goods in industrial society lags too far behind industrial production, and benefits from improved technology accrue excessively to a small class of investors.

technology, the activities of the industrial arts and their study; especially, applied science as expressed in modern material civilization, involving large-scale and complex manufacturing. Technology is concerned not only with techniques and skills of the sciences but with social and historic changes resulting from industrial innovations. The institutional aspects of technology have come to occupy the social scientists and loom large in critical analyses of Western civilization, which is held by some to favor technological accomplishments at the expense of spiritual values.

Tecumseh, 1768-1813, Shawnee Indian chief. He tried, with his brother Tenskwatawa, to unite the Indians of the Mississippi and adjacent areas in one great confederacy to resist the white man's

Tecumseh (falling at left) dies in Battle of the Thames in southern Ontario.

advance. A large Indian force under Tenskwatawa was brought to battle and defeated by an American army under William Henry Harrison at the Battle of Tippecanoe, 1811. Tecumseh joined the British in the War of 1812 and was killed in the Battle of the Thames, 1813.

Tedder, Arthur William, 1st **Baron Tedder,** 1890- , British air chief marshal. Rising to prominence in the Royal Air Force and holding offices in the air ministry, he was important in building and directing British air power in World War II. As R.A.F. commander in the Middle East, 1940-1, he scored against Gen. Rommel's forces in North Africa. Made air commander in chief of the Allies in the Mediterranean, 1943, he was deputy supreme commander during the invasion of France and the defeat of Germany, 1943-5. He was British chief of air staff, 1946-9 and chairman, British Joint Services Mission, Washington, D.C., 1950-51. He was the author of *Air Power in War*. Tedder was made chancellor of Cambridge University in 1951. In 1954, he became an executive of an automobile manufacturing company.

Tees River, 70 mi. long, N England, rising in Cumberland and flowing along the Westmorland-Durham and Yorkshire-Durham borders to the North Sea. Navigable up to Stockton-on-Tees, it is an important commercial waterway for an iron-working district. Teesdale, its upper valley, is a high moorland.

Tegucigalpa, capital of Honduras, S central Honduras; pop. 72,385. Largest city of the republic, it was founded 16th cent. and became the capital, 1880. Nearby are gold and silver mines.

Teheran or **Tehran,** capital of Iran, N Iran; pop. 1,512,082. It lies at the foot of the Elburz Mts., near the Biblical town of Rages. The city, founded in medieval times, is now a major trade and communication center in a productive agricultural region. There are metallurgical, textile, lumber, and food industries. The city became important after 1788, when it was made capital by Aga Mohammed Khan. The university was founded in 1934. The city is built about several imposing palaces.

Teheran Conference, Nov. 28-Dec. 1, 1943, in World War II between Roosevelt, Stalin, and Churchill at Teheran, Iran, to concert war plans and agree upon future operations, especially the opening of a second front in Europe. This conference, which involved the first meeting between Roosevelt and Stalin, incidentally guaranteed the territorial integrity of Iran.

Tel Aviv-Jaffa, largest city and Mediterranean port of Israel, W Palestine, c.35 mi. WNW of Jerusalem; pop. 380,000. Tel Aviv is an entirely Jewish city, founded 1906 as a suburb of Jaffa, and now one of the world's fastest growing communities. It has a modern aspect, and dominates the new nation's financial and industrial life. There are fine theaters and other cultural institutions. In 1948 it became the provisional capital of the country. It was joined with Jaffa, 1950. Jerusalem became the official capital of Israel, Dec. 1949, but much of the government's business is transacted in Tel Aviv. Several large beach front hotels were begun in the 1960s as Tel Aviv became a major Mediterranean resort.

telegraph, process of sending messages by means of electrical impulses transmitted through a wire. The first needle telegraph was patented by Cooke and Wheatstone, 1836, and in the following year was tried out successfully. In this form of the instrument a magnetic needle at the receiving station is deflected by an electric current sent by a conducting wire from the transmitting station. The Morse telegraph involves the principle of the electromagnet, producing an audible signal, and is in general use for most land lines. The Morse code is used for telegraphic messages of the normal type within the U.S., and the Continental code in all radio telegraphy, the dots and dashes being represented by short or long periods during which the current is kept on. A record of the message is made automatically on a tape or by means of a perforated ribbon, and in one type of instrument by printing the message. In submarine telegraphy a siphon recorder invented by Lord Kelvin acts as a receiving instrument and marks the message upon a traveling tape in a series of irregular waves. The so-called wireless telegraph is radio (*q.v.*). See *cable*.

Teleki, Paul, Count, 1879-1941, Hungarian statesman and geographer. At the Paris Peace Conference, 1919, he vainly used extensive ethnic and economic maps to support Hungary's attitude as to frontiers. While premier under Admiral Horthy he secured Hungarian acceptance of the Treaty of Trianon, 1920. As premier again, 1939, he attempted to mollify the Axis powers while suppressing fascist organizations in Hungary. The country was finally forced into the Axis, 1940, and compelled to join in the invasion of Yugoslavia, 1941. Teleki, who had signed a mutual assistance pact with Yugoslavia, 1940, committed suicide.

telepathy, transference from one person to another of unspoken thought, sometimes called mind reading. Scientific experiments in telepathy are recorded as early as 1871. Interest was revived in the 1930s by experiments in U.S. colleges, particularly by J. B. Rhine, with results greatly exceeding those ordinarily ascribable to chance. See *psychical research.*

telephone, electrical system for converting sounds into electrical energy and reproducing them at a distance. Invented by A. G. Bell, 1876, a telephone circuit consists basically of a source of electric current; a microphone which translates sound waves into electric-current variations; a wire line to transmit the currents; and the receiver, usually a light metal diaphragm which is vibrated by an electromagnet to translate the electric signal into sound. Complex modern telephone systems use electronic amplifiers so that signals can be sent for long distances. Since 1927, when the first transatlantic telephone circuit was inaugurated, radio "links" have been used where wire transmission lines are impractical. However, since the late 1950s, undersea cables have taken over much international telephone traffic. In turn, the late 1960s were expected to see much radio telephone traffic routed via space satellite relay stations. The development of reliable switching systems makes it possible for telephone subscribers in some areas to connect their instruments to those of other subscribers automatically. Such dial telephone systems, originally limited to local areas, are now being extended to cover entire districts and even whole countries. Most of the U.S. is expected to be so connected by the late 1960s. See *cable.*

telescope, optical instrument for viewing distant objects. The first probably was made in Holland c.1608. Galileo's instruments, made a few years later, were the first used in serious astronomical studies; they enabled him to discover four satellites of Jupiter, sunsposts, and other celestial phenomena. The simple refracting telescope

Since Alexander Bell's first model, the design of the *telephone* has changed many times. One of the latest improvements is the unit for offices with extension lines at the bottom right.

Bell Telephone

TELESCOPE

Due to the drawbacks of the refracting *telescope*, Isaac Newton finally devised this reflecting telescope in 1668. Most telescopes in use today are still of the reflecting type.

(the type made by Galileo) consists of two lenses at opposite ends of a tube. In passing through the convex outer lens (the objective), light rays from the distant object are made to converge and form a small inverted image in front of the other lens, a magnifying eyepiece through which the observer looks. In the simple reflecting telescope a slightly concave mirror at the bottom end of the tube receives the light rays from the open end and, in reflecting the rays, causes them to converge toward a prism or diagonally placed mirror (in the center of the tube), which in turn directs the rays toward the eyepiece (at the side of the tube). Large telescopes have equipment for varying the magnification, eliminating undesirable color effects due to refraction, and other purposes. Large astronomical telescopes may be equipped also for automatic sighting on celestial objects, for following a celestial object across the sky, and for photography and spectroscopic studies. Opera and field glasses are binocular modifications in

The giant radio *telescope* of Manchester Univ., in Cheshire, Eng., is the largest rotating model in the world. Pushbutton operation makes the parabolic bowl reflector (1700 tons) swing in any direction.

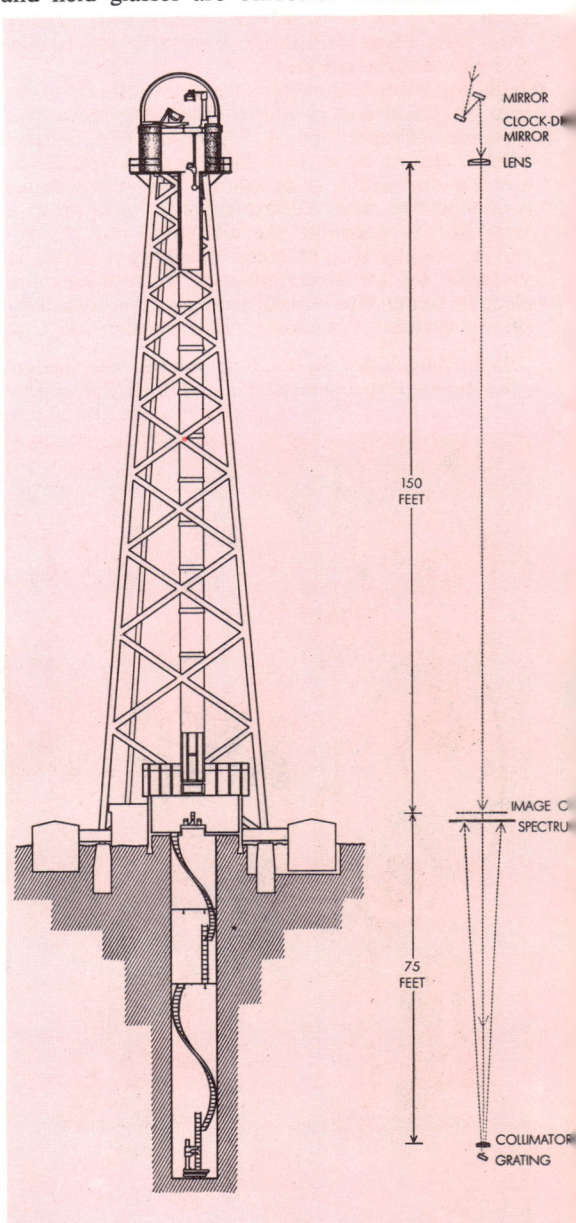

This is the tower *telescope* used for magnetic observations at the Mount Wilson Observatory. Its optical system is diagrammed at right: a clock-driven mirror tracks the sun, the solar image is formed at ground level, and light passes to a diffraction grating beneath. It is then reflected upward and dispersed into a spectrum on a screen at ground level.

which there are two parallel refracting telescopes. Refractors are generally somewhat superior to reflectors in revealing detail, but reflectors render truer colors and, since they can be built much larger, can gather more light and thus detect fainter objects. The largest telescopes (see *observatory*) enable astronomers to explore the universe to distances up to 2 billion light years. So-called radio telescopes, increasingly used in astronomy, are giant, saucer-shaped instruments designed to detect radio waves emitted by nebulae and stars in outer space. They make possible the detection and analysis of objects whose radiation is either invisible or obscured by cosmic dust. It is expected that radio telescopes will be mounted on space satellites. See *spherical aberration*.

Telesio, Bernardino, 1509-88, Italian Renaissance philosopher. He founded the Academia Telesiana (Cosentina) at Naples, where he taught his materialistic empirical philosophy in opposition to Aristotelian Scholasticism. His basic tenet was that the physical world is ruled by the opposing forces of heat and cold. Telesio's chief work is *De Rerum Natura juxta Propria Principia* (1565).

teletype, electrical device for simultaneously printing a message at a point remote from the place of origin. Teletype machines, first developed 1904, have keyboards like those of typewriters. When a key is struck, the machine generates a pattern of electrical impulses which may be transmitted by a telegraph line or by radio. At the receiving end the impulses actuate the proper type bars and spacing mechanisms to print the incoming message on a paper roll or tape. Teletyping is quicker than telegraphy and, unlike telephony, produces a permanent record of messages. By teletype techniques, printing type also may be set by an operator far from the composing machine.

television, transmission of moving images by electrical means, either by wire or, more commonly, by radio. The basic components of a television system are devices to transform the light energy of a projected image into electrical impulses and a receiving device to transform these impulses back into light energy. The cathode-ray tube (*q.v.*) is used in almost all television receivers. The most common transmitting device is the iconoscope, developed by V. K. Zworykin, 1925. This type of vacuum tube contains a plate of photoelectrically sensitive material such as selenium. A moving beam of electrons scans this plate, moving from side to side and from top to bottom according to a regular controlled pattern. When a visible image is focused on the plate of a lens, the electrical output of the tube varies from moment to moment depending on whether the small area of the plate being scanned is black, gray or white. This varying output, amplified, is transmitted together with synchronizing pulses and accompanying sound as the television signal. Workable television systems using mechanical scanning were demonstrated as early as 1925, but practical commercial television was not introduced into the U.S. until 1946. In 1951 electronic color television was publicly demon-

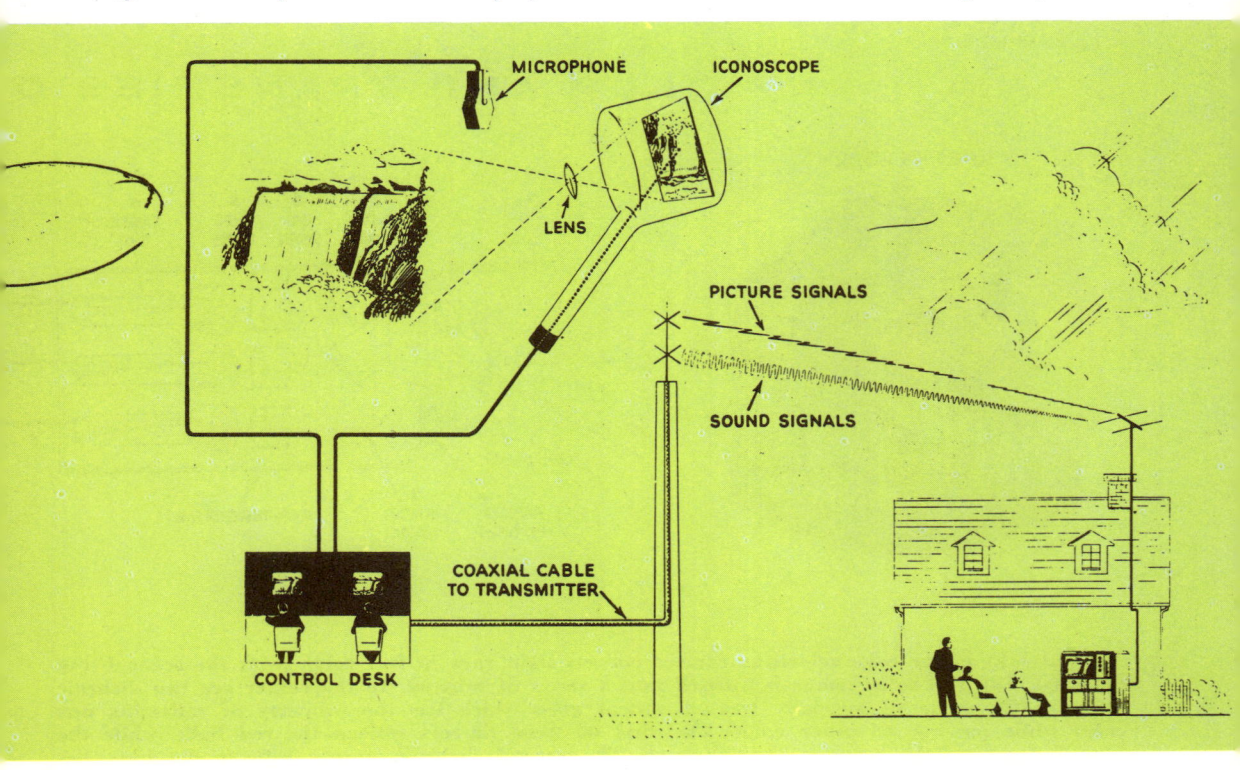

Radio Corporation of America

This simplified diagram shows how a telecast of Niagara Falls would reach the home. The iconoscope is a kind of electron tube formerly used in a television camera for transmitting the picture; it has recently been replaced by the image orthicon.

TELEVISION

In a more detailed drawing, the main elements in sending a *television* program over the airways from the studio to the amplifiers of an individual set are indicated. Before being transmitted, both picture and sound pass through the monitor booth; then sound and picture signals are separately sent but are picked up by the same antenna. The kinescope is the picture tube in the television set.

Radio Corporation of America

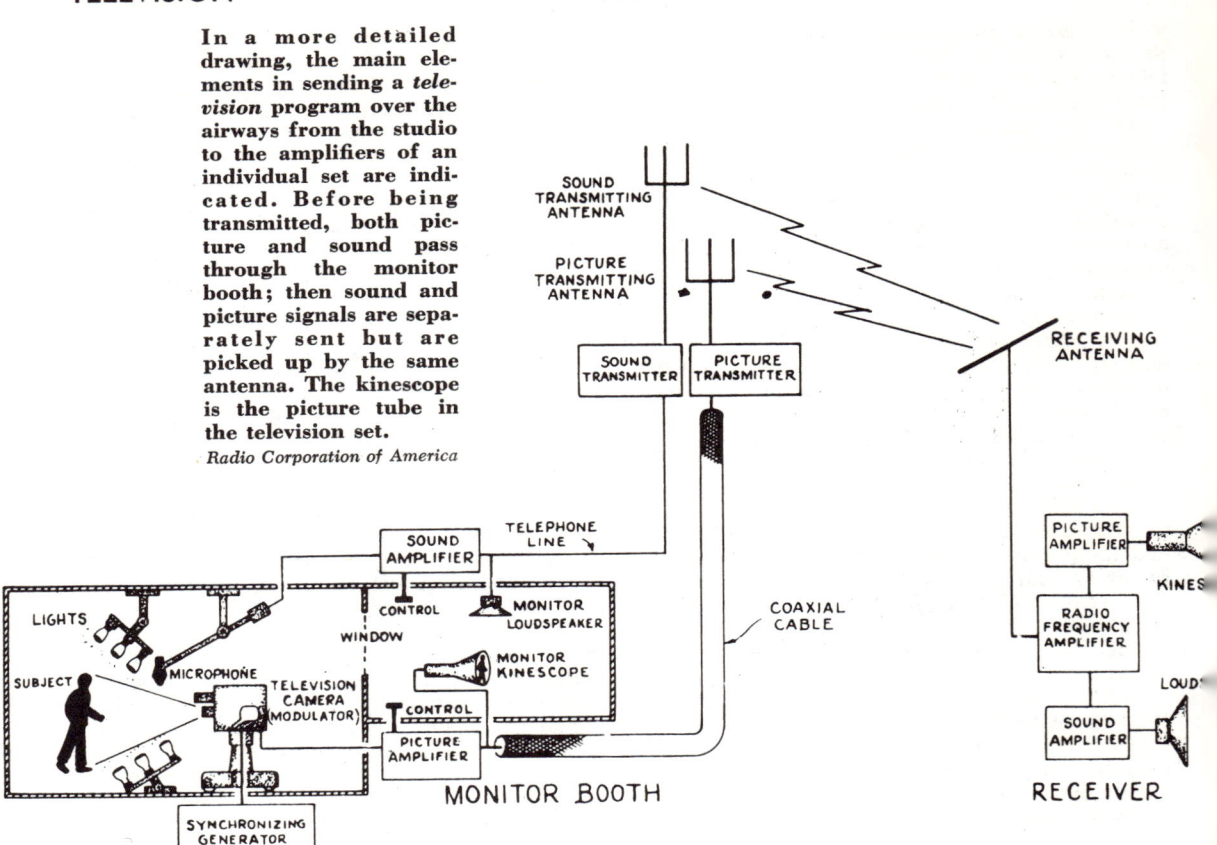

PICKUP AND TRANSMISSIO

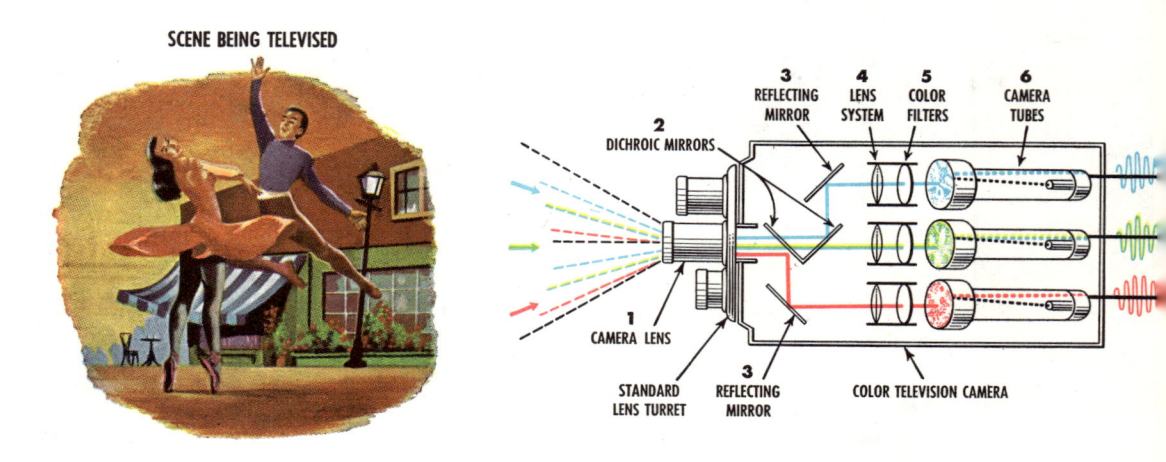

SCENE BEING TELEVISED

The lens (1) of the color *television* camera collects light rays in full color from the scene being televised. The full color image is focused into a series of mirrors. In the center are two dichroic mirrors (2) made of specially treated optical glass which has the property of reflecting one color while passing all other colors. The first of these mirrors reflects the red light, while the blue and green light pass straight through. The second dichroic mirror reflects the blue but passes the green. Thus three images, one in each primary color, are created. With the aid of regular reflecting mirrors (3) and a lens system (4) the three primary images are focused on the faces of three television camera tubes (image orthicons). In front of the camera tubes are color filters (5) which assure that the color quality of each primary has the precise value for the sys-

This tri-color picture tube is the heart of color TV receivers for the home. The cutaway drawing at bottom shows how three different electron beams combine to produce a color image on the tube face. Many tiny color dots on the screen make up the total image.
Radio Corporation of America

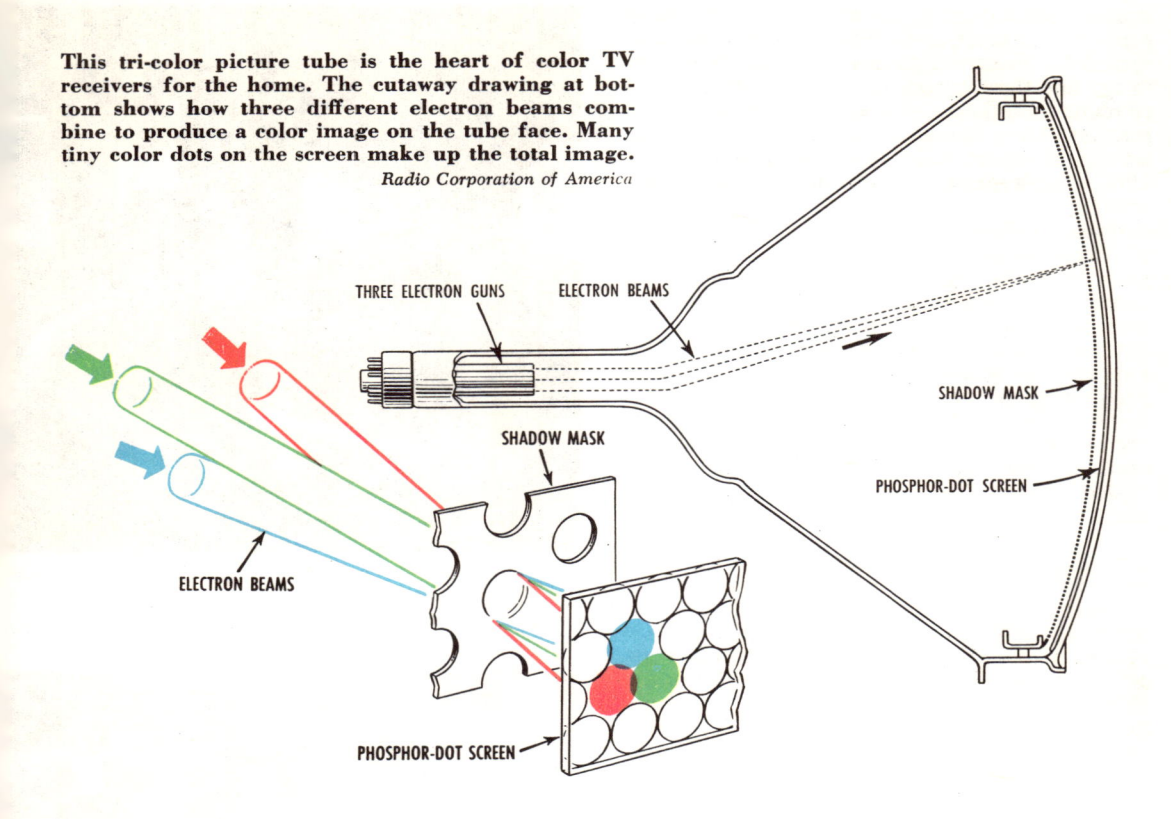

OF COLOR TELEVISION

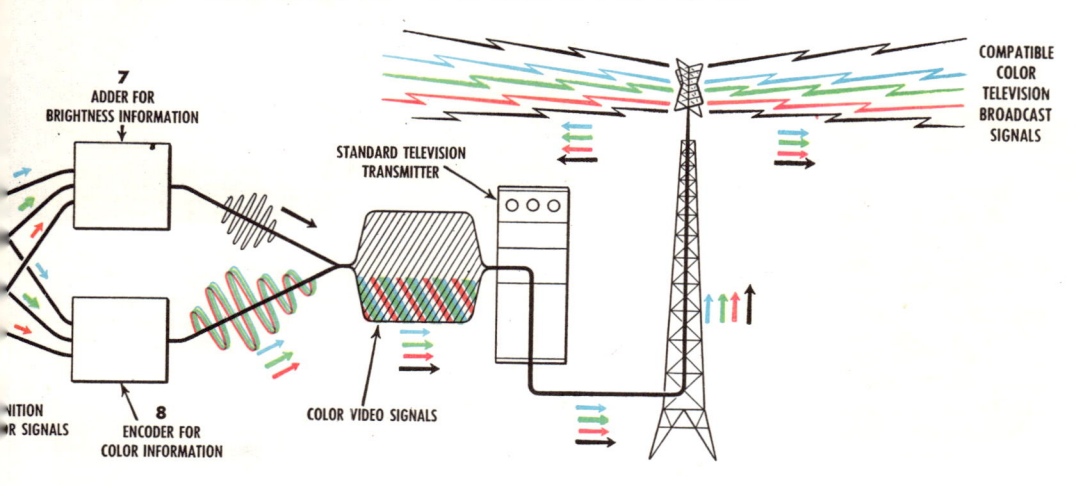

Radio Corporation of America

tem. The electron beam in each camera tube (6) scans the image pattern which has been formed in the tube screen, thereby producing a primary color signal. The three primary color signals from the three tubes are now processed for transmission. Samples of these signals, in proper amounts in relation to each other, go to an electronic adder (7) which combines them to make the brightness, or black-and-white signal. At the same time, samples of the three primary signals are fed to another unit (8) which encodes or combines them to produce a signal carrying the hue and saturation information. This color-representing signal is then combined with the brightness signal to form the complete color television signal. Although the brightness signal and the color-representing signal are transmitted together they do not interfere with each other.

TELEVISION

strated. Television in color involves the same principles as black-and-white television, but uses optical or electronic means to break down the image into three images in primary colors and to combine these into a single colored image at the receiver. Long limited to one network and one set manufacturer, color TV took a new step in 1961 when a second manufacturer brought out a color set.

television production, the technique and practice of preparing and presenting an audio-visual program over the airwaves. In general, the main concern is with live programs or those recorded on magnetic tape; filmed programs are produced much the same way as any other motion picture (see *motion picture production*). As in other performing mediums, the first order of business is the script. In this case, after the script has been written, the author, producer, and director break it down into two parts, called "audio" and "video," describing respectively what is to be heard and what is to be seen. These two parts are then printed on a new script, the audio on the left hand side of the page, and the video on the right. The cast is then chosen by a casting director who works in conjunction with the producer, the director, and the commercial sponsor of the program. Rehearsals are held daily for one or two weeks before the actual presentation or "taping" of the show. During the first week only the actors and the director are involved; following this period, the technical aspect of the broadcast comes into play. Sets are constructed in the television studio; they are usually very simple and, except for color broadcast, are drab in color. Moreover, they are mostly representative of small portions of an area—the corner of a room, the wall in an alleyway, the portion of a back yard, etc.; the television cameras are thereby able to switch from one scene to another as quickly as possible if the show is being broadcast live. Once the sets have been put in their proper places, the lights are distributed in such a way that at the flip of a switch any set can be illuminated in several ways, according to the mood desired. The foregoing refers to a performance to which no studio audience is invited. When an audience is present, there must, of course, be concessions in favor of the more traditional forms of "stage" production.

About a week before the scheduled broadcast, the dramatic and technical aspects of the television program are combined. The cast, which usually rehearses elsewhere up to this time, moves into the studio, and, under the director's guidance, there is a "technical run-through." Here the actors "walk through" their parts very slowly as the director sees that the lights, the cameras covering the various actions, and all other technical aspects of the production proceed effectively. The director sits in a glass-enclosed room that overlooks the studio, perhaps ten or fifteen feet above the studio floor; he is thus able to see at one glance everything that is occurring, and he has access to a public address system by which he can speak to all the people in the studio and make his decisions known. In addition, all the cameramen are equipped with headphones by which the director and his assistants can speak to them and give them instructions

Radio Corporation of America
In the master control room of a modern *television* studio, a director studies monitor screens while supervising a broadcast.

Revolving at high speeds, the color wheel above is used for tests of fast motion. With such devices, engineers may simulate difficult transmitting conditions. The telecast of "Carmen," below, was a color TV milestone.
Radio Corporation of America

Right: A memorable color *television* broadcast was the production of "Peter Pan," which starred Mary Martin in the title role, as well as her daughter, Heller Holliday.
Radio Corporation of America

Below: Educational television, both in schools and in the home, is becoming an important medium of instruction. Here a professor of geography uses a conic-projection skirt map in the series, "Russia: Faces of a Giant."
University of Michigan

At right the *television* camera is focused on an operating table while a surgical team performs an actual operation for a one-hour videotape presentation. This documentary show was produced as a part of a series of medical programs.
Screen Gems

without interrupting the continuity of the program.

Rehearsals are held on succeeding days with increasing frequency until the program is to be aired or taped. During the last stages, the commercial announcements are integrated into the program, and the sponsor or one of his representatives is invited to watch and suggest changes, usually so that material which might be considered "offensive" to prospective customers may be altered or deleted. During the actual presentation of the live program, absolute silence is necessary (except, of course, in the case of "audience participation" shows), and everything that happens must not take any more or less time than had been planned on beforehand. As in radio, a television program must fill out the allotted time exactly, and finish "on the nose." See *radio broadcasting*.

Tell, William—see *William Tell*.

TELLURIUM

tellurium, chemical element no. 52 (sym. *Te*; at. wt. 127.6; m. p. 452° C; sp. gr. 6.25) and boils at 1390° C. It is a soft, brittle, silver-white semimetal discovered in 1782 by Reichenstein. It normally occurs in ores of gold, silver, copper, lead and nickel.

Telugu—see *Dravidian languages.*

Temesvár—see *Timişoara.*

Tempe—see *Olympus.*

tempera—see *painting; water-color painting.*

temperance, moderation, especially in use of alcoholic beverages. The temperance movement aims at reducing or ending consumption of alcohol as a beverage. It advocates total abstinence, disseminates literature concerning effects of alcohol

The cartoon above, which appeared in the 1920s, was "A Dedication to the *Temperance* Society—O'er All the Ills of Life Victorious." The temperance pledge below called for signers to refrain from imbibing alcohol.

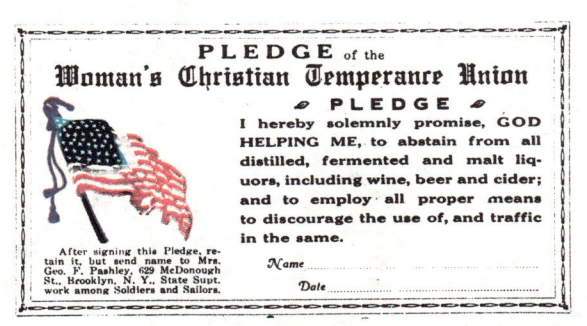

as a narcotic drug, and attempts to influence legislation. Temperance organizations, mainly of women, were started in the U.S. early in the 19th cent. The movement became a strong power with the formation of the Woman's Christian Temperance Union (founded 1874) and the Anti-Saloon League (founded 1893). It helped to bring about Prohibition, which lasted 1919-33. Prominent in the movement were Carry Nation and Frances Elizabeth Willard (1839-98). See *Alcoholics Anonymous; Prohibition.*

temperature, condition of hotness or coldness of a body that determines the transfer of heat energy to other bodies—always, according to the second law of thermodynamics, to those of lower temperature. Two bodies are at the same temperature when the mutual interchange of heat is the same, but if one body transmits more heat than it receives from the other, the first body is said to be at a higher temperature. The thermal range is measured in units or degrees of temperature by means of a thermometer (*q.v.*). As regards the human body, the temperature in health is about 98.6°F, but in fevers may rise to 106°F or higher, while in collapse it may fall to 80°F or even lower. Only a limited range of temperature of the air is endured by the body in comfort, the normal for a room being about 71°F. Absolute zero, the theoretical point at which all molecular activity is at a standstill, corresponds to a temperature of —273.16°C (—459.6°F). See *weights and measures.*

Templars, Knights—see *Knights Templars.*

temple, building for worship or for the shrine of a god or sacred figure. The Egyptians built many huge temples, notably that to Amen-Ra, at Karnak. Their temples had great pylons, courts, and sacred inner chambers open only to monarchs and priests. Terraced temples were built by the Assyrians, Babylonians, and Aztecs. In India great temples were hewn out of rocks and caves. In China, too, temples were built in caves and later of wood, with brilliant tiles and lacquer. Japanese temples were similar but simpler. The earliest Jewish temple was that built by Micah; the most famous was that of Solomon at Jerusalem, built of stone and cedar with gold decorations, destroyed and reconstructed several times before all traces of it disappeared. The Greeks built many fine temples, notably the Parthenon, dedicated to Pallas Athena. The Romans built temples early in their history; their later great Pantheon dates from A.D. 2nd cent. With the spread of Christianity, pagan temples were replaced by Christian churches in the West, but the earlier term is still occasionally used, as for the Mormon Temple at Salt Lake City.

The golden Phra Chedi shrine is one of the many Buddhist *temples* in Thailand.

TEMPLE

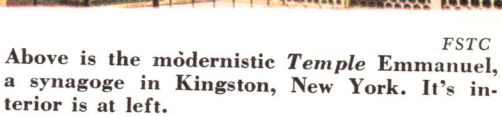

Above is the modernistic *Temple* Emmanuel, a synagoge in Kingston, New York. It's interior is at left.

Among the most famous *temples* of the West are those built in classical times. Above is the Greek temple dedicated to the goddess Ceres; it is located at Segesta, Sicily.

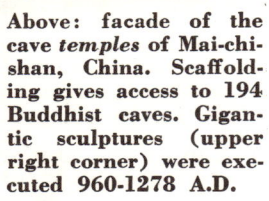

Above: facade of the cave *temples* of Mai-chi-shan, China. Scaffolding gives access to 194 Buddhist caves. Gigantic sculptures (upper right corner) were executed 960-1278 A.D.

Right: The *Gopura* (gate pyramid) of the Mylapore Temple in Madras, India, is adorned with thousands of deities and sacred personages from Hindu mythology.

Temple, Sir William, 1628-99, English diplomat and writer. He was Charles II's envoy to the Netherlands and arranged the marriage of Charles' niece Mary to William of Orange. His proposal that the king accept councilors reflecting parliamentary opinion was a step toward responsible government. In later years he composed esays and memoirs, aided by Jonathan Swift, who was his secretary.

Templewood, Samuel John Gurney Hoare, 1st **Viscount,** 1880-1952, British statesman. Becoming foreign secretary in Baldwin's coalition government, 1935, in the League of Nations he advocated sanctions against Italy for aggression against Ethiopia, but soon agreed with Premier Laval of France to concede Ethiopian territory to Italy. Violent popular protest forced Hoare and Laval out of Office, but Baldwin made Hoare first lord of the admiralty, 1936, and Chamberlain appointed him home secretary, 1937-9, and air secretary, 1940. In World War II he was special envoy to Spain. He wrote extensively on international affairs.

tempo, in music, the speed or pace at which music is performed. The tempo may be thought of as an objective standard (so many notes in a given unit of time) or as a subjective impression of faster or slower movement. In actual performances, both considerations apply. Various conductors of orchestras have been timed, and widely different speeds recorded for the same work. But other factors, such as room acoustics, precision in the playing of instruments, accentuation of rhythm, etc., may make an objectively slow tempo sound fast, and *vice versa*. Tempo, then, in an actual musical sense is relative, a factor interdependently related to many other musical considerations. The standard notations a composer uses to indicate tempo are Italian, and originated in the 17th cent. They are not precise, and indicate ranges to stay within, rather than specific speeds. Many composers have indicated tempos during composition which they later revised after hearing performances, since the slow rate of composition itself often subjectively influences choice of tempo, or the mechanical metronome may be inexact. The interpretive choices of a conductor may lead him to alter the tempo as scored.

General limits on tempo are the physical capacity of the musical instruments. An orchestral work arranged for organ, if originally very swift in tempo, must be slowed in order to register distinctly to a listener. The actual indicated tempo of some vocal music (*e.g.*, Beethoven's choral movement in the *Ninth Symphony,* and some early Baroque experimental vocal composition) is almost physically impossible for singers. Tempo as an expressive device assumed new importance with the 17th-cent. development of harmony and non-modal scales, emphasizing vertical techniques in composition, rather than horizontal elaboration, by counterpoint, of melodic lines. Various means of punctuating musical composition, rather than reliance on a relatively flat, but multi-stranded, melodic tapestry, introduced a new concern with tempo.

The principal Italian terms used to indicate tempo include: *presto* (very fast), *vivace* (lively), *allegro* (fast), *moderato* (moderate), *andante* (moderate, literally a "walking" tempo), *adagio* (slow), *lento* (slower than *adagio*), and *largo* (very slow); *accelerando* (increasing the speed) and *ritardando* (slowing down) are directions to alter the tempo momentarily, and are canceled by *a tempo*.

Temuchin—see *Genghis Khan.*

tenancy, holding or occupying of property belonging to a landlord, who in return receives rent. The relationship between landlord and tenant is usually stipulated in a lease or contract; its legal implications vary greatly in different countries and social systems (see *feudalism; manor; share cropping*). The relationship is usually reflected in the kind and amount of rent demanded. Tenant-farming is a world-wide institution, which has increased sharply in the U.S. since the depression of the 1930s. The tenant farmer, cultivating land owned by another, pays rent in legal tender or produce, or both. By 1933 nearly half the farmers in the U.S. were farming on land they did not own; the absentee owners were individuals, mortgage companies, banks, etc. In the South the tenant farmer is rapidly replacing the share cropper, who, without land or capital, bargains to till land in exchange for tools, materials, provisions, and a fixed share in the harvest.

Ten Commandments, in the Bible (Exodus), the injunctions traced by the finger of Jehovah on two tables and given to Moses on Mt. Sinai.

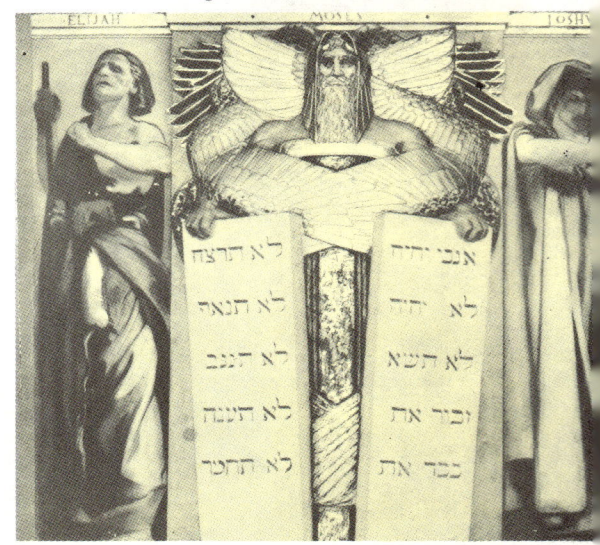

John S. Sargent's "Frieze of the Prophets" shows Moses at center with tablets bearing Hebrew inscriptions of the *Ten Commandments.* Elijah is at the left, Joshua at right.

They prohibit any worship other than that of Jehovah, and especially that of idols; they prohibit the false use of Jehovah's name; they command that the Sabbath be kept holy; they command the honoring of one's parents; they prohibit murder, adultery, theft, the bearing of false witness, and the coveting of the wife or property of one's neighbor. Variations in the enumeration of these commandments occur among the various Jewish and Christian traditions, but the sanctity of the commandments, known as the Decalogue, is basic to all Christian faiths and to the Jews and Moslems.

tendril, a twining or grasping organ of a climbing plant. Many tendrils are modified branches, but may arise from tips of leaves. Tendrils wrap around objects they contact by growth movements which are partly controlled by auxins (*q.v.*).

tenebrism, a style of painting marked by a calculated murkiness of form and color. Commonly referring to artists in Spain and Italy in the early part of the 17th cent., the term has also been used to describe later works reminiscent of that earlier period.

Tenerife—see *Canary Islands*.

Teniers, David, the elder, 1582-1649, Flemish painter. He studied with Rubens and lived for a while in Rome. His pictures were usually rustic in subject. He was the teacher of his more famous son, **David Teniers,** the younger, 1610-90, a landscape and genre painter. Extremely popular, he painted for the Spanish governor and king. Like his father's work, many of his pictures were small and featured rural scenes. He was one of the last great Flemish painters.

Tennessee, state, S central U.S.; land area 41,761 sq. mi.; pop. 3,567,089; capital Nashville; largest city Memphis; other large cities Chattanooga and

Tennessee's capitol at Nashville — Dexter Press

The flag of *Tennessee*; the state flower is the iris.

Knoxville. Tennessee is bounded N by Kentucky and Virginia, E by North Carolina, S by Georgia, Alabama and Mississippi, and W by the Mississippi River, the state's boundary with Arkansas and Missouri. In the east are the Great Smoky Mts. and the ranges of the Appalachian system, with elevations up to *c.*6000 ft. The general slope of the land is down toward the west, which is low-lying. Through the state flow the Cumberland and Tennessee Rivers and many lesser streams, and there are several important dams and reservoirs of the Tennessee Valley Authority. Agriculture is the principal occupation, although industry (largely due to TVA stimulus) has a greater earning power. The leading crops are cotton, tobacco, hay, other grains, fruit, and corn. Livestock is extensively raised. Principal industrial products are textiles, chemicals of many kinds, metal products, foods, and wood products and lumber. Forests (mainly hardwoods) are valuable; also pyrites and clay. Mineral resources include coal, zinc, phosphate, limestone, and marble.

The region of present Tennessee was contested for by the Spanish, who based their claim on the explorations of De Soto; by the French, who claimed the whole Mississippi Valley; and by the English, who regarded the area as the westward extension of the Virginia and Carolina grants. France relinquished all rights to the English in 1763, and in 1768 the Indians, by treaty, granted rights to the white men. Settlement began 1769. In the American Revolution the region was the scene of the Battle of King's Mountain, 1780. When North Carolina ceded its western lands to the U.S., 1784, the short-lived, 1784-8, State of Franklin was formed in the frontier region. In 1790 the U.S. formed the Territory South of the Ohio; in 1796 this region was admitted to the U.S. as Tennessee, the 16th state (slaveholding). Hardy settlers came overland and by river to Tennessee, which, especially in the mountain regions, long ket traditions of independence and hardihood. Strong antislavery feeling prevented Tennessee from seceding from the Union until after Fort Sumter had been fired upon; later it became a major battleground in the Civil War. Readmitted to the Union, 1866, in the 1870s it suffered a series of devastating epidemics and plagues. In 1933, with the establishment of TVA, many new industries sprang up and the cultural and economic level of the state rose.

The Hermitage, home of Andrew Jackson, is near Nashville, *Tennessee.* Often called the Mount Vernon of the South, it was built in 1804 while he was a state officer.

Dexter Press

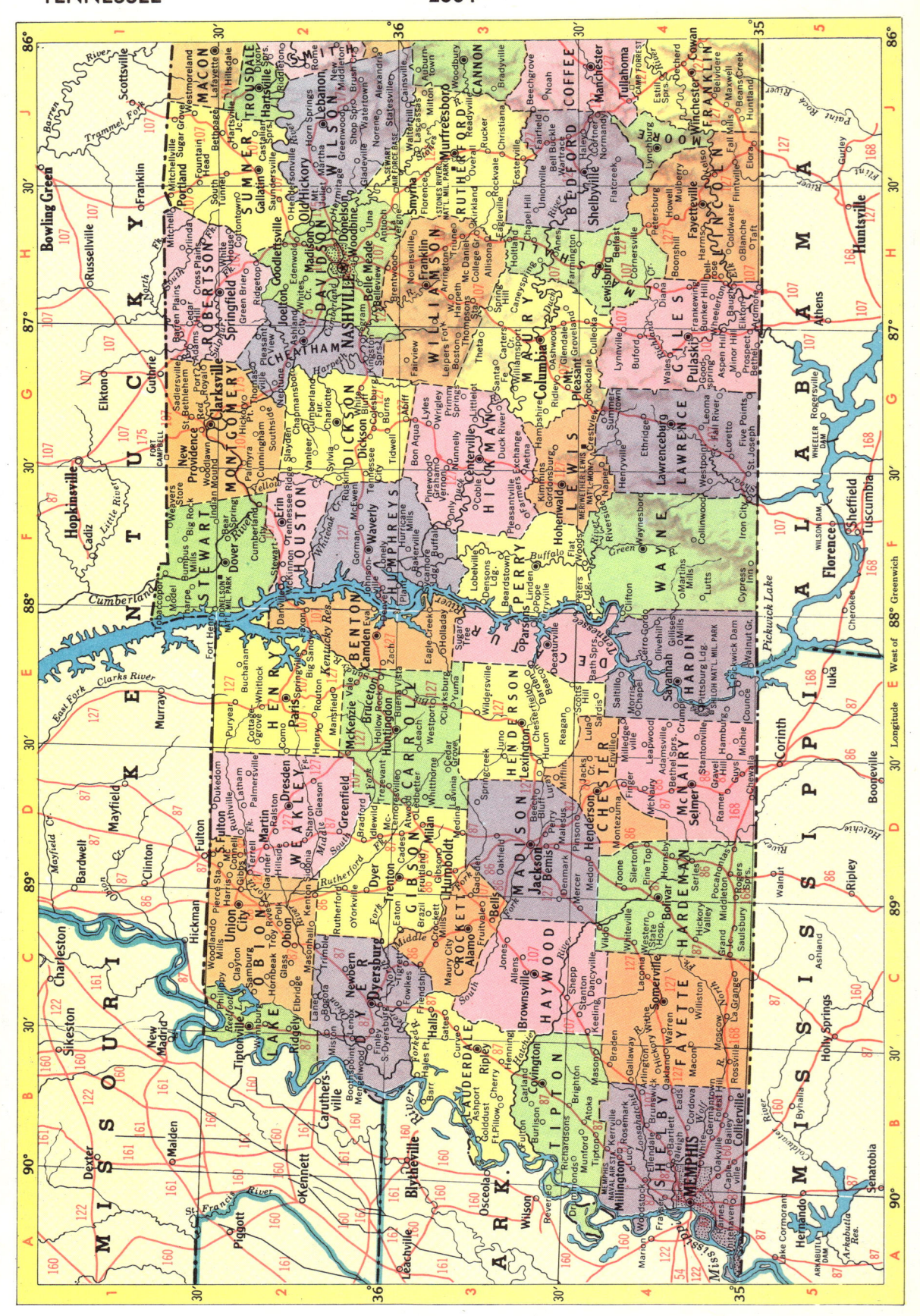

TENNESSEE 2564

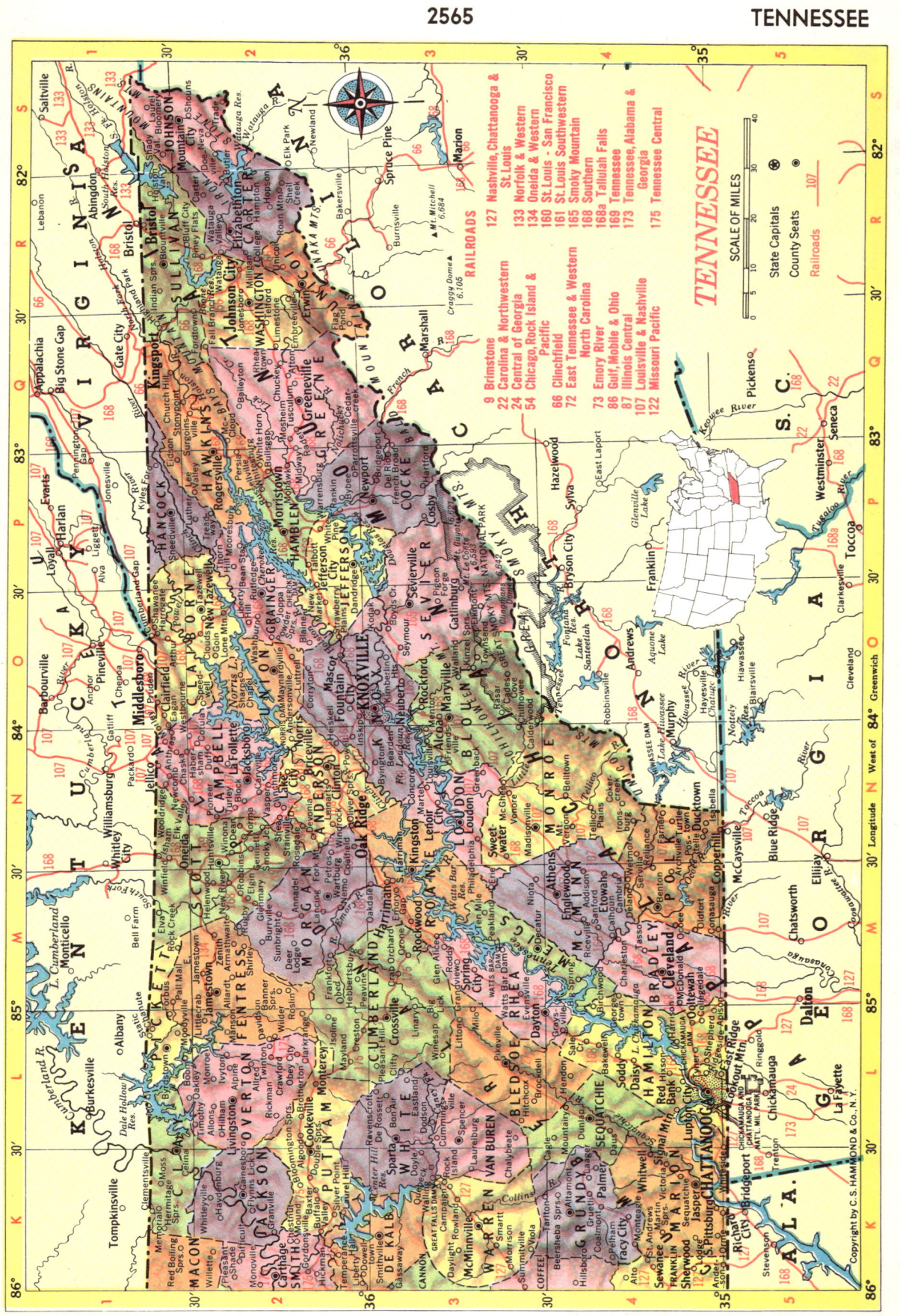

TENNESSEE

RAILROADS

9	Brimstone	127 Nashville, Chattanooga & St. Louis
22	Carolina & Northwestern	133 Norfolk & Western
24	Central of Georgia	134 Oneida & Western
54	Chicago, Rock Island & Pacific	160 St. Louis - San Francisco
66	Clinchfield	161 St. Louis Southwestern
72	East Tennessee & Western North Carolina	165 Smoky Mountain
73	Emory River	168 Southern
86	Gulf, Mobile & Ohio	168a Tallulah Falls
87	Illinois Central	169 Tennessee
107	Louisville & Nashville	173 Tennessee, Alabama & Georgia
122	Missouri Pacific	175 Tennessee Central

SCALE OF MILES

State Capitals ⊛
County Seats ◉
Railroads ───

TENNESSEE

Tennessee Information Service

This national cemetery was established near Nashville, *Tennessee,* for Union soldiers who were killed during the Civil War.

Leading educational institutions include Univ. of Tennessee and Knoxville College at Knoxville, and Fiske Univ. and Vanderbilt Univ. at Nashville. State flower, iris; motto, Agriculture, Commerce. See *Tennessee Valley Authority.*

Tennessee River, 652 mi. long, flowing through E Tennessee, N Alabama, W Tennessee, and W Kentucky. Formed in E Tennessee by junction of the Holston and French Broad Rivers, it empties into the Ohio. Previously unnavigable, it has many reservoirs created by Tennessee Valley Authority dams (Wilson, Wheeler, Ft. Loudoun, etc.), designed for hydroelectric power, flood control, and improvement of navigation. The river is navigable from Knoxville to the Ohio, *c.*560 mi.

Tennessee Valley Authority (TVA), independent corporate U.S. federal agency, created for the conservation and preservation of the soil, the control and use of water resources, the production of greater electrical power in the vast region drained by the Tennessee River. Although its projects are centered in Tennessee, they extend also into parts of Alabama, Kentucky, Mississippi, Georgia, North Carolina, and Virginia. Established 1933, TVA was authorized to take over and operate previously built government dams and other installations, and to undertake large-scale regional planning. Among the 24 major dams, most of them built since 1936, are included Wilson, Wheeler, Pickwick, and Norris Dams. These dams create huge reservoirs of

Tennessee Valley Authority

The *Tennessee Valley Authority*'s experimental fertilizer plant at Muscle Shoals, Alabama. It was constructed during World War I and assigned to the Authority in 1933.

water available for power and improvement of navigation, and aid in flood control. TVA-owned plants also produce chemical fertilizers. Constitutionality of TVA was upheld by the U.S. Supreme Court, 1936. In World War II, TVA supplied power to the Oak Ridge atomic project. Atomic plants still use about half of TVA power. One of the most extensive social experiments in the U.S., TVA has been much criticized by some private power interests and others as socialistic.

Tennessee Valley Authority

TVA projects have provided not only inexpensive electric power, but also many new recreational facilities. Above is Wheeler Dam in Alabama. At left is Tennessee's Norris Dam and Lake.

Tenniel, Sir John, 1820-1914, English caricaturist and illustrator. Tenniel became famous through his long connection, 1850-1901, with *Punch,* for which he drew political cartoons. He also illustrated many books, the most notable being Lewis Carroll's *Alice's Adventures in Wonderland* and *Through the Looking Glass.*

tennis, outdoor game played by two or four persons (called respectively singles or doubles) with rackets and balls on a court divided by a net. "Tenez" was first played in France during the reign of Louis XII, 16th cent., on an indoor walled court. Modern lawn tennis was developed c.1873 at the All-English Croquet Club grounds, Wimbledon, England, the first tournament being held in 1877. It was introduced in the U.S., 1874, when a court was laid out on Staten Island, N.Y. At first tennis was a sport available only to the rich, but today millions play, on hard or turf courts. The U.S. Lawn Tennis Association, founded 1881, is the governing body, with more than 800 affiliated clubs. The international trophy is the Davis Cup, offered 1900 by Dwight Filley Davis, American sportsman and statesman. The United States, Great Britain, and Australia have dominated Davis Cup play, except for the year 1927-32, when France ruled the courts. The Wightman Cup, a trophy awarded to the winner of tournaments between the U.S. and British women teams, was first offered 1923. American women have usually overpowered their opposition in Wightman Cup play. Among the great names of tennis are Bill Tilden (*q.v.*), Helen Wills (see *Moody, Helen Wills*), Donald Budge, Ellsworth Vines, Bill Johnston, Molla Mallory, Alice Marble, Helen Jacobs, Maureen Connolly, Althea Gibson, Vic Seixas, Pancho Gonzales, and Chuck McKinley of the U.S.; René LaCoste, Henri Cochet, Jean Borotra, and Suzanne Lenglen of France; Hugh Doherty and Fred Perry of England, Norman Brooks, Frank Sedgman, Lew Hoad, and Ken Rosewell of Australia.

Tennyson, Alfred Tennyson, 1st **Baron,** 1809-92, English poet, b. Lincolnshire. His first work, *Poems, Chiefly Lyrical,* appeared while he was a student at Cambridge, 1830. After *Poems* (1832), which included "The Lady of Shalott," he ceased publishing for 10 years out of respect to his friend, Arthur Henry Hallam, who died in 1833. Publication of his next *Poems* (1842),

Althea Gibson, the first Negro woman tennis champion of international stature, carries the winner's plaque after defeating Angela Mortimer of England for the women's singles title at Wimbledon in 1958.

Court games such as tennis have been popular for centuries. Above are English tennis players on a 15th-century court. Modern tennis tournaments attract huge crowds; below is a tournament match at the West Side Tennis Club in Forest Hills, New York.

Graphic House

containing such poems as "Locksley Hall," "Ulysses," and "Morte d'Arthur," brought recognition and, in 1845, a large annual pension for life. The great success of his *In Memoriam* (1850), elegies inspired by Hallam's death, probably caused his appointment as poet laureate that year. In this capacity he wrote *The Charge of the Light Brigade* (1854). *Idylls of the King* (1st series, 1859; complete series, 1885), based on Arthurian legend, had a universal appeal and were exceeded in popularity only by the narrative poem *Enoch Arden* (1864). Subsequently he wrote several plays, but was not at his best as a dramatist. One of his last volumes was *Demeter and Other Poems* (1889), which included "Crossing the Bar." His genius lay in the short, singing, generously felt lyric poem, although he wrote many longer poems setting forth elements of Victorian morality. He was raised to the peerage in 1884.

Tenochtitlán, ancient city, capital of the Aztec, central Mexico. It was founded c.1325 on an island in Lake Texcoco. Here occurred sacrifices at the great pyramid of Huitzilopochtli. Cortés reached the city 1519 and was repulsed 1520, the Aztec ruler Montezuma being killed. In 1521, after capturing the new ruler, Cuauhtémoc, Cortés took the city and razed it. Mexico City was built on the ruins.

tenor—see *vocal music; voice*.

tent caterpillar, larva of various moths of the genus *Malacosoma*. Widely distributed, it feeds generally on deciduous forest trees. The larvae of some species spin silken tents in the crotches of tree branches, becoming a serious pest. A variety that does not build tents, despite its name, is the U.S. forest tent caterpillar.

Ten Thousand Smokes, Valley of, area, 72 sq. mi., in Katmai National Monument, N Alaska. This region, in a volcanic section, not far from Mt. Katmai, is filled with vents in the surface of the earth, from which are emitted steam and volcanic vapors. Some of the ground near the vents is too hot to stand on. The valley was discovered by R. F. Griggs, 1916.

Tenure of Office Act—see *Johnson, Andrew*.

Ten Years' War, 1868-78, revolt in Cuba for independence from Spain. Trade restrictions and lack of Cuban representation in the government were main causes. Reforms promised in the treaty which ended the war were never forthcoming. Revolt broke out again in 1895 and ended with the Spanish-American War, 1898.

tepee or **tipi,** tent of the American Indians of the plains. It was set up by arranging long poles in a circle at the base, coming together at a point at the top; the cone was then covered with sewed skins, bark, or mats, a vent being left at the top. A door of skin was provided at one side.

terbium, chemical element no. 65 (sym. *Tb.*; at. wt. 159). Discovered in 1842 by Mosander, it is a member of the yttrium (*q.v.*) sub-group of rare earths.

Ter Borch, Gerard, 1617-81, Dutch genre and portrait painter. He traveled in England and on the Continent, working for a time for Philip IV in Spain before settling finally in Holland, 1650. *The Peace of Münster* is one of his best-known pictures. Most of his work was in miniature, exquisite in detail and color.

teredo, genus of mollusks known also as the shipworm, found in the submerged wood of ships, piers, etc., to which it may do great damage. The small annular shell is open at each end, and the mollusk establishes itself when small in the timber, perforating it in numberless directions by means of two small valves. The common shipworm is *teredo navalis*.

Terence (Publius Terentius Afer), c.195-c.159 B.C., Roman writer of comedies, b. Carthage. Brought to Rome as a slave, he was educated and freed. His chief comedy, *Andria*, 166 B.C., was followed by five others. The French comedy by Molière and the English Restoration drama were influenced by Terence's use of situation devices and realistic humor.

Teresa, Saint—see *Carmel, Mt*.

Terman, Lewis Madison, 1877-1956, U.S. psychologist, b. Indiana. For many years (until 1942) head of the psychology department at Stanford Univ., he was best known for his Stanford Revision of the Binet intelligence tests, widely used in schools.

termite, any of various social insects of the order Isoptera, also called white ant, but differing from ants in having thorax and abdomen united in their full width. Chiefly tropical, they feed mostly on dead wood; only a small proportion attack living wood and roots. Some in Africa build nests more than 20 ft. high. In one Australian species the nests are rather flattened, and the edges always point north and south. Familiar U.S. species include five castes: the large queen, which lays thousands of eggs; the king; soldiers;

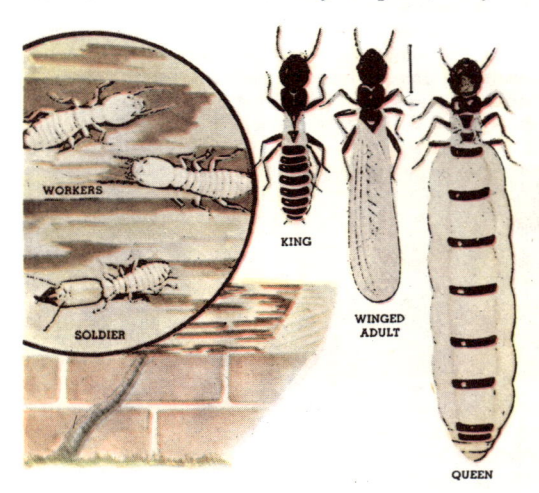

Apache *tepees* on an Arizona reservation

workers; and black-winged reproductives. To avoid light, termites sometimes build mud tunnels between their underground nests and the wood they eat. Hence they may remain undiscovered until wood structures have been badly damaged. Annual damage in the U.S. totals about $40 million. Control is effected by placing anti-termite shields on foundations and poison around the underground nests.

tern, water bird of the gull family (Laridae), belonging to the genus *Sterna* principally. Most terns are smaller than the true gulls and have a deeply forked tail. From their swift, graceful flight they have been termed "sea swallows." The common tern found on the Atlantic Coasts of America and Europe is pure white except for a black cap and grayish back and wings, the bill is orange with a bluish black tip. The legs are red. The tern feeds for the most part on small fish and crustaceans but also eats insects.

terra cotta, a reddish or buff ware made of fine clay and sometimes sand, baked at a high temperature. In architecture it was used in ancient Assyria and Persia in the form of glazed roof tiles and ornamental reliefs. The Greeks and especially

Terra cotta is used for both artistic and functional purposes. The terra cotta statuette at right was executed by Antonio Pollailo. Below are terra cotta tiles for buildings.
Architectural Terra Cotta Institute

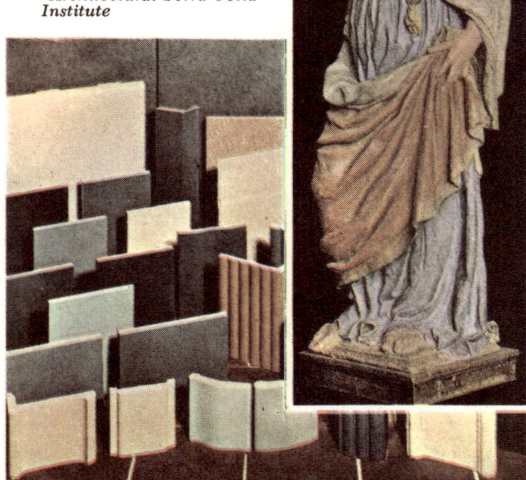

the Etruscans also used it in large, modeled decorations, and passed their art on to the Romans. Since the Renaissance its chief architectural use has been as a construction and fireproofing material. In art the use of terra cotta goes back to earliest times, in both East and West, where it was used in the figures placed in graves. The Greeks modeled small figures, *e.g.,* the Tanagra figurines, but it was the Etruscans who made the greatest use of this medium—in busts, sarcophagi, and urns. In the Renaissance such work was usually glazed and is not commonly spoken of as terra cotta. Terra cotta sculpture was revived in 18th-cent. France in the large figures of Clodion, and it is still used occasionally for portrait busts.

terramycin—see *antibiotics.*

terrapin, an amphibious turtle (family Testudinidae) widely distributed in the Americas and Eurasia, living in fresh or brackish water. The diamondback terrapin (*Malaclemmys*), found in marshes along the Atlantic Coast and Gulf of Mexico, is valued as food. It is so called from markings on the shell. Other common U.S. species are the chicken and slider terrapins and the painted, map, pond, wood, spotted, and Blanding's turtles.

Terre Haute, city, co. seat of Vigo co., W Indiana, on Wabash River; pop. 72,500. It is commercial center for a mining and farming area; the chief industries deal with coal, clay, iron and steel, paint, and glass. The city was founded 1816.

terrier, dog of any of several widely varying breeds, originally much used to catch burrowing animals. The Airedale is the largest, up to 20 in. high and 35 to 45 lb. It is probably a cross between Scotch terrier, otterhound, and bull terrier. The wiry coat is usually black or dark brown on the sides and back, and tan elsewhere. The Bedlington terrier, of lamblike appearance and weighing from 22 to 24 lbs., is a game hunter. The Boston terrier, deriving from a now extinct white English terrier and the English bulldog, ranges from under 15 lb. to 25 lb. Bull terrier, too, is a cross of bulldog to white English terrier, with some pointer blood. It was formerly bred for fighting and as a ratter. It has a long, wedge-shaped head, small, dark eyes, erect ears, and a broad chest, and weighs 15 to 50 lb. Cairn terrier, from Scotland, a good house dog and useful in sport, varies from gray to black, or is sandy or brindled. The hair is wiry, tail and legs short, shoulder height about 9 in. Dandie Dinmont, with short legs, pendulous ears, a rough but not wiry coat, and a silky topknot, ranges from black to light gray. It stands 8 to 11 in. at the shoulder and weighs 14 to 24 lb. Fox terrier, up to 15 in. high, may be smooth-coated or wire-haired. Both are usually black, white, and tan and are capable of prolonged exertion. They kill rats and other pests, but make intelligent and companionable house dogs. Irish terrier, deriving from an old English black and tan terrier, is ordinarily friendly and brave; it weighs 18 to 24 lb., has a

West Highland *terriers*

wiry, red-brown coat. Kerry blue terrier, originally from Ireland, where it was used both for hunting and as a herder, has a silky, bluish gray coat, is about 18 in. high, and weighs 30 to 38 lb. Schnauzer is a rough-haired, heavily built German terrier, unchanged for 500 years. The head is long, with small ears and a kind of beard on the chin. The color varies from grayish to grizzled, or black and tan; the shoulder height, 1 to 2 ft. Scotch (more properly Scottish) terrier, a small, rough-haired dog, is hardy, intelligent, and a first-rate companion and a splendid ratter, once in demand for fox hunting in the Scottish Highlands. It is black, gray, or brindled, stands 9 to 12 in. high, and weighs 16 to 20 lb. Sealyham terrier, developed 19th cent. at Sealyham, Wales, is now popular as a lap dog but was bred for hunting. It is wiry, with white coat; it stands 8 to 12 in. high, weighs 16 to 22 lb. Skye terrier, originally bred on the Isle of Skye and used for hunting, has an extremely long, silky coat, fawn or blue-gray. It has a long body, only 9 in. high, and weighs 14 to 20 lb. There are lob-eared and prick-eared types. Welsh terrier, resembling Airedale except for size, is about 15 in. high, weighs 20 lb.

territorial waters, waters within a nation or surrounding its coast and coming under its sovereignty. In international laws the waters within three mi. of a country's coast are considered territorial. During the 1950s disputes arose over the definition of territorial waters so far as fishing rights are concerned. The matter became the subject of international negotiation and continued in dispute. Some countries, such as Iceland, which were highly dependent on fisheries, wished to extend the limit to 12 mi. Waters leading through the territory of more than one nation are regulated by international agreements, as those for the Dardanelles, the Bosphorus, and the Danube.

territory, in the U.S., formerly a political subdivision not included in any state, but usually having its own legislature and a governor appointed by the President. Territorial status often preceded statehood. Territories, which could send delegates (non-voting) to Congress, could receive statehood after they had petitioned Congress for that status, submitted constitutions, and proved adequate population. Congress could also prescribe special conditions for admission. By the Ordinance of 1787, Congress organized the land northwest of the Ohio River into the Northwest Territory. Territories were formed from the vast lands of the Louisiana Purchase of 1803. All but 19 of the present states were once territories or parts thereof. Hawaii and Alaska were the last territories to become states. Puerto Rico, Virgin Islands, Canal Zone, and some Pacific islands are possessions without territorial status. Puerto Rico is a commonwealth that enjoys certain privileges of territories. The Virgin Islands is an organized but unincorporated territory. Some parts of Canada and Australia have territorial organizations like those of the U.S.

Terror, Reign of—see *Reign of Terror*.

Terry, Ellen Alicia, 1847-1928, English actress, mother of Edward Gordon Craig. Making her debut at age 8, she was chosen 1878 as leading lady of Henry Irving to portray Olivia in a dramatization of Goldsmith's *Vicar of Wakefield*. Their 20-year association at the Lyceum was marked by her unrivaled performances in many Shakespearean roles. After Irving's death, 1905, she continued to act under her own management. The G. B. Shaw-Terry letters form a famous and delightful correspondence. Her stage jubilee, 1906, excited world-wide interest. In 1925 she was made a Dame of the British Empire.

Tertiary Period—see *Cenozoic Era*.

Tertullian (Quintus Septimius Florens Tertullianus), *c.*160-230, Christian theologian, b. Carthage. Converted in his 30s, he devoted himself to writing defenses of Christianity against the pagans and the Jews. Many of his writings are extant, including the *Apology, To the Nations, To the Martyrs,* and tracts on baptism, patience, and penance. Critical of Church practices, he departed from orthodoxy long before his death. His writings, lucid and in excellent Latin were extremely influential.

Tesla, Nikola, 1857-1943, U.S. electrical engineer, b. Austria-Hungary. He migrated to the U.S., 1884, and became one of the foremost inventors of dynamoelectric machines; his researches are largely responsible for the development of modern alternating-current generators, transmitters, and motors. He experimented with high-frequency currents and developed an air core transformer called the Tesla coil.

testes or **testicles,** the male reproductive glands, corresponding to the ovaries in the female. They produce the sperms (spermatozoa) and male sex hormones (androgens). In mammals they are suspended in a pouch called the scrotum, to which they normally descend from the abdomen prenatally or at any time up to adolescence.

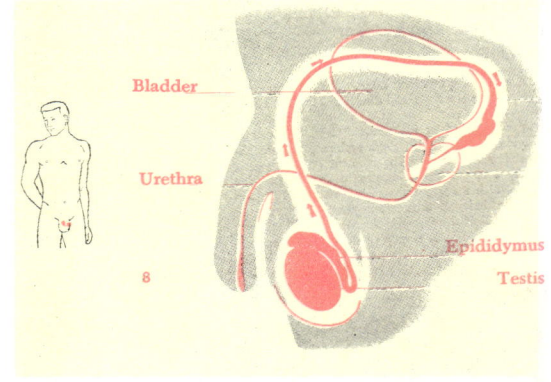

testosterone—see *hormone*.

tetanus or **lockjaw,** infectious disease caused by a toxin produced by the tetanus bacillus. It affects muscle and nerve tissue, resulting in muscle spasms, which often involve the jaw muscles, and in convulsions. The bacillus is a normal inhabitant of the intestine, where it is harmless. Since it flourishes in an atmosphere low in oxygen, tetanus occurs chiefly in deep wounds containing dead tissue and lacking fresh air. Wounds contracted in fields or streets, because they may be contaminated by animal excretions, are the most likely sources. The disease can be prevented after such a wound by tetanus antitoxin, or before injury by prophylactic immunization with tetanus toxoid. Formerly a frequent complication of war wounds, tetanus was virtually eliminated from the American armed forces in World War II by immunization. Treatment is both surgical and medical.

Teton Range, part of Rocky Mts., in NW Wyoming and SE Idaho. Teton Pass, crossed by an overland party to Astoria, 1811, is S of the Grand Teton National Park (established 1929; 299,580 acres). The park includes Grand Teton (13,766 ft.), highest peak of the range.

Tetrazzini, Luisa, 1874-1940, Italian opera singer. A popular coloratura soprano, she toured the U.S., 1910-3, and was a member of the Chicago Opera Co., 1913-4.

Dexter Press

Grand *Teton* Peak (13,766 ft. high) is characteristic of Wyoming's rugged Teton Range.

Tetuán, city, Morocco, near the Mediterranean; pop. 101,155. It is an industrial center as well as a commercial center for an agricultural region. It was taken by the Spanish, 1860, and ceded to Morocco, April 1956, with the establishment of that kingdom.

Tetzel, Johann, *c.*1465-1519, German preacher. A brother of the Dominican order, he opposed Luther in the controversy over indulgences. When Luther published his 95 theses attacking the abuse of these remissions of punishment, Tetzel replied with 106 theses defending the practice of indulgences.

Teutonic Knights, military-religious order, founded 1190 as a fraternity of German knights of the Third Crusade. In the 13th cent. the knights conquered the territory later called East Prussia, forcibly converting some of its pagan inhabitants to Christianity. Ruling as feudal lords, they later came under domination of Poland. Through one of their commanders, a member of the Hohenzollern family, East Prussia became part of Brandenburg and ultimately of Germany. The order, abolished 1809 by Napoleon, was restored 1834 as a religious order of charity in Austria.

Teutonic languages—see *Germanic languages.*

Teutons, ancient people of Germany. Together with the Cimbri they invaded Italy 2nd cent. B.C. and were finally defeated (101 B.C.) by the Roman general Gaius Marius. Their name is used to refer to a great subfamily of the Indo-European linguistic family, but it is not known whether the Teutons spoke a Teutonic or Celtic tongue. The name is loosely used to describe a hypothetical part of the Caucasian (*q.v.*) race characterized by tallness and blondness, and otherwise erroneously termed Nordic or Aryan. The name is today used figuratively for Germans and Scandinavians.

Tewkesbury, municipal borough, Gloucestershire, SW England, at confluence of Avon and Severn Rivers; pop. 5814. It is a market town with some manufacturing. There are the remains of a Roman military camp and a fine 12th-cent. church. Near here was fought the Battle of Tewkesbury, 1471, which resulted in final defeat of the Lancastrians in the Wars of the Roses.

Texas, state, southwestern U.S., 2nd only to Alaska in size, with a land area of 262,840 sq. mi. (its dimensions are 775 by 800 mi. at its widest points); pop. 9,579,677; capital Austin; principal cities Houston, Dallas, San Antonio, Fort Worth, and El Paso. Texas is bounded N by Oklahoma, E by Arkansas and Louisiana, S by Mexico and the Gulf of Mexico, and W by Mexico and New Mexico. There are low plains along the Gulf Coast; the lower Rio Grande Valley, along the boundary with Mexico, is semitropical. Texas has vast semiarid regions in the west, including coastal plains, plateaus, and the high plains. Central and N Texas have rich farm lands. There are rugged mountains and canyons, timber regions, fertile valleys, and huge cattle ranches, both on the plains and along the Gulf. In addition to vast oil and natural gas resources, minerals include coal, sulphur, granite, limestone, asphalt, salt, mercury, and cement; and the chief source of helium is here. Besides the Rio Grande, the principal rivers are the Colorado, the Red, the Trinity, and the Brazos. Oil production, agriculture, and cattle raising are the principal enterprises, but great industries have also been developed, particularly the petroleum and mineral-based chemical and metallurgical industries of the booming Gulf Coast region. Texas leads the nation in beef production, in sheep raising, and in wool and mohair output. Chief crops are cotton, corn, grain, rice, potatoes, peanuts, truck, citrus fruits, and nuts. At Tyler more roses are grown than anywhere else in the world.

The flag of *Texas*; state flower is the bluebonnet.

Spanish explorers wandered into Texas during the 16th cent. La Salle, looking for the mouth of the Mississippi, reached Texas 1685. The Spanish founded only missions and sparse settlements, 17th-18th cent. Filibustering Americans, supporting revolts against restrictive Spanish authority, entered the region after 1800. In 1821, the year Stephen F. Austin led U.S. colonists into the

TEXAS 2572

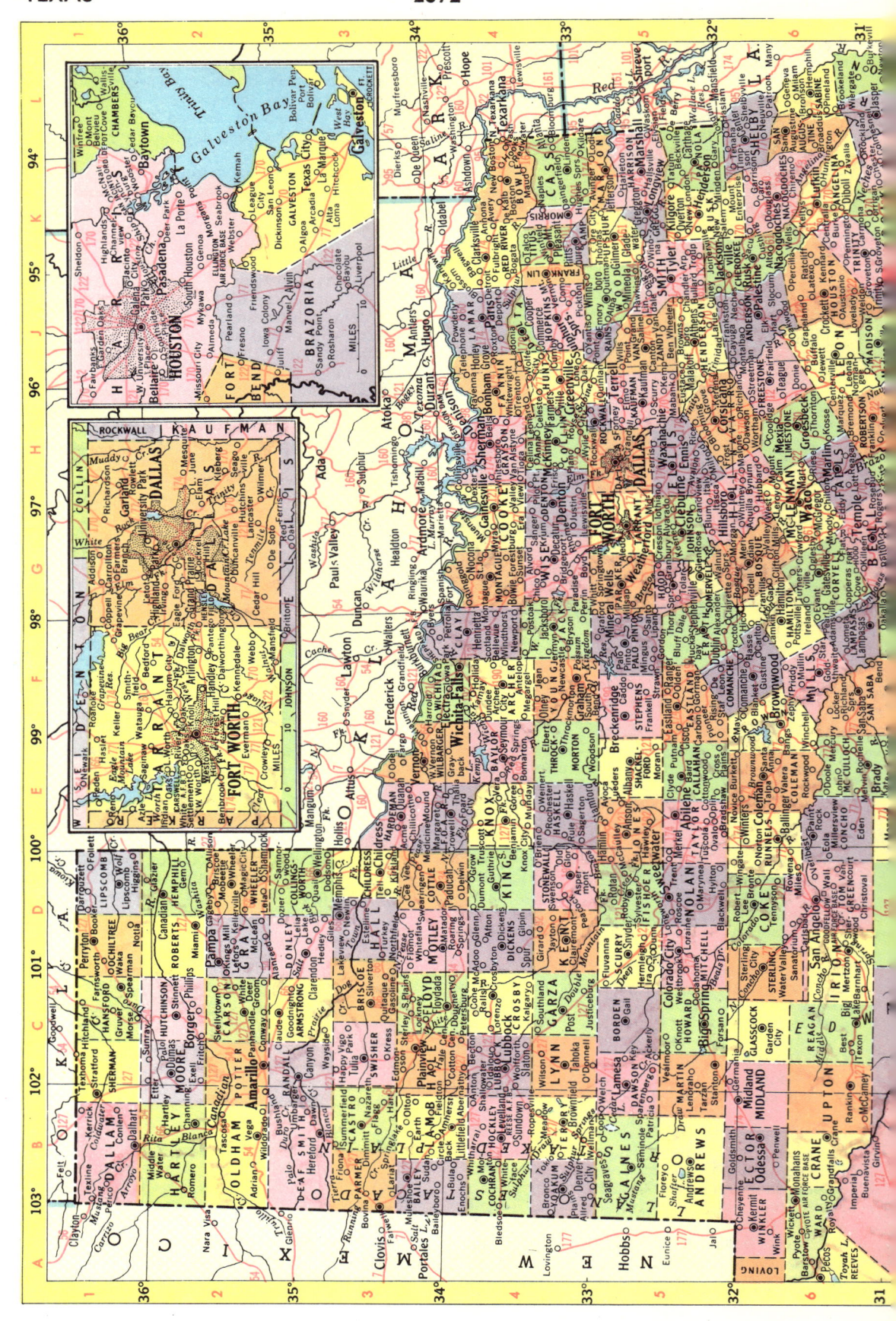

TEXAS

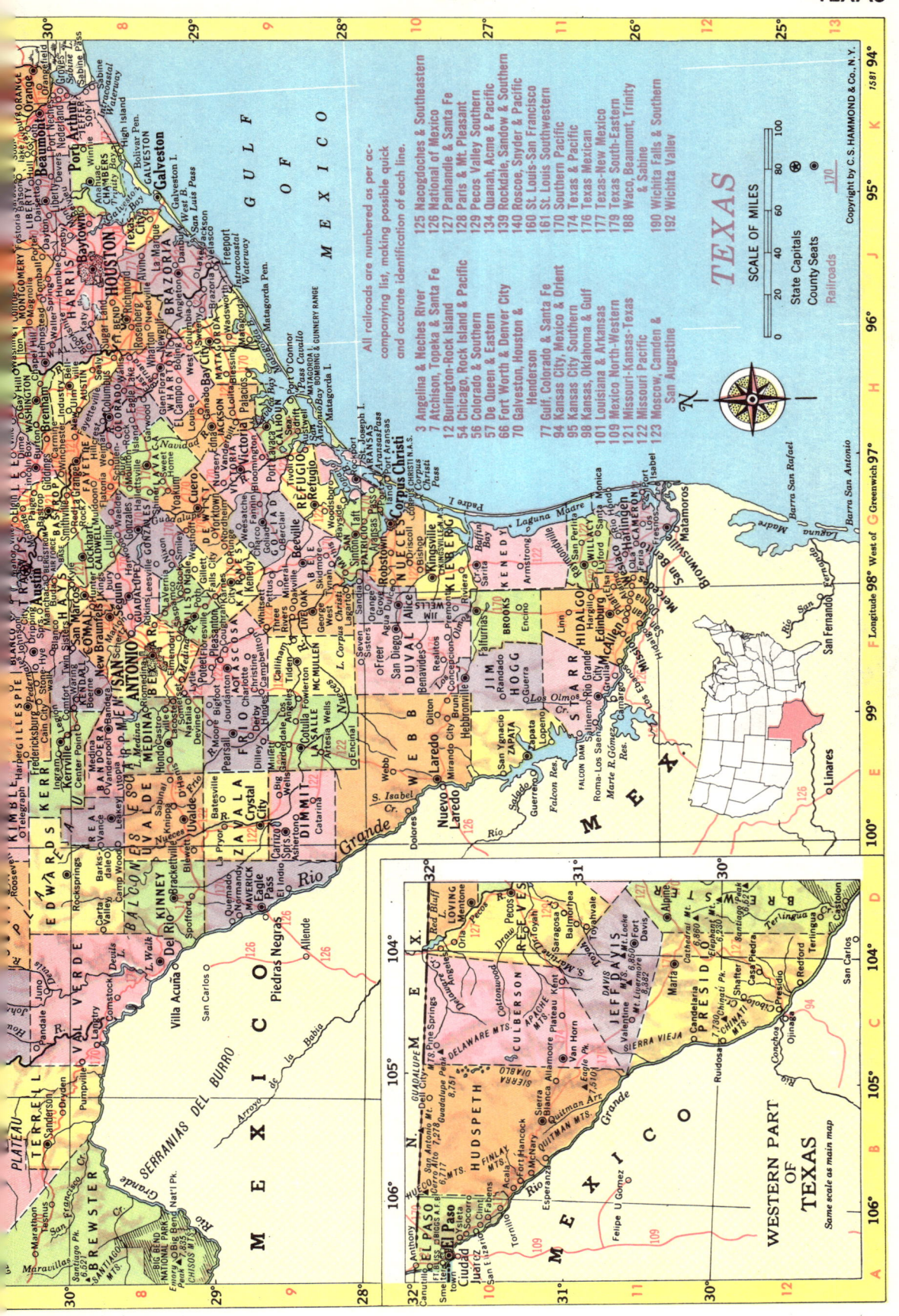

SCALE OF MILES

● State Capitals
◎ County Seats
— Railroads

All railroads are numbered as per accompanying list, making possible quick and accurate identification of each line.

3 Angelina & Neches River
7 Atchison, Topeka & Santa Fe
12 Burlington-Rock Island
54 Chicago, Rock Island & Pacific
56 Colorado & Southern
57 De Queen & Eastern
66 Fort Worth & Denver City
70 Galveston, Houston & Henderson
77 Gulf, Colorado & Santa Fe
94 Kansas City, Mexico & Orient
95 Kansas City Southern
98 Kansas, Oklahoma & Gulf
101 Louisiana & Arkansas
109 Mexico North-Western
121 Missouri-Kansas-Texas
122 Missouri Pacific
123 Moscow, Camden & San Augustine
125 Nacogdoches & Southeastern
126 National of Mexico
127 Panhandle & Santa Fe
128 Paris & Mt. Pleasant
129 Pecos Valley Southern
134 Quanah, Acme & Pacific
139 Rockdale, Sandow & Southern
140 Roscoe, Snyder & Pacific
160 St. Louis-San Francisco
161 St. Louis Southwestern
170 Southern Pacific
174 Texas & Pacific
176 Texas Mexican
177 Texas-New Mexico
179 Texas South-Eastern
188 Waco, Beaumont, Trinity & Sabine
190 Wichita Falls & Southern
192 Wichita Valley

Copyright by C.S. Hammond & Co., N.Y.

WESTERN PART OF TEXAS
Same scale as main map

TEXAS

Above: *Texas'* state Capitol at Austin. Right: the city of El Paso in western Texas.

Dexter Press
American Airlines

Above: the skyline of Houston, *Texas,* as seen from the steps of the City Hall.

Right: monument to American humorist Will Rogers in Fort Worth, Texas. *Dexter Press*

region between the Brazos and Colorado rivers, Mexico broke away from Spain. Friction between U.S. colonists and Mexicans increased, and revolt against Mexican rule began in the 1830s. A declaration of independence from Mexico was issued by the non-Mexican colonists Mar. 2, 1836. War followed, and the tragic siege of the Alamo at San Antonio occurred the same month. After Mexican forces under Santa Anna were defeated, Apr. 21, 1836, at the Battle of San Jacinto by the Texans under Gen. Sam Houston, Texas was recognized as an independent republic and remained so for 10 years. Houston was twice its president. Meanwhile many Texans, as well as people in the U.S., favored annexation of Texas to the U.S., but this was opposed by anti-slavery factions, who feared admission of another slave state. Partly because of British and French ambitions in the area, Texas was finally admitted to the Union, 1845, becoming the 28th state. This event helped precipitate the Mexican War. In 1861 Texas joined the Confederacy, but little fighting occurred in the state. Afterward cattle raising flourished. The coming of railroads stimulated development of more ranches, farms, and cities, and German, Czech, and other European immigrants arrived in substantial numbers. The Mexican population also increased. Discovery of great oil fields has greatly enriched Texans since 1901, and this wealth has been heavily invested in industry and commerce, which were stimulated also by World War II. Texas' coastal cities—Galveston, Houston, Port Arthur, and Corpus Christi—are great seaports for both foreign and local trade. The chief educational institutions are Univ. of Texas at Austin, Texas Agricultural and Mechanical College at College Station, Southern Methodist Univ. at Dallas, Rice Institute at Houston, and Baylor Univ. at Waco. State flower, bluebonnet; motto, Friendship (from the Indian word *Tejas,* source of the state's name).

TEXTILES

Texas Rangers, mounted police of Texas, organized in the 1830s by colonists in the area mainly for defense against Indians. Later they participated brilliantly in the Texas war for independence and in the Civil War. During the early days of stock raising in Texas, they were the

General Sam Houston Monument, Houston, *Texas*

principal force for law and order and thus helped much in the development of the state. Their picturesque life in the open, their courage in the face of often overwhelming odds, and their unexcelled marksmanship have been the theme of many frontier stories.

Left: Bales of wool are tested for quality at a blanket-making factory in Witney, New Zealand.

Below: *Textile* worker mends a broken end on a section of warping machine, used to transfer yarn onto steel drums.
Wool Bureau

textiles from the Latin *texere,* meaning to weave), all woven fabrics. Textiles are made from such natural fibers as wool, flax, cotton, and silk, and such synthetic fibers as rayon, nylon, Orlon, and Dacron. They are the most commonly used materials for clothing and household linens, although industrial fabrics constitute their chief usage. Chemical filters, belts, buffers, and aircraft wing coverings are but a few of the capacities in which textiles serve industry. They are also used in the manufacture of luggage, books, automobiles, and shoes. Types of cloth are identified according to the fibers used, and the particular way in which they are woven. The three most common weaves are plain, twill, and satin. Woven cloth is made from a series of parallel yarns, called warp, interlaced with another set of yarns, the woof or weft, on a loom. The essential process of manufacturing cloth has remained unchanged since primitive times. Fragments of flax yarn found in caves indicate that Swiss lake dwellers of the New Stone Age knew the art of weaving as early as 15,000 B.C. The Egyptians had perfected the craft of weaving fine linens 4000 years before Christ. Silk was being woven in China about 2500 B.C., and cotton in India by 800 B.C. The Spanish conquerors found intricately woven textiles among the Incas of Peru. The ancient Greeks' appreciation of the aesthetic aspect of clothing resulted in refinements in textile weaving and dyeing, as well as encouraging the art of embroidery. The Romans, however, showed less interest in developing the manufacture of cloth than any other ancient peoples, and they imported not only their silks and draperies but also their weavers.

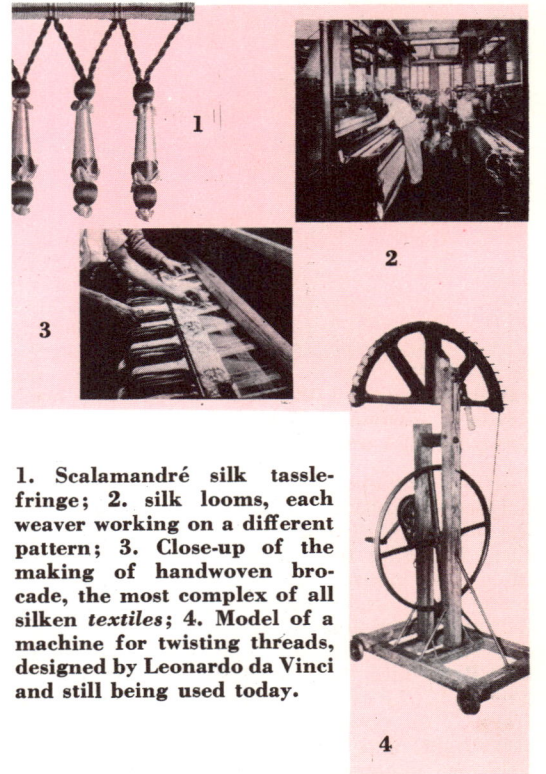

1. Scalamandré silk tassle-fringe; 2. silk looms, each weaver working on a different pattern; 3. Close-up of the making of handwoven brocade, the most complex of all silken *textiles;* 4. Model of a machine for twisting threads, designed by Leonardo da Vinci and still being used today.

TEXTILES

This gold brocade Spanish cape of the 16th century was embroidered in relief on a velvet base material.

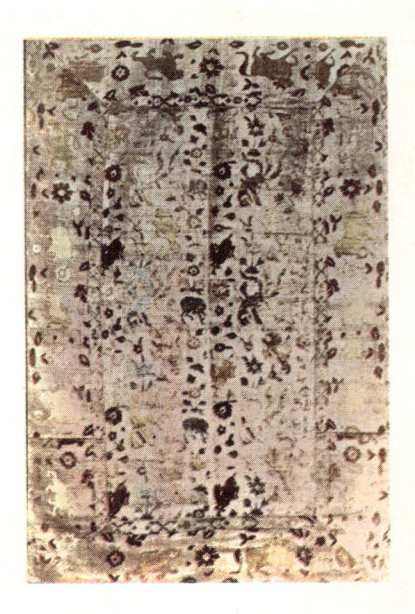

This embroidery is from a detail of a modern costume made in Manipur, India.

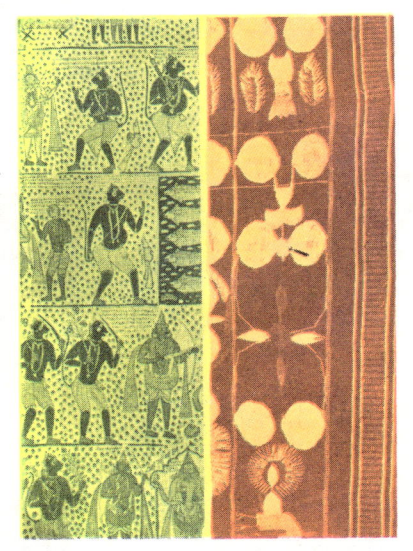

Dating from the 1700s, this Persian velvet brocade is stitched in four different patterns of varying thickness.

An embroidered cloth made by the Banjari tribesmen of Sasaram, India.

The technique of silk culture reached its heights in Europe during the Renaissance. By the 15th cent. France was manufacturing textiles, following the establishment by Francis I of a silk industry at Lyons, for centuries a center of luxurious fabrics. The modern era of factory production of textiles dates from the late 18th cent. with the onslaught of the Industrial Revolution. Such inventions as the spinning jenny (1767) of James Hargreaves, the "water frame," or power loom, (1769) of Richard Arkwright, and the cotton gin (1793) of Eli Whitney, inaugurated the age of machine-made fabrics. The types of machinery used for processing and weaving cotton and wool are similar, and synthetic fibers are processed on either system, depending on the length of fiber used. The first textile mills in the U.S. were established by Samuel Slater in 1793. Today the textile industry of America has grown into a $4 billion-a-year business, employing more than a million workers. Production of cotton, woolen, and worsted, man-made fiber, and silk broad-woven fabrics, which constitute the largest fiber-consuming branch of the textile industry, is over 13,000 million yards annually. See *synthetic fabrics*.

Thackeray, William Makepeace, 1811-63, English novelist, b. Calcutta, India. After his father, an East India Co. official, died (1819), Thackeray was educated in England. In 1834 he went to Paris to study painting; there he married and, having used up his inheritance, returned to England, 1837, supporting his family by contributing regularly to *Punch* and *Fraser's*. Years of constant production, made tragic by the insanity of his wife after 1840, finally resulted in popular acclaim with the serial publication of the novel *Vanity Fair* (1847-8). His literary reputation firmly established, in the following decade he published *Pendennis* (1850), *Henry Esmond* (1852), and *The Newcomes* (1853-5). After *The Virginians* (1859) he edited the *Cornhill Magazine* for 2 years and published in it his last novels, including the unfinished *Denis Duval*. Like Dickens he taxed his health by driving himself to give lectures in London and the U.S. At his best Thackeray develops his narrative with fine realism and acute observation of character.

Thai or **Tai languages,** a sub-family of the Sino-Tibetan languages (*q.v.*), sometimes referred to as the Kadai sub-family, consisting of Thai (Siamese), Lao (Laotian) and the Shan languages of Burma. The Thai languages are isolating, i.e. like Chinese, they are composed of primarily monosyllabic root words with a rigidly defined word order for syntactical purposes. Also like Chinese, the Thai languages are polytonal, having five basic tones; a given monosyllable will vary in meaning depending on the tone of voice used, whether even, rising, falling, etc. See *language*.

Thailand, kingdom, SE Asia, until 1949 called **Siam,** bounded E by Laos and Cambodia, W by Burma, S by Malaya and the Gulf of Siam; area 198,263 sq. mi.; pop. 22,718,000; capital Bangkok. Its S part occupies the upper section of the

Above, Becky Sharp of *Thackeray's* famed novel, *Vanity Fair*. Below, Howard Pyle's conception of Clive and Ethel Newcome, central character's in Thackeray's *The Newcomes*.

The flag of *Thailand*

Malay Peninsula, with the Isthmus of Kra. Bordered by high mountains, the country has a large interior plain with a great rice belt, watered by the Chao Phraya River. More than half the land area is forested. Teak and other woods as well as rubber, coconuts, and cotton are the chief exports. Tin and antimony are mined. Besides the native Thai, the population includes many Chinese and other Orientals. Buddhism is the predominant religion.

Siam was part of the Khmer empire, 11th-13th cent.; then a native kingdom became dominant. The Burmese began raiding the country, 15th cent.; then a native kingdom became dominant. peans to trade here, arrived, followed by Dutch, British, and French. Between 1893 and 1909 the country's boundaries shrank, Cambodia being ceded to the French, and sovereignty over four Unfederated Malay States yielded to the British. In 1932 King Prajadhipok granted a constitution, but political progress was halted, 1938, when a militarist group came into power. After the country was occupied by the Japanese, Dec. 1941,

Left, a Thai girl holds her young brother. Above left, a village in Chiang Rai province of *Thailand*, with zebu cattle; the houses, built on piles, are cool and dry. Middle, Thai rivers abound in fish; once a year great schools rush upstream and many are caught in nets. Above right, Thai merchants, in light-weight boats, travel with their produce to Bangkok; the actual selling will be done by women. Right, a Thai merchant woman offers freshly grilled bananas.

Graphic House

Pan American Airways

Above: entrance to the Temple of the Emerald Buddha in Bangkok, *Thailand*.

Right: standing Buddha in Bangkok, indicative of the importance of Buddhism in Thai life.

Graphic House

the puppet government declared war against the Allied powers and annexed parts of Indo-China, Malaya, and Burma. In 1946 a new constitution providing for a popularly elected legislature was signed by King Ananda, who soon afterward died mysteriously. He was succeeded, 1946, by his younger brother, Phumiphon Adulyadet. A constitution of 1952 provides for a unicameral national assembly, half of whose 246 members are appointed and the other half elected. For a time a military junta ruled the country after 1952.

Power, however, devolved into the hands of Field Marshal Sant Thanarat. His government was strongly pro-Western and was an important partner in anti-Communist moves in Southeast Asia.

Thales, c.640-550 B.C., Greek philosopher, statesman, and mathematician, b. Miletus, Asia Minor. Regarded as one of the Seven Wise Men of Greece, he put forward the idea that water is the first principle of the universe, everything else being but a variant of it. He was thus one of the first to suggest a scientific explanation of the facts of the universe. He is said to have foretold an eclipse of the sun that took place 585 B.C.

thallium, element no. 82 (sym. *Tl;* at. wt. 204.39; m.p. 303.5° C.; sp. gr. 11.86), a silvery-white metal, malleable, and moderately active. Its existence was first predicted by means of spectroscope in 1861; it was isolated the following year. In its physical properties thallium resembles lead; with non-metals, it forms various salts, all of which are extremely poisonous. Not generally employed in industry or commerce due to its toxic qualities, thallium appears to be widely distributed in nature, frequently occurring with such substances as raw iron, copper pyrites, native sulphur, and the like.

Thallophyta, a subkingdom of the plant kingdom including the primitive-mainly aquatic plants (*e.g.* the fungi and the algae), with no true roots, stems, or leaves. Reproduction is primarily asexual.

Thames River, c.150 mi. long, S Ontario, flowing SW, past London, to the St. Clair River. Near Chatham, Oct. 5, 1813, was fought the **Battle of the Thames** in the War of 1812. An American force, under Gen. W. H. Harrison, defeated British and Indian forces under Gen. H. A. Proctor and Tecumseh. The battle established U.S. control of the Northwest, and the death of Tecumseh destroyed the Indian confederation against the U.S.

Thames River, c.210 mi. long, S England, rising in the Costwold Hills in Gloucestershire and flowing E, mostly through pastoral country, to its estuary, which opens into the North Sea. It is the principal river of Great Britain. Among its tributaries are the Cherwell, Kennet, Mole, and

Above, boats along the *Thames* are colorfully decorated to celebrate the Festival of Britain. The famous Tower Bridge, built in 1894, is one of many that span the Thames river from Gloucester to London. *Pan American Airways*

THANKSGIVING

Medway. Oxford, Henley, Eton, Windsor, Hampton Court, and London lie on its banks. Around the Oxford area it is known as the Isis River. Canals connect it with the industrial centers of England. It is navigable by lightdraft boats to Lechlade, Gloucestershire, and by sea-going vessels to the port of London, which extends from London Bridge to Blackwall. In London the Thames is spanned by 15 bridges, most famous of which is London Bridge, 1831, which replaced a 13th-cent. bridge. In Roman times the river was called Tamesis.

Thanksgiving Day, national holiday in the U.S., the 4th Thursday in November. It marks the November day, 1621, when the Plymouth colonists, acting on a proclamation by Gov. Bradford, held a feast and gave thanks to Providence for the good harvest following the lean winter of 1620-1. From the time of Lincoln's proclamation, 1863, Thanksgiving has been proclaimed each year by the President and the state governors as a day for thanks to God for the blessings of the year. It is popularly celebrated with feasting and church-going. The last Thursday in November was the day specified by Lincoln. Pres. F. D. Roosevelt chose the 3rd Thursday, in 1939, 1940 and 1941, and Congress later specified the 4th Thursday.

Above: The "first *Thanksgiving*" day took place in New England in November, 1621, when the Pilgrim Fathers shared their repast with friendly Indians.

Below: Macy's annual Thanksgiving Day Parade in New York City.

Graphic House

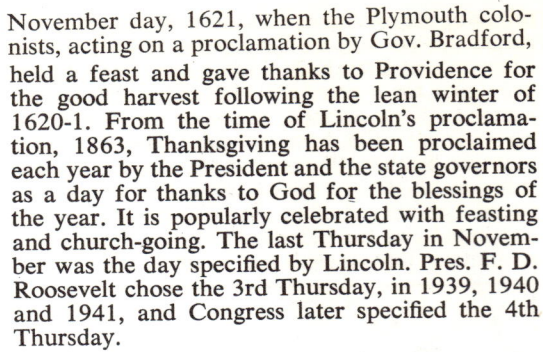

Above: In the same parade, a patriotic display passes the Museum of the New York Historical Society on Central Park West.

Below: A float in the Macy's *Thanksgiving* Day Parade representing the story of Cinderella.

Graphic House

Théâtre Français—see *Comédie Française.*

Thebes, ancient city of Egypt, now completely in ruins. Modern Karnak and Luxor are near its site on the Nile. One of the oldest cities in Egypt, it began to grow after it was made capital by the founders of Dynasty XII, and reached its peak in Dynasties XVIII and XIX, when its mammoth buildings and riches were the envy of the world. Later the seat of power moved northward, and the city never recovered from the sacking of 661 B.C. by Assyrians. One of the world's greatest collection of monumental ruins, Thebes boasts of a giant necropolis, the temples of Karnak and Luxor built for the sun-god Amen, and the tomb of Tutankhamen.

Thebes, Greek city, 33 mi. NNW of Athens; pop. 9126. According to tradition, it was founded by the "Phoenician" Cadmus; its acropolis was called the Cadmea. It was the home of Pindar, and memorable in Greek mythology as that of Oedipus and Hercules. In ancient times Thebes dominated the other cities of Boeotia (*q.v.*) and was an implacable foe of its neighbor Athens, against which it supported Persia in the invasion of 479 B.C., and Sparta during the Peloponnesian War. Thebes soon turned on her ally and became, under Epaminondas, 371-362 B.C., the leading city of Greece. The rise of Macedonia finally drew Athens and Thebes together in defense of Greek freedom; they shared the defeat of Chaeronea, 338 B.C. In 336 B.C. Alexander the Great made an example of Thebes by destroying the city and selling its citizens as slaves.

Alexander the Great reviews his troops after the sack of *Thebes*, 336 B.C. Only the citadel, the temples and Pindar's house were spared by the Macedonian armies.

theism, belief in a personal God, creator and mover of the universe, transcending the creation, yet eternally participating in it. Believers in such monotheistic faiths as Judaism, Islam, and Christianity may be characterized as theists; theism is a philosophical rather than a theological term. It is distinguished from deism, belief in a deity removed from the universe; pantheism, belief that the universe, or nature, is the expression of deity; and monotheism and polytheism, which refer to the aspects of divinity. See *God.*

Theiss River—see *Tisza River.*

theme, in musical composition, a recognizable, separate and structurally significant element in the total work, often equated with the "subject," although this latter term may include several or more themes. In a musical work, themes usually recur, or are developed, but always remain essentially identifiable. A "melody" may be a theme, but a theme does not necessarily imply the lyric quality which is usual here. It may be a rather lengthy musical statement, as in many "themes and variations," where it is the center of a specific musical form. It is an important element in much program music, such as "symphonic poems," where its significance is less that of abstract development (as in themes and variations), as that of recurrent evocation and development of an atmosphere or mood. The term "motif" denotes the shortest possible, self-existent theme. The Wagnerian "leitmotif" is a device used to announce an object, a person, or an aspect of character.

Themis, in Greek mythology, daughter of Uranus and Ge (Heaven and Earth), and like her husband Iapetus, a Titan. Prometheus, Epimetheus, and Atlas were their children. However, Themis was also a goddess of law and natural harmony, the wife of Zeus, and by him the mother of the Fates and the Hours. She is depicted holding scales and a cornucopia.

Themistocles, *c.*528-*c.*462 B.C., Athenian statesman. He founded Athenian naval power, which gave his city leadership over all Greece. Under his direction Piraeus was fortified, a strong navy was built, and the Persian fleet, on its approach, was lured into narrow waters to its destruction (Battle of Salamis, 480 B.C.). Becoming unpopular, Themistocles to save his life, *c.*468 B.C. fled to the Persians and served them during his last years.

Theocritus, 3rd cent. B.C., Greek poet, b. Syracuse. He lived first at Cos and then at Alexandria. Of his poems, 30 idyls are extant. He was the first and greatest of the pastoral poets. Virgil was influenced by his work.

Theodora, A.D. 508?-548, Byzantine empress. She was apparently a courtesan and actress before her marriage, 523, to Justinian I, shortly before he became emperor of the Eastern Roman Empire. Noted for her beauty, wit, cruelty, and resolution, for 20 years she had great influence over him.

Theodoric (Theodoric the Great), A.D. *c.*454-526, ruler of the Ostrogoths from 474, and of Italy from 493. Invading Italy, he defeated and killed Odoacer, then established Ostrogothic rule over Italy, with Ravenna and Verona as his capitals. Considering himself an officer of the empire, he recognized both Roman and Gothic law and used many Romans as administrators, including Boëthius, later executed for treason. In German legend he is Dietrich von Bern, *i.e.* Theodoric of Verona.

Theodosius I (Theodosius the Great), A.D. *c.*346-395, Roman emperor. Upon the emperor Valens' death, 378, Theodosius was made emperor of the East by Gratian. He subdued the Goths and then, 388, defeated Maximus, who had killed Gratian and usurped power in the West. Theodosius was an intimate of St. Ambrose, bishop of Milan; but after Theodosius had ordered the massacre of 7000 Thessalonians, because an official of their city had been murdered, he submitted to Ambrose's demand for his public penance, 390— an event significant of imperial subjection to church law. The last to rule the entire Roman empire. Theodosius was succeeded by his sons Honorius and Arcadius, who permanently divided it. The son of Arcadius, **Theodosius II**, 401-450, was the second Byzantine emperor, ruling from 408. He appeased the Huns with subsidies and codified Roman law (the Theodosian Code, on which the code of Justinian was later based).

theology (from the Greek word *theos*, God, and *logos*, doctrine), the science which treats with the existence of God, His attributes, and the Divine will regarding our actions, present condition, and ultimate destiny. The sources of theology are of two kinds: *natural*, or *philosophical*, in which the knowledge of God derives from nature or reason; and *supernatural, positive*, or *revealed*, as set forth in sacred writings. The contents of theology are classified into the categories of *theoretical* theology, or dogmatics, and *practical* theology, or ethics.

As comprehending the whole extent of religious science, theology is divided into four principal classes: *historical, exegetical, systematic*, and *practical*. Historical theology treats with the history of doctrine. Exegetical theology embraces the interpretation of sacred writings and criticism. Systematic theology arranges methodically the great truths of of religion. Practical theology consists of an exhibition, first, of precepts and directions; and second, of the motives from which we should be expected to comply with these. Apologetic and polemic theology belong to several of the above-mentioned classes at once.

Theology is a part of the religious tradition of all sophisticated societies. In the western world, it usually connotes Christianity, although Islam and Judaism both have elaborate theological systems. In Christianity, theological systems grew out of the conflict with heresies within the church and the challenges of religious groups without it. The greatest early conflict within the church was the Arian controversy, which was largely responsible for the convening of the Council of Nicaea. A major theological opponent of early Christianity outside the church was Manichaeism (*q.v.*). St. Augustine was originally a Manichaean, and much of the impetus for his theological formulations derived from his later opposition to this group. Augustine was greatly influenced by Platonism, and especially by the Neo-Platonism of Plotinus (*q.v.*). His systematic theological formulation rested on an essentially emotional apologia for his faith; this approach remains one of the two major Catholic traditions to this day.

The second is Scholasticism which was essentially a review of Christian theology that took place in the 12th and 13th cents. It questioned the Augustinian dependence on Platonic philosophical categories, and debated its mystical, or "irrational" emphasis. Many Scholastics insisted that philosophy should avoid the area of the revealed and the assumed. St. Anselm (*q.v.*), a rationalist, was a major 12th cent. scholastic. Duns Scotus, and preeminently St. Thomas Aquinas (*qq.v.*) represented the 13th cent. in the controversy between revelation and reason.

The Protestant Reformation, theologically speaking, was Augustinian, or anti-rational, in nature. It doubted the possibility of rational vindication of religious truths, and shunned dialectical or speculative approaches to religious belief. Eighteenth-cent. "enlightenment," as exemplified by Kant, raised questions as to the nature or existence of God, examined basic assumptions of faith, and, in a Thomistic sense, was philosophy improperly employed rather than true theology. (The Scholastics conceived of theology as the systematic investigation of revealed truths, while philosophy proceeds always from reason and does not investigate truths that transcend reason.)

In the 20th cent., neo-Scholasticism is a significant movement, as exemplified by the work of Jacques Maritain. Contemporary Protestant thought continues in the Reformation anti-rationalist, Augustinian approach; thus the theological direction of such men as Reinhold Niebuhr, Karl Barth, and Paul Tillich derives from the Danish philosopher-theologian Soren Kierkegaard. The major theological controversy of contemporary western Christianity is that which it has always been: rationalism *vs.* irrationalism. But perhaps the major common effort of most modern theologians, no matter what their position on this question, is their attempt to reconcile the new physical and social sciences and the new speculative techniques with the essential articles of their religious faith.

Theophrastus, *c*.372-287 B.C., Greek philosopher, He studied under Plato and Aristotle, succeeding the latter as head of the Peripatetic School. Two treatises on botany, *On the History of Plants* and *On the Causes of Plants*, are his important works, most of his copious writings having been lost. His *Characters*, sketches of individual types, as "The Chatterer," etc., influenced later writers, particularly in France.

theorbo—see *stringed instruments*.

theorem, a statement of truth or fact. In mathematics, a theorem defines certain absolute relationships between various algebraic or geometric terms or functions; the theorem, however, must be proved step by step in order to have any validity. The well-known **Pythagorean Theorem**, which states that the square of the hypotenuse of a right triangle is equal to the sum of the squares of the two other sides, may be demonstrated through an indefinite number of examples to be true, but this does not prove the rule as being absolute for all cases. A "proof" must be devised which, step by step, brings the inevitable generality that the theorem always must hold true. This may be done by purely geometric means, or with the use of algebraic equations. The theorem differs from the *axiom* and *postulate*, which are considered self-evident and are incapable of being proved in the above manner. See *algebra; geometry; mathematics*.

theosophy, religious system based on intuitive knowledge of God. The name, meaning divine wisdom, is applicable to such teachings as those of ancient Hindu philosophers, Neo-Platonists, Gnostics, and Buddhists. An important early modern theosophist was the German Jakob Boehme, whose writings, notably *Aurora* (1612, pub. 1634), influenced Spinoza and Hegel. Theosophy in its modern form is represented by the Theosophical Society, founded 1875 by Mme

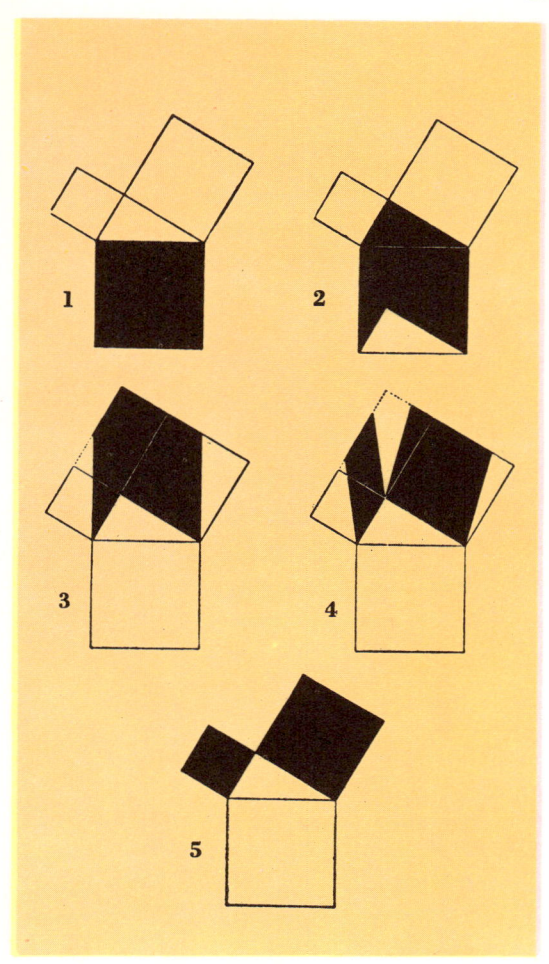

A geometric proof of the Pythagorean *theorem*: 1. The square of the hypotenuse is marked in black; 2. a triangle is constructed on top of the square, and then an equal triangle is omitted at its base; 3. the form of the black area is not changed, but is moved upward until its base line is lifted to the height of its top line; 4. the black area is split—each of the two parts taking the form of a parallelogram and moved sideways; the bases and heights are unchanged, so that the areas remain precisely the same; 5. this process can be continued until the black areas reach their last phase and become identical with the squares of the other two legs; 6. this completes the derivation of the theorem.

Elena Blavatsky. The world center of this society, which claims a membership of c.50,000, is near Madras, India; its U.S. headquarters is at Wheaton, Ill.

therapy or **therapeutics**, in general, the medical science which treats of the application of remedies for diseases. **Drug therapy** refers to the use of a variety of chemical substances to alter the functioning of the body in such a way that the health of an individual is stimulated and/or pathological conditions of all sorts are dissipated. Some drugs are inorganic compounds, while others are substances taken from plants or animals; recently such organic drugs have been synthesized in both laboratories and factories. Sulfa, adrenalin, vitamins, and antibiotics, as well as antitoxins and other vaccines and sera, are all examples of drug therapy as it is practiced today.

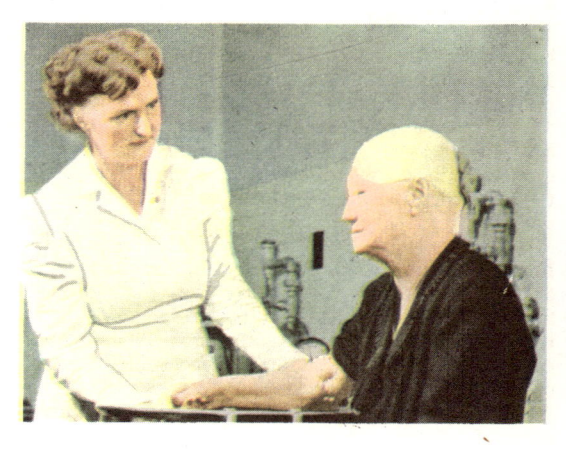

Above: Physical *therapy* has recently been applied to the treatment of older persons with chronic ailments such as arthritis. However, the traditional application of this technique is still the rehabilitation of children and young adults, such as the polio victims below.

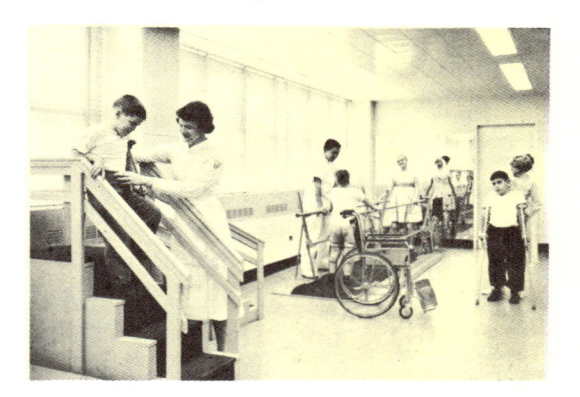

Electric shock therapy is the use of high voltages of electricity in the curing of psychopathological conditions. In use since the late 19th cent., the usual method of treatment is the introduction of the electric current into the brain by means of two electrodes. It was found during World War II, that many soldiers who had been rendered incapable of fighting, or even totally incapacitated by traumas resulting from battle (*i.e.* "shell shock"), would show remarkable recovery of their senses after this method of therapy. However, it soon became apparent that such recoveries were only of a transitory nature, as most patients treated in this manner sooner or later relapsed to their former state, sometimes in only a matter of days or weeks. It is now believed that electric shock is not in the strictest sense a "therapy" at all, but merely a means of putting the patient "within reach" of other psychotherapeutic methods dealing with his particular problems.

THERMODYNAMICS

Chemotherapy is the use of drugs to destroy or inhibit the growth of alien micro-organisms in the body which cause disruption in its normal functioning. In addition, gains are being made in the use of chemicals for treatment of such conditions as cancer and heart disease, neither of which is believed to be caused exclusively (if at all) by "germs." Real or artificially produced hormones, for example, have been shown to affect greatly the growth of tumors, both malignant and benign.

Any electrical instruments used to diagnose or relieve illness in general are part of the discipline called **electrotherapy.** Examples include the electrocardiagram and the electroencephalograph (*qq.v.*).

Physiotherapy is a term which refers to combination of "physical" treatments to stimulate a patient's health. Unlike the previously mentioned therapies, which seek to destroy or seek out unhealthy influences on the body, physiotherapy is usually employed in the rehabilitation of patients after basic recovery from a pathological condition (*e.g.*, paralysis, stroke) has been affected. Heat (**thermotherapy**), light (**phototherapy**), water (**hydrotherapy**), and **occupational therapy** (*q.v.*) may all be employed to help a person speed his recovery from serious illness. See *medicine*; *radiotherapy*.

thermodynamics, in physics, the study of heat relative to mechanical and other forms of energy. Joule was first to determine the mechanical equivalent of heat, asserting that heat is a form of energy. Other important early-19th-cent. pioneers were Rumford and Davy. Maxwell, Lord Kelvin, and others studied heat in relation to molecular motion. Of the so-called laws of thermodynamics, the first states that a definite amount of heat is absorbed for every unit of work done and that a given quantity of work produces a definite amount of heat. The second law states that heat energy is transferred always from a place of high to one of low temperature. An additional third law of thermodynamics maintains that the absolute zero of temperature can never be reached. A special field of thermodynamics applied to the heat mechanism of chemical reactions is thermochemistry.

thermometer, instrument for measuring variations in temperature. The common household thermometer consists of a sealed glass capillary tube, ending in a bulb at the bottom containing alcohol or mercury, and with a vacuum in the upper part. As the temperature rises, the liquid expands and rises in the tube, on which graduations give the reading; correspondingly, a drop in temperature causes the level of the liquid to fall. Electrical thermometers that measure temperature in terms of varying electrical resistance are used for very high and very low temperatures. For various purposes other types of thermometers are used, such as the bimetallic type, in which temperature change is indicated by the difference between the change in length of one metal strip and the change in length of another (having a different coefficient of expansion) resulting from a change of temperature. In English-speaking countries the Fahrenheit temperature scale is ordinarily used, with freezing point at 32° and boiling point at 212°. For scientific purposes the centigrade (*q.v.*) scale is almost universal, with freezing at 0° and boiling at 100°. Also used for scientific purposes are the Kelvin or "absolute" scale, with zero at absolute zero (—273.1°C) and using the centigrade degree as the unit, and the Réaumur, with freezing point at 0°C and boiling at 80°C. These various scales can be converted as follows (C = number of degrees centigrade, F = Fahrenheit, R = Réaumur):

$$F = 9 \times C \div 5 + 32$$
$$C = 5 \times (F - 32) \div 9$$
$$F = 9 \times R \div 4 + 32$$
$$C = R + (R \div 4)$$
$$R = 4 \times (F - 32) \div 9$$

See *weights and measures.*

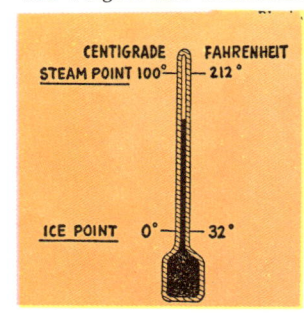

Above: *thermometers* with Centigrade and Farenheit scales.

Right: the first thermometer, devised by students of Galileo.

At left is an eighteenth-century French room *thermometer*. Center is a nineteenth-century thermometer-barometer combination. The instrument at right is an hygrometer as well.

One of the most recent developments is the *thermometer* attached to a thermostat, thus facilitating control of room temperature.

"*Theseus* and the Minotaur," a 20th-cent. French tapestry designed by Marc Saint-Saëns.

thermonuclear bomb—see *fusion, nuclear; nuclear weapons*.
Thermopylae, mountain pass, E Greece, between Mt. Oeta and Gulf of Lamia. There, 481 B.C., during the Persian Wars (*q.v.*), a heroic band of Greeks under King Leonidas futilely resisted a gigantic force of invading Persians. The latter, expected to follow a coastal road between cliffs and sea, where the Greeks were stationed, reached the Greek rear by a mountain trail. Leonidas with his 300 Spartans and 700 Thespians, who refused to retire with the main body of the Greek army, remained fighting in the pass until they were annihilated. The encounter had no effect on the war's outcome, but was considered symbolic of Greek courage.
thermos bottle—see *vacuum bottle*.
thermostat, appliance for automatically indicating changes in temperature by the expansion of metals. It is used for regulating steam pressures or temperatures, as in homes or incubators. A common type consists of a strip composed of dissimilar metals which have different coefficients of expansion. The strip bends with temperature changes and, in bending, makes or breaks an electrical contact.
Theseus, in Greek legend, an early king of Athens, son of Aegeus. Reared in his mother's house at Troezen, as a man he journeyed to Athens, slaying Procrustes and other brigands on the way. One of seven youths and seven maidens doomed to be fed to the Minotaur, Theseus with Ariadne's aid slew the monster. On the way home he forgot to change the sails from black to white to announce victory, and Aegeus, seeing the black, killed himself, whereupon Theseus became king. He conquered the Amazons and made their queen, Hippolyta, his wife; their son was Hippolytus. After Hippolyta died Theseus kidnaped Helen, but her brothers rescued her. He tried to help his friend Perithous kidnap Persephone from Hades, but both were held there until Hercules rescued Theseus alone. In his absence Phaedra, his last wife, fell in love with Hippolytus and, repulsed, killed herself, casting blame on the youth. Theseus cursed Hippolytus, and Poseidon caused the death of the boy. A tyrant in later years, Theseus was driven from Athens and murdered in distant Scyros.

Thespis, 6th cent. B.C., Greek dramatist. Regarded as the founder of tragedy, he introduced an actor outside of the chorus who conversed with the leader of the chorus, thus developing dialogue and converting the choral song into rudimentary drama.
Thessalonians, Epistles to the—see *Epistles*.
Thessalonica or **Thessaloniki**—see *Salonika*.
Thessaly, department of Greece; area 5395 sq. mi.; pop. *c.*694,461. In ancient times, as the region of Greece south of Macedonia, it was a fertile plain noted for its grain and horses, ruled by feudal lords, and played no part in Greek affairs until Jason of Pherae (374-370 B.C.) ruled it as a kingdom and invaded S Greece. Falling under Macedonian control, Thessaly was liberated by Rome, 196 B.C., but later became part of the Roman province of Macedonia. Its chief city was Larissa, now capital of the department, pop. *c.*55,733.
Thetis, in Greek legend, a sea-nymph, daughter of Nercus and Doris. Zeus, Poseidon, and other gods wooed her until they learned the prophecy that her son would surpass his father. The mortal Peleus became her husband, and all the gods attended the wedding except Eris (*q.v.*), who incited strife among them. Her son was the hero Achilles.
thiamine—see *vitamins*.
Thiers, Louis Adolphe, 1797-1877, French statesman and writer. Prominent in bourgeois opposition to Charles X, as author of the 10-vol. *History of the French Revolution* (1823-7) he helped induce Louis Philippe to accept the French crown during the July Revolution, 1830. Failing to gain support for aggressive foreign policies while foreign minister, 1832-4, and premier, 1836, he opposed the conservative ministry of Guizot, 1847-8, and helped precipitate the February Revolution, 1848. Forced to withdraw from politics after the *coup d'état* of the later Emperor Napoleon III, Dec. 1851, he devoted himself to his 10-vol. *History of the Consulate and the Em-*

pire (1845-62). Allowed to return, he became leader of the Liberal opposition. As such, after the fall of the empire in the Franco-Prussian War, he was elected chief of the executive power of the provisional government, Feb. 1871, which office became that of president of the republic, Aug. 1871. In constitutional battles between royalists and republicans from which the Third Republic emerged, his own sentiments gradually became republican. After he made peace, suppressed the revolt of the Paris Commune, Mar. 1871, and arranged payment of the German indemnity, 1872, he was judged insufficiently conservative by a predominantly royalist assembly, 1873, and resigned.

Third Republic—see *France*.

Thirty-Nine Articles, major formulation of the official creed of the Anglican Church. They were finally approved, 1571, in the reign of Queen Elizabeth I, and ratified, 1604 and 1628, under James I and Charles I. They were based on 42 articles of faith originally drawn up by Archbishop Thomas Cranmer, 1551, under Edward VI. The approved articles are accepted also by several Episcopalian Churches.

Thirty Tyrants—see *Critias*.

Thirty Years' War, 1618-48, European War, initially religious, later predominantly political, directed against the Hapsburg power. In a revolt by Bohemian Protestant nobles, 1618, against their Catholic king, Ferdinand (later Emperor Ferdinand II), the Bohemian crown was offered to Frederick V (*q.v.*). After Frederick's defeat, 1620, the extirpation of Protestantism in Bohemia, and victories for the imperialist forces, leadership of the Protestants devolved, 1625, on Christian IV of Denmark, who had territorial ambitions in Germany. But repeated victories of Wallenstein and Tilly for the imperialists resulted in the Edict of Restitution, 1629, returning to the church all ecclesiastical estates secularized since 1552, and proscribing all Protestant sects in the empire other than the Lutherans. Gustavus II of Sweden, fearful of Hapsburg control of the Baltic, now came forward as champion of the anti-Hapsburg forces. With the aid of subsidies from Cardinal Richelieu of France, the tide was turned against the imperialists, despite Gustavus' death at Lützen, 1632. Richelieu took France actively into the war in 1635. Peace negotiations began 1643, and peace was finally secured, 1648, by the Treaty of Westphalia (see *Westphalia, Treaty of*). This war, a major crisis in German history, devastated much of Germany, ended her medieval commercial eminence, and also ended Hapsburg attempts to unify Germany.

Thisbe—see *Pyramus and Thisbe*.

Thomas, Augustus, 1857-1934, U.S. playwright, b. St. Louis. His first successful play, *The Burglar* (1889), was followed by many others, of which perhaps the best known, such as *Alabama* (1891), *In Mizzoura* (1893), *Arizona* (1899) and *Colorado* (1902), have original backgrounds. He also wrote *The Witching Hour* (1907).

Thomas, Dylan Marais, 1914-1953, Anglo-Welsh poet, b. Swansea. His first volume of verse, *Eighteen Poems,* (1934) aroused quick interest. *Twenty-Five Poems* (1936), *Deaths and Entrances* (1946) and *Collected Poems* (1952) fol-

Under Milkwood, a lyrical drama by Dylan Thomas depicting a day in the life of the Welsh village Llareggub, was first a radio play. Since then it has been adapted for stage and successfully produced in the U.S.

lowed. His verse is characterized by rich assonance and alliteration; he generally scans his lines by counting the syllables in a line rather than the feet. His style depends heavily on mixed symbolism and a language thick with rare words. A love-poet, he has been characterized as a "new romantic." His stories include the whimsical collection, *Portrait of the Artist as a Young Dog* (1940), and his best play is *Under Milk Wood,* written for the BBC shortly before his death. He spent many years in America giving poetry readings, and several records of his recitals are available. His wife, Caitlin Thomas, wrote a biography of their marriage, *Left-Over Life to Kill,* in 1958.

Thomas, Norman Mattoon, 1884- , U.S. Socialist leader, b. Marion, Ohio. An ordained Presbyterian minister, he early turned to the cause of socialism, finally resigning from the ministry, 1931. He founded the magazine *World To-Morrow,* 1918, was associate editor of the of the *Nation* 1921-2, and was associated with the Fellowship of Reconciliation, League for Industrial Democracy, and American Civil Liberties Union. Thomas was Socialist Party candidate for President in every Presidential election from 1928 to 1948, winning his highest vote, 884,781, in 1932. An ardent opponent of both fascism and communism, he wrote *America's Way Out* (1930), *Human Exploitation* (1934), and *The Test of Freedom* (1954). He also wrote *Mr. Chairman, Ladies and Gentlemen* (1955), and *Great Dissenters* (1961).

Thomas, Saint, one of the 12 apostles. The fact that his name is Aramaic for twin, while his other name, Didymus, is Gr. for twin, led to speculation on his actual name. He is characterized in the Bible as loath to believe until convinced (John xx:24-29), hence is known as "doubting Thomas." According to ancient tradition, he became a missionary in Parthia or India; and existing Christian sect in Malabar, called Thomas Christians, claims to have been founded by him. His day is Dec. 21.

Thomas à Becket, Saint—see *Becket, Saint Thomas à.*

Thomas à Kempis (Thomas Hamerken), 1380-1471, German monk and religious writer, b. Kempen, Prussia. He became an Augustinian monk, 1407, and spent his entire life in the monastery, writing devotional and other religious works. His *Imitation of Christ* (1471), outlining a way of life for the devout, ranks as one of the most widely read works of Christian spirituality.

Thomas Aquinas, Saint, 1226?-74, Italian theologian, b. at Roccasecca near Aquino of a noble family. He gained the epithets Doctor Angelicus

Detail from Nicolaus Manuel Deutsch's "St. Thomas Aquinas and St. Louis of France."

and Prince of the Scholastics. He became a Dominican friar, a student under St. Albert (Magnus) at Cologne, then a famous teacher in Paris and several cities of Italy. He is best known as the greatest scholar of the medieval church; his philosophy is often called Thomism and has been revived as neo-Thomism in recent times. His two great works were the *Summa contra Gentiles,* a commentary on Aristotle's teachings, and the *Summa Theologiae,* in which Aristotelian and Christian theories were successfully synthesized; the latter remains a basic theological text for Christians. He was canonized 1323. His day is Mar. 7.

Thomism, philosophical system based on the teachings of Thomas Aquinas (*q.v.*).

Thompson, David, 1770-1857, English explorer and fur trader in Canada. A Hudson's Bay Co. fur trader, 1784-97, he later made many trips of exploration for the North West Co. In 1807 he was the first to cross the Rockies to the source of the Columbia River and travel its length, and in 1810 he explored its whole system. His careful record keeping, surveying, and map making became of great, though not immediately recognized, geographic importance. His map of W. Canada is still, in part, used. He served on the commission that surveyed the U.S.-Canada boundary, 1816-26.

Thompson, Francis, 1859-1907, English poet. He studied for the Roman Catholic priesthood, then for a medical career, but finally went to London to write. Rescued from poverty and illness by Wilfrid Meynell, editor of *Merry England,* to whom he sent his first poems in 1888, Thompson became famous with the publication of *Poems* (1893), which contained his masterpiece. "The Hound of Heaven." Later came *Sister Songs* (1895) and *New Poems* (1897), and a biography of Loyola.

Thomson, James, 1700-48, British poet, b. Scotland. Son of a clergyman, he went to London, 1725, and supported himself as a tutor. His literary reputation was established by the publication, 1726, of *Winter,* the first book of his most popular poetic work, *The Seasons* (published complete 1730). In its celebration of nature the poem preluded the romantic movement. Thomson wrote with David Mallet the masque *Alfred,* which contains the ode "Rule Britannia." His most mature work was the rhymed allegory *Castle of Indolence* (1748).

Thomson, James, 1834-82, British poet and essayist, b. Scotland, pseudonym B.V. (Bysshe Vanolis). Raised in a charitable institution in London, he was from the first unhappy. He was an army teacher in Ireland from 1851 until his dismissal, 1862. Thereafter, he struggled to live by his writing in London, where amid poverty and loneliness that drove him to drugs and alcoholism, he produced his best poem, *The City of Dreadful Night* (first published in the *National Reformer,* 1874).

Thomson, Virgil, 1896- , U.S. composer and critic, b. Kansas City, Mo. His most famous work, the opera *Four Saints in Three Acts,* to a libretto by Gertrude Stein, caused a sensation at its performances, 1934, by the Friends and Enemies of Modern Music. Other compositions include the opera *The Mother of Us All,* music for films (*The Plough That Broke the Plains, The River, Louisiana Story*), chamber music (including *Five Portraits*), and piano and vocal pieces. Since 1940 he has been a newspaper music critic.

Thomson, William—see *Kelvin, William Thomson, Baron.*

Thor, in Norse mythology, the mighty son of Odin, and god of the storm, war, and strength. He was called the Thunderer; as his chariot rolled, thunder resounded. When he threw his magic hammer, a thunderbolt followed, and the hammer returned to his hand. He had an iron glove to hold the red hot hammer, and a magic belt to double his strength. He loved to fight the giants. Most widely worshiped deity in the northern lands, he was called Donar by the Germans and

THORAX

In Norse mythology, it was Thor's lightning which brought a decisive victory to the gods in their great battle against the giants.

Thunaer by the Anglo-Saxons. Thursday is derived from his name.

thorax or **chest,** part of the body containing the heart, large blood and lymph vessels, and the lungs. In mammals it is separated from the abdomen by the diaphragm, and protected by the ribs, spine, and breastbone. Its cavity is lined with a membrane called pleura. When referring to insects, the thorax is considered to be the three segments behind the head, bearing legs and sometimes wings.

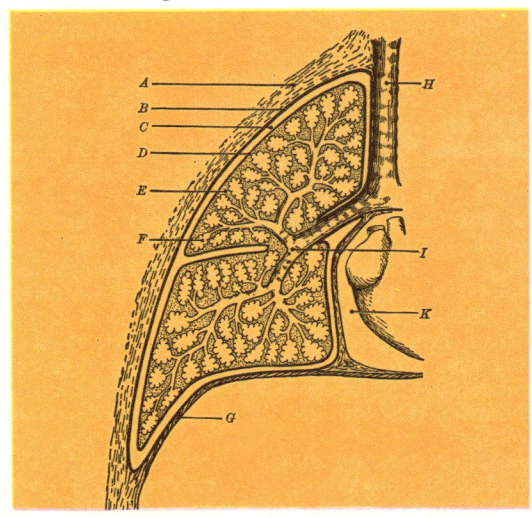

Vertical sections of the thorax: A. muscles, ribs, etc.; B. pleura, lining same; C. pleural space or cavity; D. pleural covering of the lung, E. connective tissue of the lung; F. alvioli or air-spaces of the lung; G. diaphragm; H. trachia; I. bronchus; K. pericardial space in which the heart lies.

thorazine—see *tranquilizers.*

Thoreau, Henry David, 1817-62, U.S. essayist and naturalist, b. Concord, Mass. Graduating, 1837, from Harvard, he briefly tried business and school-teaching, then devoted himself to "plain living and high thinking." Believing that man fritters away his life with details and is tyrannized by social customs and institutions, he minimized his possessions and affairs, earning a bare living by odd job and spending much of his time as an observer of nature. To demonstrate the simple life he built a small cabin at nearby Walden Pond and lived there two years, 1845-7. His first book, *A Week on the Concord and Merrimack Rivers* (1849), was a complete publishing failure. *Walden, or, Life in the Woods* (1854), his account of the Walden experiment, now a classic, also enjoyed little fame. As a strong antislavery man and as the most vigorous of the Transcendentalists, however. Thoreau was prominent in the Concord circle, which included among others his close friends Emerson and Hawthorne. After his death from tuberculosis his reputation gradually grew, until with the 20th cent. his pungent style and aggressively individualistic philosophy became fully appreciated. His posthumously published works include *The Maine Woods* (1863), *Excursions* (1863), *Cape Cod* (1865), and voluminous journals.

Thorez, Maurice, 1900- , French Communist leader. The French Communist Party's major theoretician, he assisted in the organization of the Popular Front, 1936, and guided Communist activities in the chamber of deputies, 1936-9. Fleeing to Moscow early in World War II, he returned after the liberation of France and held cabinet posts, 1946-7 and 1951, before leading the party into opposition. Though an ardent Stalinist, he survived the anti-Stalinist purges of the mid-1950s.

thorium, chemical element no. 90 (sym. *Th;* at. wt. 232; m.p. 1845°C.; sp. gr. 11.13). It is a radioactive metal having a half-life (*q.v.*) of 13,-900,000,000 years, decaying by alpha emission. It is the first in a radioactive disintegration series ending in lead and including radium, actinium, polonium, radon, bismuth, and thallium. Discovered by Berzelius in 1828, the dark gray metal is an important fuel in nuclear reactors (*q.v.*).

thorn, also called spine, sharp-pointed protective structure of plants. Thorns arise in various ways: some are outgrowths of the bark or epidermis; others are modified branches, stipules, or leaves. Thorns are especially common among plants growing in desert conditions.

Thorndike, Edward Lee, 1874-1949, U.S. psychologist and educator. He taught at Teachers College, Columbia Univ., 1899-1940. He gained a reputation by his tests to measure intelligence and learning ability. He is well known also for his graded lists of words understood by children and for his dictionaries.

Thorpe, James (Jim Thorpe), 1888-1953, U.S. athlete. Five-eighths Indian, of Sac and Fox ancestry, he was a great football star at Carlisle Institute and later played professionally. In the 1912 Olympic Games he won the decathlon but was declared ineligible to receive the medal because of professional activities. From 1913 he played baseball with New York, Cincinnati, and Boston in the National League. He has been rated by many as America's greatest athlete.

Thorvaldsen or **Thorwaldsen, Bertel,** 1770-1844, Danish sculptor. In 1797 he went to Rome, where most of his work was done, and became a leader of the classic revival. Although he designed and executed other works, he was most successful in his *Jason, Cupid and Psyche, Venus,* and other subjects from classical mythology. His heroic figures of the *Lion of Lucerne* at Lucerne, Switz., are notable.

Thothmes—see *Thutmose.*

Thousand and One Nights—see *Arabian Nights Entertainments.*

Thousand Islands, group of c.1500 islands in the upper St. Lawrence, near Kingston, Ontario. The U.S.-Canada boundary passes among them. This is a favorite vacation region. The Thousand Islands International Bridge (completed 1938) crosses several of the islands and connects New York with Ontario.

Thrace, region, E Balkan peninsula, divided 1923 between Greek W Thrace and Turkish E Thrace. In ancient times Thrace was inhabited by a primitive people speaking an Indo-European language. It was held by the Persians, c.512-479 B.C. Thereafter a kingdom arose which constantly menaced Greek colonies on the Thracian coasts from the Strymon (Struma) River east to Byzantium, including the Thracian Chersonesus (Gallipoli Peninsula). Philip and Alexander of Macedonia subdued Thrace, 4th cent. B.C., acquiring its mineral wealth. In the 3rd cent. B.C., Thrace was overrun by Celts, who drove the Thracians north toward Scythia. Annexed by Rome as a province, A.D. 46, the land was the last part of the Byzantine empire to fall to the Turks, 1453.

thrasher, any of various birds, resembling the thrushes, of the family Mimidae and principally genus *Toxostoma.* A familiar species of eastern U.S. is the brown thrasher, sometimes called the brown thrush, closely related to the mockingbird. It is a slender, rufous brown species, common in shrubbery. The song is unusual in that each phrase is repeated two or three times. Several species of thrashers inhabit the deserts of southwestern U.S., such as the curve-billed and the crissal thrasher. They are adapted for digging with their bill in the sand for food.

thread, thin cord made of twisted fibers. Stronger than yarn (*q.v.*), it is used for sewing and lacemaking. Thread is generally made of cotton, linen, silk, and synthetic fibers such as nylon.

Three Rivers, Quebec—see *Trois Rivières.*

thrips, any member of the insect order Thysanoptera, of wide distribution. Most adults have four broadly-fringed wings; some are wingless; all are minute. Many are pests of vegetables and flowers, but a few feed upon other thrips and even smaller insects.

throat, muscular structure in the upper neck, chiefly concerned with the function of swallowing. It has two sections: the fauces and the pharynx. The throat lies at the back end of the mouth, from which it receives food, and partially below and behind the nose, from which it receives air. It transmits food to the esophagus (food tube) and air to the larynx (voice box or Adam's apple), whence it goes to the windpipe. Food is kept from entering the larynx by a valve (epiglottis) which closes during swallowing. Sore throat is due to inflammation of the pharynx or of the tonsils, which lie in the fauces. See *tonsils.*

thrush, bird of the family Turdidae, of small or medium size, and varying much in color. Many thrushes are fine songsters. They live on insects, worms, and berries, make their nests on trees, bushes or the ground, and lay five or six eggs. The young are usually spotted below. The robin (*q.v.*) is a common American species, as also are the bluebird (*q.v.*) and the veery or Wilson's thrush. Other American species are the wood thrush, famous for its song; the hermit thrush, considered the finest songster in North America; and the varied thrush, also called the Alaska robin, found on the Pacific Coast. The nightingale (*q.v.*) is a European species.

Thucydides, c.460-c.400 B.C., Athenian historian. During the Peloponnesian War he commanded an Athenian naval squadron on the Thracian coast, 424 B.C., but was exiled after failing to relieve Amphipolis from the Spartans. He then traveled, visiting the countries of the Spartan allies, and thus became able to take the impartial view for which his *History of the Peloponnesian War* is famous. In 404 B.C. he was recalled to Athens.

Thule, Eskimo settlement on coast of Hayes Peninsula, NW Greenland; pop. 498. It was founded,

Graphic House

Eskimo women and children near their settlement on the outskirts of Thule, Greenland.

THULIUM

1910, as a Danish trading post. It is capital of the Thule colony district. During the 1950s a great U.S. airbase and radar early-warning station were built at Thule. A nuclear reactor went into operation here in 1960 to supply the base with heat and electric power. The name Thule applies also to the form of Eskimo culture found here as well as in other arctic regions.

Above: A U.S. Air Force rescue helicopter departs from Knak, near *Thule* Air Force Base, Greenland.

Left: The map room of the Fifty-fifth Air Rescue Squadron, based in *Thule*.

Below: Eskimos worship within a modern Danish Church on the outskirts of *Thule*.

Graphic House

Graphic House

At a Danish hospital in *Thule*, two tubercular Eskimo patients are busy with their knitting.

thulium, element no. 69 (sym. *Tm;* at. wt. 169.4), a rare earth metal of no commercial use. Discovered in 1879, thulium occurs in several natural ores, and forms a few compounds characteristically light green in color.

thunder, the sound produced when a flash of lightning (*q.v.*) passes throught the air, heating the adjacent air and causing it to expand and send out a wave. This wave is heard as a crash of thunder. Rolling thunder occurs when there is a long flash of lighting, for sound waves from the farther parts are heard later than waves from the nearer parts. When clouds, mountains, differing layers of air, or other obstructions cause echoes and reverberations, rolling thunder is also heard. The distance between a lightning flash and an observer may be calculated on the principle that sound travels *c.* a mile in five seconds; the observer has only to count the seconds between the sight of the lightning flash and the sound of the thunder. Some lightning is so far distant that no thunder reaches the observer.

thunderstorm, rainstorm with lightning and thunder (*qq.v.*). Common during summer months, it is caused by the rise of hot, moisture-laden air currents from the earth and the sudden condensation of the moisture in the colder upper atmosphere. The electrical charges that collectively form lightning result from the agitation and breaking up of raindrops by violent air currents. The thunder is caused by the explosive expansion and contraction of the atmosphere when it is suddenly heated by lightning.

Thurber, James Grover, 1894-1961, U.S. writer and cartoonist. In 1926 he began to contribute his humorous drawings and essays to *The New Yorker*. Collections of his work include *The Owl in the Attic* (1931), *The Seal in the Bedroom* (1932), *My Life and Hard Times* (1934), *My World—and Welcome to It* (1942), *The Thurber Carnival* (1945), and *Thurber Country* (1953). *The Male Animal* (1940), a comedy written with Elliott Nugent, was made into a motion picture. Thurber's other works include *The Wonderful O* (1957) and *The Years with Ross* (1959). The

THUNDERSTORM

CUMULONIMBUS

Direction thunderstorm is moving

General width - several miles

latter deals humorously with his work under Harold W. Ross, eccentric editor of *The New Yorker* magazine. *The Thurber Carnival* (1960) was a Broadway staging of some of his works. *Battle of the Sexes* appeared in 1960 and *Lanterns and Lances* in 1961.

Thuringia, former state, central Germany, surrounded by Bavaria (S), Hesse (W), Lower Saxony (NW), Saxony-Anhalt (N), and Saxony (E), area 6022 sq. mi.; pop. 2,927,497. Its capital was Weimar; other towns Jena, Erfurt, Gotha, Gera, and Eisenach. The Saale is the chief river. The Thuringian Forest lies in its S section. Thuringia was originally tributary to Attila, the Hun, and to the Franks under Charles Martel. Charlemagne set up the Thuringian Mark. In the 16th cent. Thuringia was a stronghold of the Reformation. Following World War I, the free state of Thuringia was formed, 1920, by the union of Saxe-Weimar-Eisenach, Saxe-Meiningen, Saxe-Altenburg, Saxe-Gotha, Reuss, Schwarzburg-Rudolstadt, and Schwarzburg-Sondershausen. Over half of the area is agricultural. Manufactures include textiles, glass, porcelain, machinery, optical and scientific instruments, and toys. Under Russian occupation after World War II, Thuringia was reconstituted and enlarged by the addition of former Prussian territory; however, it ceased to exist, 1952, when by an administrative realignment along the Soviet pattern, the East German states were replaced by 14 economic districts.

Thutmose or **Thothmes,** name of four pharaohs of Egypt, of the XVIIIth dynasty, ruling 16th-15th cent. B.C. They established Egypt as a great empire and built some of its most splendid structures (see *Karnak; Luxor*). **Thutmose I** (ruled *c.*1540-1493 B.C.) led an army as far as the Euphrates River, but he extent of his conquests is not certain. The brief reign of **Thutmose II,** who ruled jointly with his father, was overshadowed by that of his sister, **Hatshepsut** (ruled *c.*1501-1481 B.C.). She was the first important queen in history; during her reign Egypt's trade and public works thrived. She was succeeded by her son, stepson, or half-brother, **Thutmose III** (ruled *c.*1482-1447 B.C.). One of the great pharaohs, he crushed the lesser rulers of Palestine and Syria at Megiddo, making them vassals of Egypt. He also defeated the powerful kingdom of Mitanni, and made treaties with the Kassites and Hittites. **Thutmose IV** ruled *c.*1420-1411 B.C.

thymus, mass of tissue resembling lymphoid tissue in the upper portion of the chest. Often called a gland, it has never been definitely proved to have endocrine activity. The thymus is largest in infancy, gradually shrinking almost to the point of disappearance in adults. It enlarges in certain thyroid and muscle disorders, but its exact function is unknown. Formerly, certain cases of sudden death were believed associated with thymus enlargement, but this theory has been discredited.

thyroid gland, ductless (endocrine) gland consisting of two lobes, which lie on each side of the trachea, joined by an isthmus. Its internal secretion, or hormone (thyroxin), increases combustion in the body and stimulates growth. The thyroid is functionally interrelated with the pituitary, sex, and adrenal glands. Normal thyroid function requires small amounts of iodine, usually present in food, but absent in certain areas of the world (*e.g.,* Switzerland and part of the Great Lakes area). In such iodine-deficient regions the gland may swell, producing goiter. Excessive thyroid function is called hyperthyroidism, or Graves' disease. Decreased function is hypothyroidism (cretinism in infants). Both conditions can now be satisfactorily treated. Radioactive iodine has proved a potent aid in diagnosis and treatment of disorders of thyroid function and in certain unusual types of thyroid cancer.

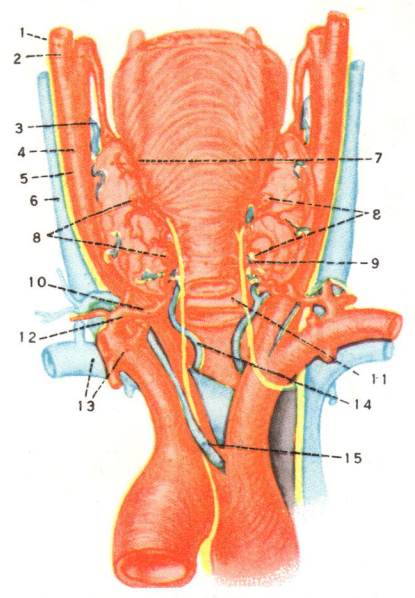

Thyroid and parathyroid, back view: 1. internal carotid artery; 2. external carotid artery; 3. superior thyroid vessels; 4. common carotid artery; 5. vagus nerve; 6. internal jugular vein; 7. thyroid gland; 8. parathyroids; 9. esophagus; 10. inferior thyroid vessels; 11. trachea; 12. thyroid axis; 13. subclavian artery and vein; 14. recurrent laryngial nerves; 15. thoracic duct.

Thyssen, Fritz, 1873-1951, German industrialist. As head of a powerful steel trust he financially assisted Hitler's rise to power in Germany. Quarreling with Hitler, he fled the country, only to be brought back to a concentration camp. After World War II he went to Buenos Aires, where he died.

Tia Juana, Mexico—see *Tijuana*.

Tiberius (Tiberius Claudius Nero Caesar), 42 B.C.- 37 A.D., second Roman emperor. The emperor Augustus, after four heirs-apparent had died, adopted Tiberius as his son and heir. Tiberius had been a successful general and for 16 years the husband of Julia, daughter of Augustus, when he succeeded as emperor, 14 A.D. Though he ruled with wisdom and moderation, he acquired a reputation, discredited by modern historians, for cruelty and lechery. In A.D. 26 he retired to Capri, leaving the pretorian prefect Sejanus, his adviser, in charge at Rome. Persuaded later of Sejanus' treachery, Tiberius ordered his execution. Tiberius was succeeded by his grand-nephew, Caligula.

Tiber River (Ital.: *Tevere*), central Italy, rising in the Tuscan Apennines and flowing generally south about 24 mi. to the Tyrrhenian Sea. The strategic location of Rome at the ford of the Tiber between ancient Etruria and Latium accounted for its early importance.

Tibesti, extensive mountain massif in the Sahara, running south from Libya into Chad and rising above 11,200 ft. The volcanic range is of a jagged, deeply eroded shape. There are a few scattered oases, due to relatively frequent rainfall, and the natives are primitive and nomadic. Some of the region was first explored, 1952.

Tibet, country, central Asia, bounded N by Sinkiang, China, S by Nepal and India; area 471,660 sq. mi.; est. pop. 1,273,969; capital Lhasa; other towns Gyangtse, Shigatse. Hemmed in by the Himalayas, Kunlun Mts., and other ranges,

Graphic House

Above, *Tibetan* soldiers march on patrol duty near the Indian border. Below, a Tibetan nobleman rides through the town of Lhasa.

Tibet's Pass of Jelep La, *c*.14,500 feet high, is in the Himalayas of southwest Assam.

These *Tibetan* women are eating "ysamba," a native dish, out of home-made crockery.

Tibet consists of a high plateau (average altitude *c*.16,000 ft.). The Ganges, Indus, Salween, Mekong, and Yangtze Rivers have their headwaters here. The chief river is the Brahmaputra, which rises here as the Tsangpo; its valley is the main agricultural region of the country. Transportation facilities are primitive, yaks and horses being used for carrying export goods over the mountain passes. There are, however, motor roads between Lhasa and Yatung via Shigatse and Gyantse, and between Nagchukna and Gartok (completed 1956), from northern to western Tibet. In 1957 Sinkiang and Gartok were linked by a 1000-mile highway. Since 1957 there has been air service between central Tibet and China. Stock raising is the chief occupation. The dominant religion is Lamaism (a form of Buddhism).

From the 7th cent., when Buddhism was introduced, Tibet held itself apart from the rest of the world. Until the 1900s it was virtually closed to all foreigners. Controlled by the Chinese from 1720, Tibet continued to be claimed by China despite Tibet's declaration of independence, 1913. In 1950 the Chinese Communists sent armies into Tibet, and in 1951 the country was incorporated into China as an autonomous province, nominally ruled by the Dalai Lama and the Chinese-supported Panchen Lama. There is a national assembly composed of the bulk of Tibet's officialdom. In 1959 the Dalai Lama, who had long opposed Communist Chinese interference in Tibetan national affairs, sought asylum in India following an abortive rebellion against Chinese rule. The Panchen Lama was installed as the ostensible ruler of the country.

Tibetan languages, a sub-family of the Sino-Tibetan languages (*q.v.*), spoken by some 5 million speakers in Tibet, parts of Kashmir and the Chinese provinces of Szechwan and Yunnan. The Tibetan languages are most closely related to the Burman languages (*q.v.*), with which they are frequently grouped under the heading of Tibeto-Burman languages. Tibetan is written with an alphabet based on the Sanskrit alphabet of the 7th Cent. A.D., when writing was first introduced into Tibet. The language is largely tonal, like Chinese. There exist two separate words for each expression, the one honorific for addressing the nobility, the other non-honorific for speaking to inferiors. Among the nobility there are frequently even two honorific terms, the one for use when speaking to the high nobility, the other for use among peers. A learned Tibetan may thus occasionally have to master three separate vocabularies. Modern colloquial Tibetan depends largely on word order and particles to indicate syntactic relationships. See *language.*

tic, habitual repetitive twitching of a muscle or a muscle group, usually of psychogenic origin. Tics most commonly involve the face (*e.g.,* blinking, mouth movements), but may include jerking of the neck and habitual sneezing, coughing, or hiccuping. *Tic douloureux* or Trigeminal neuralgia, a disorder of the fifth cranial nerve characterized by recurrent, intense, lancinating pain in one or more areas of one side of the face supplied by that nerve. The paroxysms of pain are often accompanied by fleeting contractions of the facial muscle causing the victim to grimace horribly. This disorder produces one of the most excruciating and intolerable pains experienced in medical disease. Occasionally, the source of irritation can be traced to a diseased tooth or a tumor of the fifth cranial nerve. In most cases, however, the cause is unknown. Although vasodilator drugs (*e.g.,* carbon dioxide, histamine and nicotinic acid) may be of some help in alleviating the pain, it usually becomes necessary to use narcotics. In some cases it is necessary to inject the Trigeminal nerve with alcohol or to cut it surgically in order to control pain.

tick, small, parasitic, bloodsucking arachnid, feeding mostly on mammals. The larva has only six legs. Some ticks require hosts of different sizes; others reach maturity on the same host. They transmit a number of diseases, including Rocky Mountain spotted fever. Some kinds produce tick paralysis as a result of poison injected into the victim.

Ticonderoga, village, NE New York, at N end of Lake George; pop. 3568. It makes paper and pencils, and is a resort community. In 1755 the French built a fort here; it was captured by Gen. Jeffrey Amherst for the British, 1759. On May 10, 1775, Ethan Allen and his Green Mountain Boys captured Fort Ticonderoga from the British, who later reoccupied it. The New York State Historical Association has a museum here.

tidal wave, ocean wave of extraordinary size, formerly believed associated with the tides. Most such waves are properly seismic marine waves, resulting from submarine earthquakes; they may reach a height of 90 ft. at the shore. Considerable success has been gained since about 1950 in predicting the path and time table of Pacific tidal waves, called *tsunami*. In 1960, loss of life in Hilo, Hawaii, following earthquakes in Chile, was lessened substantially after warnings by seismographers. Exceptionally strong winds also may cause so-called tidal waves.

tide, raising and lowering of the level of the oceans due to gravitational attraction or "pull," of the moon and the sun. The lunar force is about twice the sun's. The waters are drawn into a long wave on the side of the earth directly facing the moon; here is high tide. A lesser high tide simultaneously occurs on the opposite side of the earth, this being due to the fact that the difference between the moon's pull on the enarer side and its pull on the farther side (the force lessens with distance) acts as a pull away from the moon. When moon and sun are in line with the earth, their joined attractive forces create spring tides, which show great variation between high and low phases. When moon and sun pull at right angles to one another, neap tides result; these

As the earth rotates on its axis and the moon revolves around the earth, a gravitational pull creates *tides*. When the sun and the moon pull at right angles, partly counteracting each other's force, tides are low and are called neap tides (above). During the new and full moons, the sun and moon pull together making spring tides, the highest of all (below).

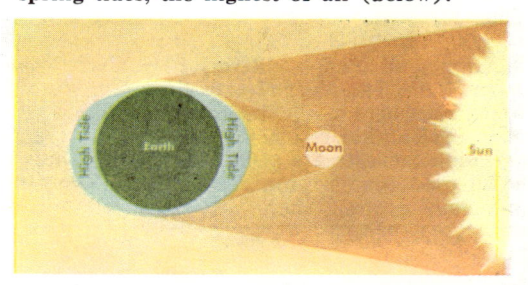

show less variation. High and low phases of the tides follow each other at intervals of *c*.12 hours, 25 min., but the earth's rotation and differences in ocean depths, continental masses, barometric pressures, and coastal features cause tidal variations along the coasts. Spring and neap tides each occur twice monthly. The Bay of Fundy is famous for its high tides. Tidal flow sometimes sets up strong local coastal currents. Newton, with his theory of gravitation, was the first to postulate an acceptable scientific explanation of tides.

Tientsin, city, Hopei province, NE China, at junction of Pei River and Grand Canal; pop. 3,100,000. A port, communication center, and manufacturing city, it produces steel, textiles, food, glass, and porcelain ware and is an outlet for the products of N China and Inner Mongolia. It was made a treaty port, 1860, and sections of the city were subsequently granted to several countries as foreign concessions. These were finally abolished, 1946. Badly damaged during the Boxer Rebellion, 1900, Tientsin was largely rebuilt in western style. The city was held by the Japanese, 1937-45, and taken by the Communists, Jan. 1949.

Tiepolo, Giovanni Battista, 1696-1770, Venetian painter. Inspired by the rich colors and majestic scenes and skies of Veronese, Tiepolo's luminous scenes of miracles, triumphs, and apotheoses, historical, religious, and allegorical are lighter, more brilliant, more ethereal against clear pale blue skies and floating, rose-tinged clouds, seen in daring perspective. He was a great and prolific ceiling painter, whose frescoes decorate many churches and palaces in and around Venice, the palace of the archbishop in Würzburg, 1750-3, and the royal palace in Madrid, where he worked from 1763. His son **Domenico Tiepolo,** 1727-1804, assisted him on many decorations and was a painter of note.

Tierra del Fuego, archipelago, S South America. Divided between Chile and Argentina, it consists of one large and several small islands, separated by the Strait of Magellan from the mainland. They were discovered by Magellan, 1520. The southern point is Cape Horn. The land is steep and windswept with a few fertile areas on which inhabitants raise sheep.

Tiffany, Charles Lewis, 1812-1902, U.S. jeweler, b. Killingly, Conn. He founded Tiffany and Co., which became a leading international jewelry and silverware firm. His son, **Louis Comfort Tiffany,** 1848-1933, b. New York City, was an artist. He turned from painting to manufacture of stained glass, inventing a new type known as Favrile glass, which was used for windows, mosaics, and small *objects d'art*.

Tiflis, capital of Georgian Soviet Socialist Republic, SE Georgia, U.S.S.R., on Kura River; pop. 694,000. The southern terminus of the Georgian Military Road (*q.v.*), it has long been a vital link between Europe and Asia. As an industrial center for the Caucasus, it produces cotton and silk, tobacco and wine, and machinery. It has a university, technical schools, theaters, museums, and an opera house. Tiflis means "warm springs," and its sulphur springs have made it a health resort. It became the capital of Georgia, 5th cent., and was a seat of Persian power on the ancient trade route between East and West. The Russians captured it, 1799. In 1921 it became capital of the Transcaucasian Federation, and in 1936 of the Georgian Soviet Socialist Republic.

tiger, largest member (*Felis tigris*) of the cat family. Widely distributed in Asia, it inhabits jungles and forests, preying on deer, pigs, and other mammals, and sometimes attacking domestic cattle and man. The body is 5 to 7 ft. long, with a 3-ft. tail; the shoulder height is 3 ft. The rough tongue assists the teeth in tearing off flesh. The fur is orange above, with black striping on head, limbs, body, and tail. The underparts are white.

tiger beetle, any of some 2000 kinds of insect-eating beetles of the family Cicindelidae. Most have almost parallel-sided bodies, ¼ to 1 in. in length, and long legs, which carry them rapidly. Many are brilliantly colored, but the few nocturnal ones are generally blackish. The larvae live in tunnels in the ground, usually not far from water, and catch passing prey. The larval life usually lasts two or three years; pupation takes place in the burrow.

Tiglath-Pileser—see *Assyria*.

Tigris River, c.1150 mi. long, SW Asia. Rising in the mountains of Kurdistan, it flows through Iraq, past Baghdad, to join the Euphrates River and form the Shatt-al-Arab (*q.v.*). Its Biblical name is the Hiddekel, and along its course are ruins of the once great ancient cities of Nineveh, Ashur, and Ctesiphon.

Tihwa—see *Urumchi*.

Tijuana, city, Lower California, NW Mexico; pop. 137,644. Just below the U.S. border, it is a resort town, famous for its racetracks and gambling casinos at Agua Caliente. It was popular during the U.S. Prohibition era. In 1961-62 a program to rehabilitate the city was inaugurated.

Tilburg, city and inland port (Wilhelmina Canal), North Brabant province, S Netherlands, c.35 mi. SE of Rotterdam; pop. 136,991. A leading industrial center, it produces textiles, machinery, and chemicals.

Tilden, Samuel Jones, 1814-86, U.S. lawyer and political leader, b. New Lebanon, N.Y. A prominent lawyer in New York City and state Democratic leader, he was responsible for the destruction of New York's Tweed Ring, 1868-72. In 1875 he became governor of New York; in 1876, Democratic candidate for President. He won 250,000 more popular votes than the Republican, Rutherford B. Hayes, but his electoral majority was questioned because of a dispute over returns from Louisiana, Florida, South Carolina, and Oregon. The electoral commission appointed by Congress gave the vote to Hayes, Mar. 2, 1877. Tilden was convinced that he had rightfully won the Presidency, but in the interest of national unity he let the issue drop. Retiring to the country, he left most of his fortune to found a free public library in New York.

Tilden, William Tatum, II (Big Bill Tilden), 1893-1953, U.S. tennis player. Called almost universally the world's leading player, he won the first of his eight U.S. National titles in 1920, and dominated the tennis world for the first two-thirds of that decade. Greatest player in the U.S. for 10 consecutive years, he won 70 American and International titles and was the mainstay of the U.S. Davis Cup team, winning 17 victories in the Challenge Round against 5 defeats. He turned professional 1931 and was "pro" champion for many years.

tile, small slab, usually made of fired clay, used for roofs, walls, etc. It may be unfinished after firing but is more often glazed; it may be plain or incised, flat, or curved so that the joints overlap. Tiles have been used in architecture since

Colorful ceramic *tiles* embellish the façade of the Shore Road School, Bellmore, N.Y.

Above: A modern bathroom with glazed ceramic *tiles* protecting its walls.

Left: The front of the medieval Cathedral of Zaragoza is tiled in Moslem mosaic style.

Below: tile mosaic in a N.Y. public school.
FSTC

ancient times. Egyptian colored tiles from c.5000 B.C. have been found, and the Assyrians and Babylonians used them decoratively in their great palaces. The Persians made richly decorated, lustered tiles. The Greeks used tiles for roofing, and the Romans in their floors, walls, and baths. The Moors, like the earliest Persians, made vividly colored, lustrous tiles, and it is their work that may be seen in the Alhambra in Spain. The Spanish passed the manufacture and use of tiles on to Italy and America. Since 17th-cent. Holland, fine tiles have been made at Delft, the most distinctive being genre scenes sketched in blue on a white ground; these became popular throughout Europe for fireplaces and stoves and were introduced into the American colonies. Tiles are now mass-produced and used more for utilitarian than decorative purposes.

till—see *moraine*.

Till Eulenspiegel—see *Eulenspiegel, Till*.

Tilly, Johannes Tserklaes, Count von, 1559-1632, Flemish general. Commanding the Catholic League in the Thirty Years' War, he won many victories, including the battle at the White Mountain, 1620, at Stadtlohn (1623), and the storming of Magdeburg, May 1631, when over 40,000 people were butchered. In the following Sept., Tilly was routed by Gustavus Adolphus at Breitenfeld, and in Apr. 1632 was mortally wounded at the Battle of the Lech.

Tilsit (Rus.: *Sovetsk*), town formerly in East Prussia, now in NW Soviet Union, c.65 mi. NE of Königsberg (now called Kaliningrad); pop. 85,900. It is a port on the Neman River near the Baltic Sea, renowned for its cheese. The town arose from a colony of Teutonic Knights. Here, July 7, 1807, Napoleon, then at his zenith, made a treaty with Tsar Alexander I by which Westphalia was formed out of Hanover and West Prussia and placed under Jérôme Bonaparte; Prussian Poland was given to Russia and Saxony; and Alexander agreed to join France against Britain.

timberline, the elevation on mountains of sufficient altitude above which trees do not grow, or the boundary of the zone in the arctic regions north of which trees are not found. In a general way, a rise of altitude is equivalent to an increase in latitude, so that the equivalents of the lichen, mosses, and low shrubs of the tundra (*q.v.*) north of the arctic timberline are found growing in the Alpine meadows above the timberline even in equatorial regions. Just below the timberline is usually found the coniferous forest, although there is a transition zone in which stunted trees grow. Even in the arid U.S. Southwest, there is sufficient rainfall to support the coniferous forest below the *c*.11,500 ft.-timberline and the Alpine meadows above it.

timbrel—see *tambourine*.

Timbuktu, city, Republic of Mali; pop. 7000. It is on the edge of the Sahara, near the most northerly point of the Niger. Formerly an immense walled city, it was an important trading center and terminus for camel caravans bringing salt, gold, slaves, etc. It flourished 11th-16th cent., when its pre-eminence was destroyed by a Moroccan army. It was taken by the French, 1893.

time, duration of an event, or period during which something happens. Time was measured by early man by the passage of days, by phases of the moon, by seasons, and by the apparent passage of sun and stars overhead. Shorter periods were measured by the sundial in Egypt as early as 1500 B.C., and later by the water clock. The modern clock came into use in Europe in the 13th cent., the watch in the 15th cent. The modern chronometer and other timekeeping devices, used in connection with observations of celestial bodies, have greatly facilitated time measurement. The calendar (*q.v.*), which makes possible reasonably accurate measurement of time from year to year, has been improved periodically since its beginnings in ancient Babylonia. Measurement of time takes into account changes in the earth's position with respect to the sun throughout the year. Mean solar time, or civil time, which is the time used in ordinary civil affairs, represents a compromise, the *mean* solar day of 24 hours being the *average* length of the solar day throughout the year. On any given date the *apparent* solar day, which is the day as measured by the sun's positions as actually observed on that day, may be as much as 30 sec. shorter or longer than the mean solar day, which has the same length throughout the year. For astronomical purposes the *sidereal* day is used; this begins when the vernal equinox (see *equinox*) is at the meridian and lasts until (the earth having rotated once) it is again at the meridian. Since the earth rotates through about 360° in each 24 hours, each degree of longitude represents 4 min. of time. To avoid the inconvenience of changing the time whenever one travels a short distance east or west, the earth has been divided into 24 longitudinal time belts. Within each belt, time is the same everywhere, so that one's watch needs to be reset only when one moves into the next time zone, which is exactly 1 hour later or earlier. Under this arrangement each new day begins at the International Date Line (*q.v.*). The time used in each of the time belts by custom or law is known as standard time.

Earth *time* is calculated by the rising and setting of the sun. If a watch's hour hand points to the sun, due south will always be the mid-point between the hand and the number 12.

Under so-called daylight saving time, which is intended to facilitate maximum use of the daylight hours during summer and was first adopted in the U.S. during World War I, clocks are 1 hour ahead of standard time; *e.g*, when it is 10 a.m. standard time, it is 11 a.m. daylight saving time. Daylight saving time is ordinarily adopted only in mainly nonagricultural states.

Ship time, formerly used by ships at sea, determined by the sun's actual position, has now been generally superseded at sea by zone time. However, aboard ships (and in military establishments also) the designation of zone time begins with 0000 (midnight) and runs up through the succeeding 24 hours to the next midnight; *e.g.*, 0125 is 1:25 a.m., and 2250 is 10:50 p.m. Time may be indicated aboard ship by means of striking a bell from 1 to 8 times. The 24 hours are divided into six 4-hour watches; each watch is divided into 8 half-hour periods, the beginning of each being identified by the number of bells struck, progressing from 1 (at 12:30, 4:30, 8:30) to 8 (at 4, 8, 12 o'clock). Einstein introduced the concept of time as forming a fourth dimension, as bodies moving in space (*q.v.*) must be considered relative to other bodies moving in space.

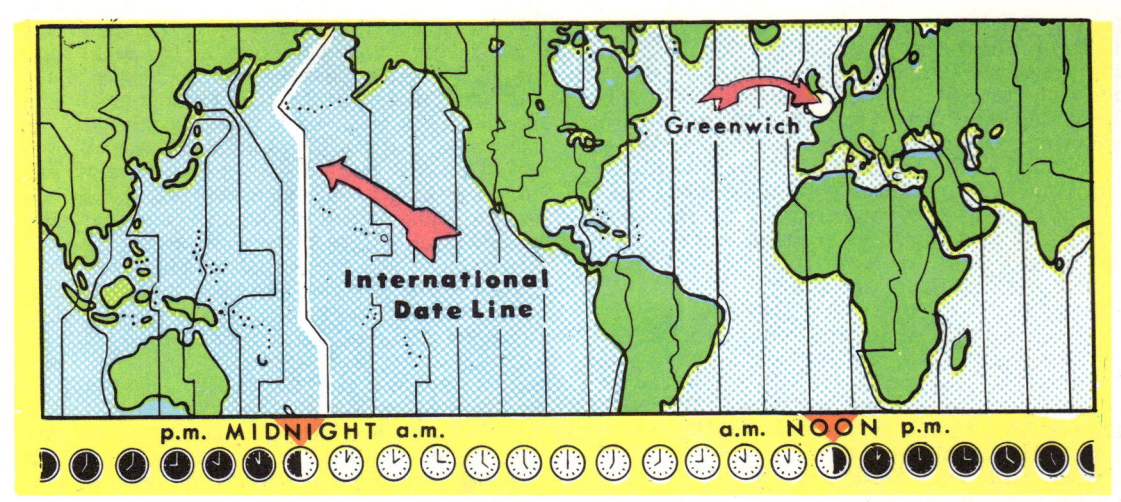

The world *time* meridians, top, evenly spaced fifteen degrees of longitude apart, determine world standard time, figuring from the zero longitude of Greenwich mean time. These zones are used only for convenience, as it makes no difference what time meridian is used in any particular area, as long as the changes in time equal twenty-four hours throughout the entire globe. The International Date Line, below, was established so that the necessary change of date would be located in a place on the earth's surface where there are no people. This is an imaginary line, but can be found on most maps. When the line is crossed a day is either lost or gained, regardless of the time of day: due west gains, while due east sets back the date.

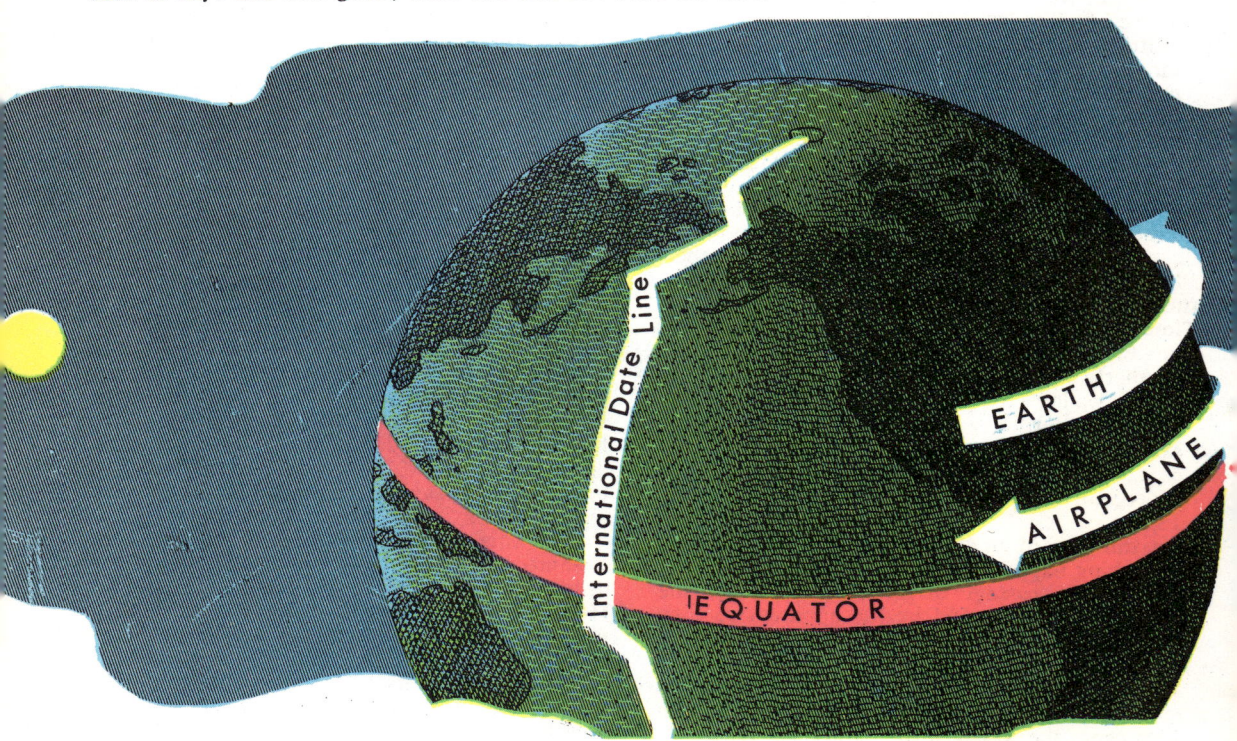

Times Square, in New York City, at the junction of Broadway, 42nd Street, and Seventh Avenue, often called "the crossroads of the world." It is the center of the city's theater district. The square and surrounding district take their name from the *New York Times* Tower.

Timisoara (Hung.: *Temesvár*), city, the Banat, W Rumania, near Yugoslav border, *c*.80 mi. NE of Belgrade; pop. 148,176. It is an important commercial and communication center with varied industries and a university. There are Roman Catholic and Eastern Orthodox cathedrals. The town was taken from the Turks, 1716, by Prince Eugène of Savoy. It belonged to Austria-Hungary until 1919, when it was ceded to Rumania. It still has large Hungarian and German minorities.

Timor, largest of the Lesser Sunda Islands, partly a possession of Indonesia; area 13,071 sq. mi. The E part of this mountainous island is the overseas territory of **Portuguese Timor** (area 7322 sq. mi.; pop. 496,000), with the capital at Dili (pop. 3321). In 1951 Portugal granted the colony financial and administrative autonomy. **Indonesian Timor** (area 6120 sq. mi.; pop. 822,915) occupies the W half of the island (capital Kupang). Before Dec. 1949 this area belonged to the Netherlands and was called Dutch Timor. The chief products of the island are copra and sandalwood. The entire island was held by the Japanese in World War II. See *Indonesia, Republic of*.

Timoshenko, Semyon Konstantinovich, 1895- , Russian marshal. Of peasant stock, after tsarist service in World War I he became a Red Army commander of cavalry during the civil wars, 1918-20, and a close associate of Stalin. Commander in the Russo-Finnish War, 1939-40, commissar for defense (1941), and in command of operations on the SW and S fronts (1941-2) he was responsible for the defense of Stalingrad, 1942-3. He was a member of the Central Committee (1939-52).

timothy, perennial, long-spiked grass (*Phleum pratense*) native to Europe and W Asia, now the most extensively cultivated hay plant in the U.S. Thriving best in northerly climates, it is raised only to a limited degree in the South. U.S. production has shrunk since farm machinery began to replace the horse.

Timothy, Saint, d. A.D. *c*.100, early Christian missionary, b. Lycaonia, of Gentile father and Jewish mother. He was circumcised in manhood by St. Paul to placate Jewish converts to Christianity (Acts xvi). Timothy accompanied Paul on many missions, visited him in Rome, and according to tradition was given charge of the church at Ephesus, becoming its first bishop. The two *Epistles to Timothy* (see *Epistles*) were addressed to him. His day is Jan. 24.

Timur—see *Tamerlane*.

tin, element no. 50 (sym. *Sn*; at. wt. 118.70; m.p. 232°C; sp. gr. 7.3), a brilliant, soft and malleable, whitish-gray metal. Its chief source is cassiterite (stannic oxide). Principal mines are in Malaya, Bolivia, Thailand, China, and Nigeria. It is largely used as a covering for iron, in tinfoil

These workers in Manima district of the Congo are extracting pure *tin* by means of water pressure from a mine containing cassiterite ore, the chief source of the metal.

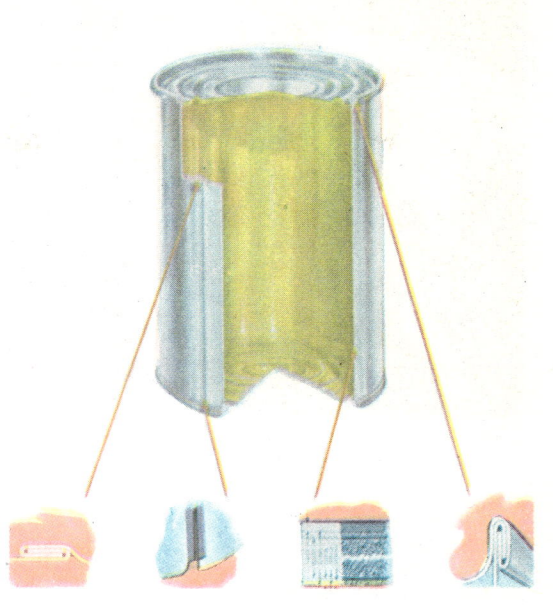

Profile of a modern *tin* can. At the bottom are details of the can's construction. From left to right: side seam, notch, thicknesses of the various tin plates, double seam.

for wrappings (though largely superseded for this use by aluminum), in mirrors, and in utensils. As an alloy with copper, it forms bronze and bell metal; and with lead, pewter and solder. Some tin compounds are used in the textile industry. **Tinfoil** consists of thin sheets of aluminum, or sometimes of an alloy of tin, used for wrapping tobacco, chocolate confections, etc. **Tinplate** consists of sheets of wrought iron or mild steel coated with tin to prevent oxidation (rust), and is used for receptacles for preserved (tinned or canned) foods.

Tinian—see *Mariana Islands*.

Tintagel, small village, Cornwall, SW England, on a cape; pop. 1234. The ruined Norman castle is the legendary birthplace of King Arthur. Remnants of an early Celtic monastery were recently excavated. There is also a Norman church with Saxon parts.

Tintoretto, 1518-94, Venetian painter; real name Jacopo Robusti. He is supposed to have entered the studio of Titian only to be shortly sent home by the "jealous" master. Thereafter he studied by himself, guided by the inscription in his studio: "the design of Michelangelo and the coloring of Titian." Most of his early work has been lost or destroyed; his first known great works are four pictures for the Scuola di San Marco, outstanding among which is the *Miracle of St. Mark,* and three pictures for the Church of Santa Maria dell'Orto: the *Worship of the Golden Calf*, the *Last Judgment*, and the *Presentation of the Virgin*. It is the Scuola di San Rocco, the decoration of which occupied him intermittently for about 23 years, that remains the shrine of Tintoretto. Of the more than 60 paintings executed for the scuola and church, there are included the great *Crucifixion,* the *Annunciation, Mary Magdalen,*

TIPPECANOE

Tintoretto's famous "Bacchus and Ariadne" is in the Ducal Palace, Venice, Italy.

and *St. Mary of Egypt*. He was also occupied in the decoration of the ducal palace, for which he painted *Origin of the Milky Way* (now in London) and the huge *Paradise,* among many others. Tintoretto was a painter of enormous energy and originality of design, which pervade his canvases in a surge of movement, color, and light, flowing in and out of the picture, distorting figures, and becoming more and more flashing and abstract until his late *Paradise,* which is a tissue of color, light, and energy. He also did an enormous number of portraits.

Tippecanoe River, *c.*200 mi. long, rising in NE Indiana and flowing SW to the Wabash. On its banks was fought the Battle of Tippecanoe, Nov. 7, 1811, when William Henry Harrison repulsed Indians led by Tenskwatawa, Tecumseh's brother.

"Christ in the House of Martha and Mary" is one of *Tintoretto's* many religious paintings.

Tipperary, urban district, Co. Tipperary, S Ireland; pop. 5149. It is a market and dairying center. Of a monastery founded by Henry III, only the gatehouse remains. County Tipperary has 5148 sq. mi.; pop. 133,313.

Tippoo Sahib or **Tipu Sahib,** 1753-99, maharaja

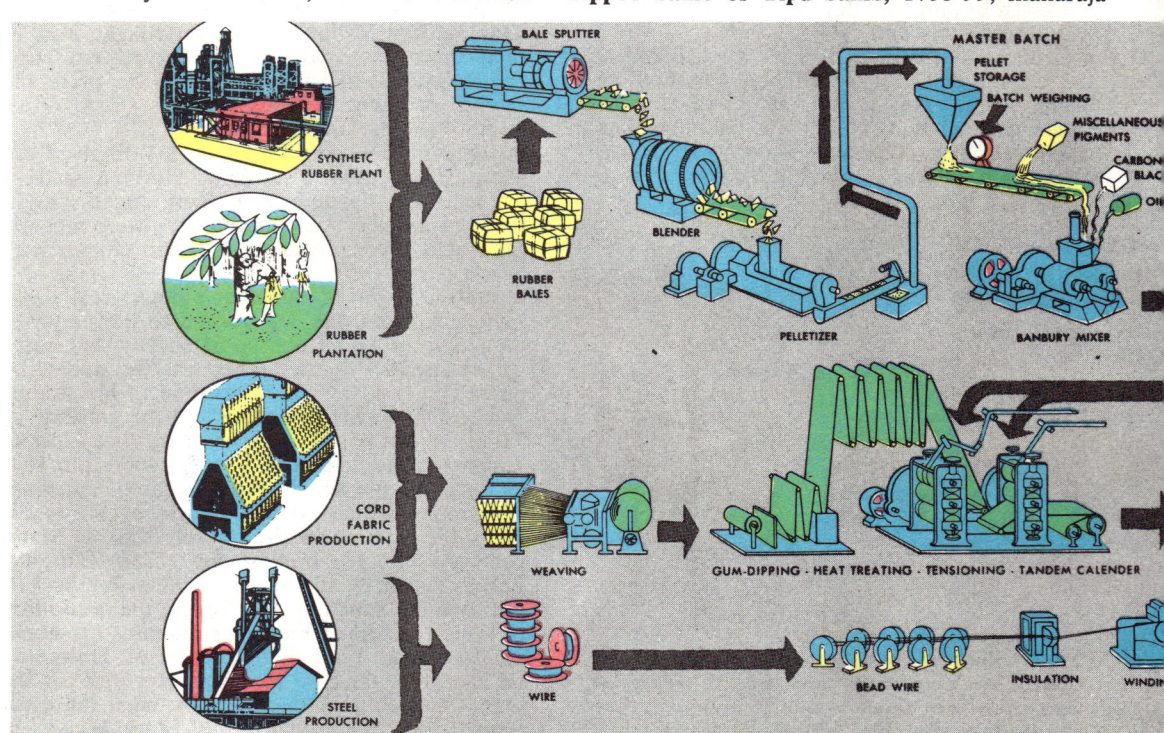

of Mysore, India. Like his father, Hyder Ali, whom he succeeded, he bitterly resisted the growth of British power in India. The British beat off his attack on Travancore, 1790, and by the treaty of 1792 he lost much of his domain. His refusal to disarm led to the storming of his capital, Seringapatam, by British troops. He was killed in the defense.

Tirana or **Tiranë,** capital of Albania, in the country's center *c.*20 mi. E of its Adriatic port of Durazzo; pop. 119,000. Albania's largest city, it has growing industries: textiles, soap, tobacco products, and foodstuffs. The population is largely Moslem. The city was founded, 17th cent., by a Turkish general.

tire, band encasing a wheel to protect or cushion it. The first tires, used for wagons and carriages, were made of leather fastened by nails, or of metal strips usually formed around the wheel while hot and suddenly watercooled to shrink to a tight fit. Later solid rubber was used, especially after the invention of the bicycle. The modern pneumatic tire, with its inner tube holding air under pressure and its outer casing composed of vulcanized rubber treads rimming a corded rubber fabric, was based on a patent granted to John Dunlop of England, 1845. Pneumatic tires were first produced by Dunlop, *c.*1889, for bicycles, and were subsequently manufactured for automobiles. The corded structure and outer treads were later improvements, as was the larger surface of the modern balloon tire. In recent years synthetic rubber has been increasingly used in tires (see *rubber*).

Tiresias, in Greek legend, a Theban soothsayer. For seeing Athena at her bath he was blinded, but having seen her inadvertently he was recompensed with the gift of prophecy. By another account, he spent part of his life as a woman, and on recovering the shape of a man was asked which sex took more pleasure from acts of love. His answer—women—so infuriated Hera that she blinded him, but Zeus rewarded him with seer's powers. Oedipus and his sons learned their fate from Tiresias, and even from the underworld he advised the visiting Odysseus.

Tirol—see *Tyrol.*

Tirpitz, Alfred Friedrich von, 1849-1930, German admiral. As secretary for the navy, 1897-1916, he helped make Germany a great naval power. He commanded the navy, Aug. 1914 to Mar. 1916, being a strong advocate of the policy of unrestricted submarine warfare against Allied sea lines of communication. Retiring in 1916, he returned to public life in 1924 when he entered the Reichstag as a nationalist deputy, a post which he held for four years.

Tiryns, ancient city, Greece, E Peloponnesus, founded as early as 2800 B.C. The ancients believed the Cyclopes had set in place the massive

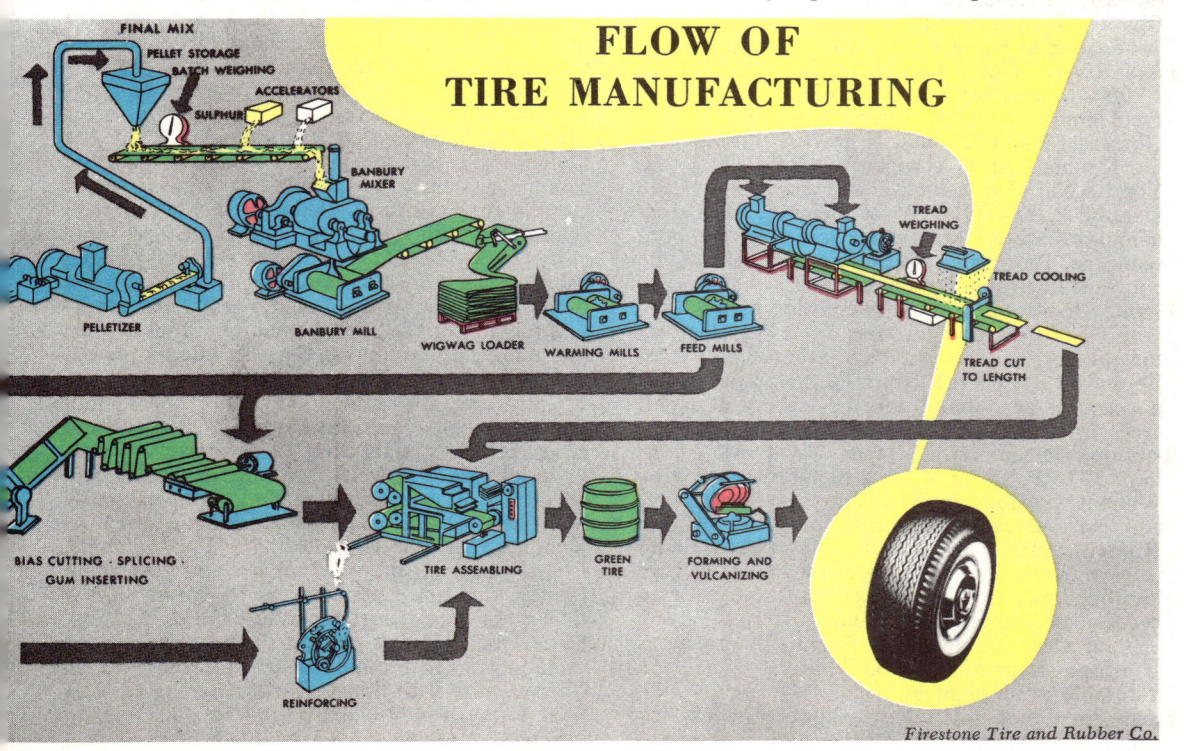

Firestone Tire and Rubber Co.
Cured *tires* being conveyed for inspection

FLOW OF TIRE MANUFACTURING

Firestone Tire and Rubber Co.

stones, many still standing today, of its walls and palace. Tiryns, like Mycenae, was a major center of Mycenaean culture, *fl.* 14th cent. B.C., and survived as an independent town until destroyed, *c.*470 B.C., by Argos.

tissue culture, the growth of small samples of the tissues or organs of animals or plants, isolated in containers of nutrient solutions. This modern technique has been extremely useful in the study of single cells and specialized tissues, and has been widely used in medical research, especially that related to cancer and senility. Tissue cultures are kept aseptic, and must be maintained at the temperature of the species from which the culture is taken. It is interesting that cells in such a culture do not grow old, but appear to endure indefinitely. Whole organs and young embryos of plants have been grown fairly successfully in such cultures.

Tisza, Kalman, 1830-1902, Hungarian statesman. Prominent in the Hungarian revolutionary government of 1848, after its overthrow by Austria he became a leader of the Calvinist Magyars, who hoped to sever all ties with Austria. He continued agitating for independence after his election to the diet, 1861, but accepted the compromise Dual Monarchy, 1867. As prime minister, 1875-90, he modernized Hungary and improved the position of Magyars within the country, meanwhile cooperating with Austria. His son, **Count Stephen Tisza,** 1861-1918, a leading agrarian economist, was prime minister twice, 1903-5, 1913-7, attempting to suppress the extreme Hungarian nationalists and renew the policy of cooperation. Opposing the war on Serbia, 1914, for fear Magyar dominance in Hungary would be threatened by the expected annexation of Slavic territories, he was overthrown, 1917, after the accession of Emperor Charles I of Austria, who opposed Magyar dominance in Hungary. Tisza was assassinated.

Tisza River, (Ger.: *Theiss;* Serbo-Croat.: *Tisa*), *c.*800 mi. long, SE Europe, a major tributary of the Danube, rising in Carpathian Mts. on SW Ukraine (Soviet Union). It flows S through fertile lowlands of E Hungary (Alföld) and NE Yugoslavia (Vojvodina), past Szeged, to the Danube *c.*25 mi. NNW of Belgrade. Principal tributaries are the Mureș and Someș Rivers, both rising in Rumania. Approximately half of its course is navigable for small vessels.

Titanic, British liner, sunk by collision with an iceberg off Newfoundland, Apr. 14, 1912. She was the greatest ship of her day, over 46,000 tons. Bound for New York from Southampton on her maiden voyage, she struck the iceberg at night. Over 1500 of the 2223 aboard died.

titanium, element no. 22 (sym. *Ti;* at. wt. 47.90; m.p. 3272°F; sp. gr. 4.5), a metal discovered by William Gregor, an English clergyman, 1791, and isolated as pure whitish metal by M. A. Hunter, 1910. Titanium ores have been found in New York and N Quebec; the metal is 10th in abundance in the earth's crust but is rare because of extraction difficulties. It is as strong as alloy steel but weighs half as much and melts at a high temperature. Titanium oxide is used as a durable white pigment in paints.

Titans, in Greek mythology, children of Uranus and Ge (Heaven and Earth). Most important were Cronus, who castrated his father; Iapetus and his wife-sister Themis, parents of Prometheus, Epimetheus, and Atlas; Rhea, wife-sister of Cronus and by him the mother of the Olympian gods. The others were Oceanus, Coeus, Crius, and Hyperion—male Titans; and Theia, Mnemosyne, Phoebe, Tethys—female Titans. The progeny of these were also called Titans. When Zeus led the Olympian gods against the Titans, only Oceanus among the elder Titans supported the Olympians. The remainder were cast into Tartarus by Zeus.

"Titan Struck by Lightning," painted in 1707 by the French artist Largillière.

tithe, originally, a levy of one tenth of a person's possessions taken for support of the church and the poor. Such levies were common among the ancient Hebrews and persisted until modern times in the Western world, first as a voluntary contribution to the church and later, in England and some European countries, as a legal tax. In 1836-60 the English Parliament, by a series of acts, established a permanent tithe rent charge payable in money. In the U.S. tithes have not been legalized, but some churches encourage their members to tithe in the sense of contributing a tenth of their annual income for religious and charitable purposes.

Titian, 1477-1576, Venetian painter, b. in the Dolomites; real name Tiziano Vecelli or Vecellio. Taken to Venice as a child, he studied under Gentile and Giovanni Bellini and worked with Giorgione, with whom he collaborated on some early works. *Sacred and Profane Love,* painted shortly after Giorgione's death, 1510, shows the dreaminess, the poetic, shimmering landscape, and feeling for the coparticipating drama of man and nature of Giorgione. Titian's middle period, while he was Venetian court painter and a man of great worldly fame and honor throughout Europe, yielded portraits and mythological and religious subjects showing great mastery of the material world: powerfully living, masterful people—their flesh, accoutrements, and personality—in such subjects as the *Assumption of the Virgin* (1518) in the Church of the Frari, Venice; *Flora* (Uffizi); the famous *Venus of Urbino* (Pitti); and such portraits as the *Man with a Glove* (Louvre). Introduced to Charles V, 1530, he executed his first portrait of the emperor and in 1554 painted for him the great *Trinity,* which Charles took with him to Yuste after his abdication. Titian was also patronized by Charles' son Philip II, for whom he painted mythological

Above: Titian's "The Virgin and Child" from the collection of Jules Bache.

Below: detail from his "Presentation of the Virgin," painted 1534-8.

Titian's "Man in a Red Cap"

subjects and the *Last Supper* (Escorial). A portrait of Philip which Titian did in 1550 was influential in winning the hand of England's Queen Mary for the prince. A magnificent *Pietà,* intended for his own tomb and finished by Joseph Palma the younger, exemplifies the intensification of emotional feeling and mysticism and flickering, translucent, almost impressionist technique which, in contrast to his robustly sensuous earlier work, make his last paintings sheets of luminous, transcendent emotion and color. Carried off at 99 by the plague, Titian was the supreme master of color of the Venetian school and the model for many of the best subsequent painters of Italy, Holland, Flanders, and France.

Titicaca, Lake, divided between Bolivia and Peru; area *c.*3200 sq. mi. It is the largest inland freshwater lake of South America and the highest navigable lake in the world (alt. 12,644 ft.). Steamers connect Puno, Peru, with Guiqui, Bolivia. Nearby Indian villages grow maize and wheat.

TITLES

titles and forms of address. As additions to a person's name, titles are indicative of some honor, office, or dignity, *e.g.,* emperor, prince, duke, mayor. Some titles are held *virtute officii, i.e.* "king"; others, like the titles of the five British orders of nobility, are hereditary; some, like that of knight, are conferred for life.

The form of address to and between persons has lost much of the ceremony that characterized the custom a few generations ago. Many of the methods and terms which are used today would then have been serious breaches of etiquette. Both spoken and written salutations differ widely, even in English-speaking countries. Because of its monarchical traditions and hereditary titles, England has many forms and a strict code of address. In the U.S., the fewer and simpler forms are not indicative of a person's birth, or family, but rather of his profession or political position. Thus in all diplomatic and official correspondence, the manner of addressing letters and invitations, as well as that of personal address, is of great importance.

The common forms of address are used for informal correspondence between personal friends and untitled persons. Special forms are required for the address and the salutation of letters addressed to persons in high governmental and ecclesiastical positions, and to members of the royalty. Doctors (M.D., Ph.D., etc.), dentists, and members of the Armed Forces also have special forms of address. In addressing invitations, the full title is used, except in the case of barons. Professional titles precede titles of rank. The use of Esquire (Esq.), formerly limited to lawyers, country gentlemen, and eldest sons of knights, is now more general. The title *Honorable* (in Great Britain and Canada, *Honourable* is the preferred spelling) is ignored in conversation, and is never used on business cards.

The following list of Titles and Forms of Address contains the most important of the commonly used forms.

TITLES AND FORMS OF ADDRESS

	ADDRESS	SALUTATION
Man	Mr. . . .	Dear Sir: or Dear Mr. . . . :
Men	Messrs. . . . and . . .	Gentlemen:
Married woman	Mrs. . . .	Dear Madam: or Dear Mrs. . . . :
Married women	Mmes. . . . and . . .	Mesdames: or Ladies:
Unmarried woman	Miss . . .	Dear Miss . . . :
Unmarried women	The Misses . . .	Mesdames: or Ladies:
Doctor (M.D., Ph.D., etc.) and Dentist	Dr. . . . (or the ordinary form of address is used with the addition of the initials M.D., D.D.S., Ph.D., etc.)	Dear Doctor: or Dear Dr. . . . :
Air Force, U.S.A.	(Officers and enlisted men should be addressed by their titles) — General . . . , Colonel . . . , Corporal . . . ,	Dear General . . . : (Colonel, Corporal, etc.). (For ranks below Second Lieutenant) Mr. . . . :
Army, U.S.A.	(Same as Air Force, U.S.A.)	(Same as Air Force, U.S.A.)
Marine Corps, U.S.A.	(Same as Air Force, U.S.A.)	(Same as Air Force, U.S.A.)
Navy, U.S.A.	(Officers and enlisted men should be addressed by their titles) — Admiral . . . , Commander . . . , Ensign . . . (For petty officers, the title is written after the name) . . . , Gunner's Mate.	(Business salutation for all ranks) —Dear Sir: (For officers of high rank)—Dear Admiral: (All ranks below Commander)— Mr. . . . :
Bishop (Methodist)	Reverend Bishop . . .	Dear Bishop . . . :
Bishop (Protestant Episcopal)	The Right Reverend . . . , Bishop of . . .	Right Reverend: or Dear Sir:
Bishop (Roman Catholic)	Most Reverend . . . , Bishop of . . .	Your Excellency:
Cardinal	His Eminence (Christian name) Cardinal (surname) (If he is an archbishop or bishop, include this title with name of the see.)	Your Eminence:
Clergyman	The Reverend . . .	Dear Sir: or Reverend Sir: or My dear Mr. . . . :
Clergyman (if a doctor of divinity)	The Rev. Dr. . . . or the Rev. . . . , D.D.	Dear Sir: or Reverend Sir: or My dear Dr. . . . :
Pope	His Holiness Pope . . . , The Vatican, Vatican City, Italy	Your Holiness:
Priest, Secular (Roman Catholic)	(The) Rev. . . .	Dear Reverend Father:
Priest, Religious (Roman Catholic)	(The) Rev. . . . (initials of his order)	Dear Reverend Father:
Rabbi	Rabbi . . .	Dear Rabbi . . . :
Alderman (Canada and U.S.)	Alderman . . .	Dear Sir:
Ambassador	His Excellency, the (country) Ambassador	Dear Mr. Ambassador:
Associate Justice of the Supreme Court	Mr. Justice . . . , The Supreme Court	Dear Mr. Justice: or Sir:
Attorney General	The Honorable . . . , Attorney General	Sir:
Cabinet Officer (U.S.)	The Secretary of (State, Labor, etc.) Washington, D.C.	Dear Mr. Secretary:
Chief Justice of the Supreme Court	The Chief Justice of the United States	Dear Mr. Chief Justice: or Dear Sir:
Congressman	The Honorable . . . , United States House of Representatives, Washington, D.C.	Dear Sir: or Dear Mr. . . . :
Governor	The Honorable . . . , Governor of . . .	Dear Sir: or Dear Governor . . . :
Governor General of Canada	His Excellency, the Governor General	My Lord: or Sir:
Judge (Canada)	The Honourable Mr. Justice . . . (if of a superior court); or His Honour Judge . . . (if of a county court, court of sessions, or district magistrate)	Sir:

	ADDRESS	SALUTATION
Judge (U.S.)	The Honorable . . . , United States District Judge (or, Chief Judge of the Court of Appeals, etc.)	Dear Sir:
King (United Kingdom)	His Majesty the King	Sir: or Your Majesty:
Mayor (Canada)	His Worship, The Mayor of . . .	Sir:
Mayor (U.S.)	The Honorable . . . , Mayor of the city of . . .	Sir: or Dear Mr. Mayor:
Member of Parliament (United Kingdom)	The Honorable . . . M.P.	Sir:
President of the United States	The President, or The President of the United States, The White House, Washington, D.C.	Sir: or (less formal) Dear Mr. President:
Prime Minister of Canada	The Right Honourable . . . , Prime Minister of Canada	Sir:
Queen (United Kingdom)	Her Majesty the Queen	Your Majesty:
Senator (Canada)	The Honourable Senator . . .	Dear Sir: or Dear Senator:
Senator (U.S.)	The Honorable . . . , United States Senate, Washington, D.C.	My dear Senator: or Dear Mr. . . . :
Senator (State)	The Honorable . . . , The State Senate	My dear Senator: or Dear Mr. . . . :
Speaker of the House of Representatives	The Honorable . . . , The Speaker of the House of Representatives, United States House of Representatives, Washington, D.C.	Dear Mr. Speaker: or Sir:
Vice President of the United States	The Vice President; or The Honorable . . . , Vice President of the United States	Mr. Vice President: or Dear Mr. Vice President:

titmouse, any of various small woodland birds of the family Paridae, of wide distribution. Their main food is small insects and insect eggs. The tufted titmouse (five to seven in. long) of eastern U.S., distinguished by its crest, is gray with buffy flanks. The plain titmouse of the Southwest has no crest but otherwise resembles the tufted titmouse. Both birds are permanent residents in their regions. The titmouse family includes the chickadee (*q.v.*).

Blue *titmice*

Tito, Josip Broz, 1892-   , Yugoslav statesman and soldier. Son of a blacksmith, he entered the Austro-Hungarian army in World War I, was captured by the Russians, and fought with the Red Army in the Russian civil wars, 1918-20. Returning to his native Croatia, where he helped organize the Communist Party, during World War II he became a leader of the Yugoslav partisans against the Germans. At this time he took the name Tito. His relations with the anti-German Serbian leader Draja Mikhailovitch soon deteriorated, and after accusing him of Nazi collaboration Tito won control of the resistance movement and fought with Russian, British and U.S. aid. In 1945 he became head of the Yugoslav government and established a Communist dictatorship with Russian affiliations. His Federal People's Republic deposed King Peter II, and Tito became marshal of the Yugoslav army and dictator. Destroying all opposition, he executed Mikhailovitch, imprisoned Archbishop Stepinac, and through the adoption of economic plans along Russian lines, prepared for the rapid industrialization of Yugoslavia. His resistance to Russian interference in domestic affairs led to a rupture with the Cominform, 1948, and his subsequent diplomatic rapprochement with the Western powers against Russian pressure. He took the title of president of Yugoslavia in 1953. Though in 1956-57 he made a tentative peace with Nikita Khrushchev, who twice visited him, he retained his independence of the Soviet bloc and gained the open enmity of Communist China. He was host to a meeting of neutralist nations in Belgrade in 1961.

Titulescu, Nicolas, 1883-1941, Rumanian statesman. As foreign minister, 1927-36, he was prominent in League of Nations activities, helping to form the Little Entente between Rumania, Yugoslavia, and Czechoslovakia and the Balkan

Entente with Yugoslavia, Greece, and Turkey to protect those countries from German, Italian, Hungarian, and Bulgarian ambitions. Forced to resign by the fascist Iron Guard, 1936, he fled to France after Rumania joined the Axis, 1940.

Titus (Titus Flavius Sabinus Vespasianus), A.D. 39-81, Roman emperor. When Vespasian, his father, competed for the throne, A.D. 68, Titus was left in command of the war in Judea and destroyed Jerusalem, A.D. 70. Succeeding his father, A.D. 79, he became popular because of his lavish gifts and spectacular games; for the latter he built the amphitheater now called the Colosseum. During his otherwise unnoteworthy reign, Pompeii and Herculaneum were buried by the eruption of Vesuvius.

Titus, Epistle to—see *Epistles*.

Tivoli, town, Latium, central Italy, c.15 mi. ENE of Rome; pop. 23,000. Beautifully situated in the Apennine foothills, it was known to the ancient Romans as Tibur, a favorite resort of the ancient world. Tivoli contains the celebrated 16th-cent. Villa d'Este, whose gardens contain some 900 fountains of all shapes and sizes, ranging from a towering hydraulic organ to sphinxes. Water for this immense architectural fantasy originally flowed through the Villa of Hadrian (reigned 125-135 A.D.) on the plains below Tivoli. Hadrian's villa was the largest and most elaborate of all the imperial residences; a great many of the works of art now in Roman museums and palaces were taken from it.

Tlemcen, town, Oran dept., NW Algeria; pop. 73,445. The city, still Moslem, was an important trading center and capital of a Berber dynasty, 13th-15th cent. It produces carpets and leather goods.

Tlingit, American Indian tribe of the NW Pacific Coast, speaking a language usually identified as Athabascan. See *Indians, American*.

T.N.T.—see *trinitrotoluene*.

toad, any of the amphibians of the family Bufonidae, related to the frogs but differing from them in that the adults are usually more terrestrial. Their warty skin is typically dry, with glands exuding an acid secretion; there are often no teeth. They do not cause warts. The family is widespread, with some species of the genus *Bufo* in North America. Toads are useful because they feed on such pests as flies and worms.

toadstool, common name applied to any umbrella-shaped poisonous fungus, particularly one which may be mistaken for an edible fungus. Notable among toadstools are the deadly amanitas, one species of which is reported to be used by Siberians as an intoxicating narcotic. See *mushroom;* chart with *poison*.

tobacco, coarse herbaceous annual (*Nicotiana tabacum*) native to tropical America. Its large

Pan American Airways

The Villa d'Este at *Tivoli*, built in the 16th century, has beautiful gardens with a fountain (above) and impressive sculptures and bas reliefs on its walls (below).

Hamilton Wright

An American *tobacco* plant

Ripe leaves of Burley tobacco, left, stand before a barn in Scott County, Kentucky. Below, tobacco workers plant or "set" tobacco on a plantation in Shelby County, Kentucky.

leaves contain nicotine and, when cured, are used for smoking and chewing tobacco, snuff, insecticides, and medicines. The U.S. raises the largest supply—over three billion lbs. annually—but Brazil, Rhodesia-Nyasaland, India, Japan, Russia, China, and Turkey also produce large quantities. Another species, *N. rustica*, is grown in Europe and Asia to a limited extent. See *smoking*.

Tobago—see *Trinidad and Tobago*.

Tobit, in the Book of Tobit, a pious Jew of Nineveh. He defied Assyrian law by burying the dead and so was deprived of his property. His son Tobias then went to Media for funds, and on the way met with adventures, was befriended by the angel Raphael, and struggled with the demon Asmodeus; the result was a fortune and a wife, and long life for Tobias and Tobit. The **Book of Tobit,** containing the tale, is considered apocryphal by the Jews and Protestants, but deuterocanonical by the Roman Catholics.

tobogganing and bobsledding, sport of sliding down a snow-covered hill or ice chute on a sled. It has lost some popularity in the U.S. because of the growing enthusiasm for skiing. Sleds, three to eight ft. long, are of several types, the fastest being the steel skeleton types and bobsleds. Both race at the winter Olympics. Most famous of all toboggan slides is at St. Moritz, Switzerland, where the 1350-yd. course is steeply banked. Center of the sport in the U.S. is Lake Placid, N.Y. Tobogganing is governed by the Amateur Athletic Union.

Tobolsk, city, W Siberia, at junction of Irtysh and Tobol Rivers; pop. 46,700. It is the trade center for a fishing and fur area. Tobolsk was founded by Cossacks, 1587, and was capital of W Siberia until 1824.

Tobruk, town, Cyrenaica, Libya, on Mediterranean; pop. 4995. An Italian garrison town, it was taken by the British early in 1941, and when they were driven out of Libya shortly after, a British garrison in the town withstood siege until June 1942, when Rommel's forces overpowered it. Tobruk was retaken by the British Nov. 1942.

Tocatins River, *c.*1700 mi. long, rising in central Brazil. It flows north into the Pará River, the southeastern arm of the Amazon.

Above, mature *tobacco* is sprayed by pipes in the fields. Below, harvested tobacco is taken from the fields by tractor; next, they will be taken into a barn to be "cured."

Reynolds Tobacco Co.

toccata, a musical form, usually in one movement, and usually for solo instrument, such as organ, lute, or harpsichord. It developed prior to the baroque period (*e.g.*, organ toccatas of Merulo), and then in the 16th, 17th, and 18th cents. became a medium for virtuoso instrumental performance, rapid scales, arpeggios, etc. Chromatic brilliance, a headlong pace, relatively free contrapuntal elaboration with an effect of improvisation, bold modulations, and rich chordal effects were characteristic. The celebrated organist and composer, Frescobaldi (1583-1644), used the form extensively. In the late 17th and early 18th cents. Buxtehude's toccatas, romantic and technically accomplished, were direct predecessors of the great toccatas of Bach, his student. Bach occasionally composed toccatas in more than one movement, and here the term became less precise in its formal significance.

Tocqueville, Alexis, Comte de, 1805-59, French writer. On a mission to the U.S., 1831-3, to study prison systems he assembled material for *Democracy in America* (1835), a treatise on the society and government of the U.S. This did much to popularize theories of democracy in Europe, particularly Great Britain. His *The Old Regime and the Revolution* (1856), emphasizing tensions during the French Revolution between centralism and localism, predicted the ultimate victory of centralism.

Togliatti, Palmiro, 1893- , Italian Communist leader. Joining the Communist Party, 1921, he went into exile, 1926, following the triumph of Fascism in Italy. He worked with the Comintern in Moscow and in Spain during the Spanish Civil War, 1936-9. Becoming chief of the Italian Communist Party, 1944, he held cabinet posts in the provisional government, 1944-5. His party, though it remained second largest in Italy, opposed the pro-Western tendencies of the government with decreasing success and popular support.

Togo, Heihachiro, Count, 1847-1934, Japanese admiral. The greatest naval hero of Japan, he was trained in England and was largely responsible for development of the Japanese navy. In the Russo-Japanese War, 1904-5, he defeated a Russian force at Port Arthur, then scored his greatest triumph in the Battle of Tsushima (1905) in the Korea Strait, which ended in destruction of the main Russian fleet. Before his death he served as chief of the Japanese naval General Staff and as member of the supreme war council.

Togo or **Togoland,** independent republic in W Africa on the N Gulf of Guinea coast, bordered by Ghana, Upper Volta, and Dahomey; area 21,853 sq. mi.; pop. 1,642,000; capital Lomé.

The flag of *Togoland*

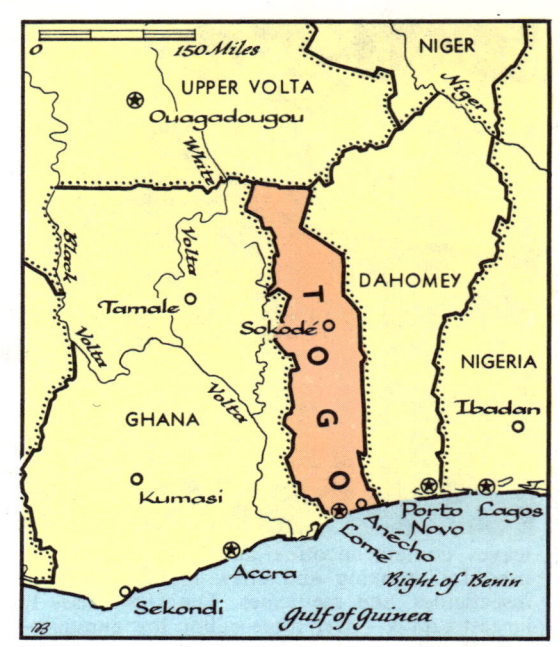

The long, narrow strip was a German protectorate until Aug. 1914, when it was invaded by Anglo-French forces. Subsequently divided between the British and French, both sections became League of Nation mandates (1922) and U.N. trust territories (1946) under administration of Britain and France. **British Togoland** was administered from the Gold Coast colony. When the colony became an independent dominion in 1957 (see *Ghana*), British Togoland was integrated into the new state as the administrative region of Trans-Volta Togoland. **French Togo** in 1958 became an autonomous republic and gained its full independence in 1960. Inland the country is hilly, with many streams and waterfalls. The land varies from forests and arable stretches to dry plains. Commerce is based on coffee, cocoa, palm oil, palm kernels, copra, groundnuts, cotton, and manioc. There are many plantations.

Tojo, Hideki, 1884-1948, Japanese general and government official. He left his post as head of the secret police in 1937 to become chief of staff of the Kwantung army. As minister of war, 1940-1, under Konoye, he spearheaded the militarists' cause. Becoming prime minister, Oct. 1941, he followed aggressive foreign policies which led to the attack on Pearl Harbor and establishment of a rigid military dictatorship at home. He resigned, 1944, under pressure from those anxious for peace, as Japan's military defeats mounted. After Japan's surrender, 1945, he vainly attempted suicide; he was then tried as a war criminal, convicted, and executed.

Tokay (Hung.: *Tokaj*), town, NE Hungary, on Tisza River, c.120 mi. NE of Budapest; pop. 5074. The town is famous for its sweet, white Tokay wine and its greenish Imperial Tokay, a liqueur made from the juice of overripe grapes.

Tokelau or **Union Islands,** group of three atolls, S Pacific Ocean, N of Samoa; area c. four sq. mi.; pop. 1929. The principal product is copra. Annexed by the British, 1889, the group was added to the Gilbert and Ellice Islands colony, 1916. In 1926, it was brought under the jurisdiction of Western Samoa, held as a mandate by New Zealand. In 1948 the islands were declared a part of New Zealand. The native population is of Polynesian stock.

Tokharian languages—see *Indo-European languages.*

Tokio—see *Tokyo.*

Tokugawa, Japanese family that held the shogunate (1603-1867). The first Tokugawa shogun (*q.v.*) was Ieyasu (1542-1616), who succeeded Hideyoshi (*q.v.*) as military ruler of Japan when he defeated the feudal lords in battle, 1601. As shogun he established his capital at Yedo (now Tokyo) and succeeded in establishing his rule by centralizing the government, controlling strategic parts of the country and by curbing the independent daimyo (landholding nobles). Under the Tokugawa shogunate, foreign influences were strongly resisted and feudalism was firmly maintained. Weakened by pressure exerted by European powers and beset by rebellion at home, the shogunate finally collapsed, 1867, and with the Meiji Restoration (see *Mutsuhito*) Japan entered her modern period.

Tokyo, capital of Japan, largest city in the world, capital of Japan, on SE Honshu and on Tokyo Bay; pop. 8,310,027. The financial and commercial center of Japan, before World War II it was important also for heavy industry. The Sumida River (*q.v.*) and various canals flow through the city, but adjacent Yokohama is used as the main port. Many of Japan's leading educational institutions are here, including Tokyo Univ. (founded 1877, formerly called Imperial Univ.). Representative buildings include the Diet and the Imperial Palace. Also notable is the earthquake-proof Imperial Hotel, designed by Frank Lloyd Wright. Yasukuni-Jinja is a shrine dedicated to the war dead and there is a shrine in memory of Emperor Meiji. The Ginza is the best known street in the city. Tokyo had its beginnings in a 12th-cent. fishing village called Yedo (or Edo) which in 1603 was made capital by Ieyasu, first Tokugawa shogun. With the Meiji restoration, 1868, which ended the power of the shogunate, Yedo became the seat of the emperor, who had formerly held court in Kyoto, and its name was changed to Tokyo ("eastern capital"). Tokyo was almost destroyed in the earthquake of 1923, in which c.150,000 died. It was rebuilt by 1930, but in World War II was half razed by U.S. bombing. It was again rapidly rebuilt.

Left: skyline of *Tokyo*, dominated by the new Electric Building.

Right: Japanese lady and her child stroll through the streets of Tokyo.

Lower left: famed Japanese Theater, Tokyo.

Lower right: gardens of Tokyo's Hotel Imperial.

Graphic House

Toledo, city, co. seat of Lucas co., NW Ohio, on a harbor formed by the Maumee River near its mouth on Lake Erie; pop. 318,003. One of the largest ports on Lake Erie, it handles coal, iron ore, oil, farm products, and a large variety of manufactured goods, and is served by an extensive railroad system. Chief industries include the manufacture of glass, steel, automobiles, chemicals, machinery, and cement. Settled 1817, Toledo was contested by Michigan and Ohio troops in 1835 (the "Toledo War") because of errors in early maps. The dispute was settled by Congress, 1836, when Ohio's possession of Toledo was made a condition for Michigan's entrance to the Union. Completion of canal systems in the 1840s accelerated industrial and commercial growth of the city.

Toledo, city, New Castile, central Spain, capital of Toledo province, on Tagus River; *c.*40 mi. SSW of Madrid, pop. 38,136. One of the most ancient and interesting towns of Spain, with only minor industries today, it is particularly known as the long-time residence of El Greco, who painted many of his best-known canvases here. Toledo is the seat of the Roman Catholic primate of Spain. Many old fortifications and gateways still stand. In 1936, during the Spanish Civil War, the Alcazar (famous palace of the Moorish rulers) was almost destroyed during the siege of Franco forces who held out here until relieved. Toledo was also celebrated for its swords. The city has one of the country's most imposing Gothic cathedrals; another noted church is Santo Tomé (with El Greco's *Burial of Count Orgaz*). Toledo dates back to pre-Roman days. The Romans called it Toletum. In 712 it was taken by the Moors and made capital of a flourishing emirate. It was reconquered, 1085. Toledo preceded Madrid as capital of Castile and Spain.

Toledo, Francisco Alvarez de, 1515?-84, Spanish viceroy of Peru (1569-81). Bringing order among the Spanish rivals for the loot of the Inca civilization, he also consolidated the Indian villages and brought them into the Spanish orbit, subordinated the authority of the Church, destroyed the power of the great landowners, and established and regulated enforced labor by the Indians on the land and in the mines. Although he adopted many Incan customs and laws and sponsored the compilation of invaluable histories of the Inca, he is criticized for his destruction of the Incan culture.

Toller, Ernst, 1893-1939, German dramatist and poet. He took an active part in the revolution in Bavaria in 1919 and was imprisoned 5 years for his political activities. In 1933 he was exiled from Germany by the Nazis. He committed suicide in New York. Besides several volumes of verse, he wrote many plays, including *Man and the Masses* (1920), *Brokenbrow* (1924), and *Pastor Hall* (1939). He was a leader of the expressionist school of German literature, which flourished after World War I.

Tolstoy, Aleksey Nikolayevich, 1882-1945, Russian novelist. One of the foremost Soviet writers, he is known for his historical novels, including *The Road to Calvary* (1918-23), *Peter the Great* (1929-34), and *Bread* (1938).

Tolstoy, Leo (Russ.: *Lev Nikolayevich Tolstoi*), 1828-1910, Russian novelist and philosopher. Born of a noble family, he spent a large part of his youth in dissipation. For a time he served in the Russian army in the Caucasus and during the Crimean War. After marrying, 1862, he settled on his estate at Yasnaya Polyana, devoting himself to the interests of the peasantry and the enjoyment of nature. Here he wrote two of the greatest of all novels—*War and Peace* (1865-9), an epic story of the Napoleonic Wars embodying Tolstoy's fatalistic view of history; and *Anna Karenina* (1875-7), a vivid picture of contemporary St. Petersburg life. Both novels are remarkable for rich detail, acute character analysis, and broad scope. Tolstoy's conversion to religion in this period is described in his *Confession* (1879). So fervent were his belief in and practice of nonviolence and extreme simplicity in living that a Tolstoyan cult developed among his followers. Later works include *What Then Must We Do?* (1886), *The Kreutzer Sonata* (1889), *What is Art?* (1897-8), *Resurrection* (1899-1900), and his play *The Living Corpse* (1910). By the time of his death he had given away almost all of his possessions in his effort to achieve complete Christian charity and simplicity.

Toltec—see *Aztec.*

Toluca, capital of Mexico state, central Mexico; pop. 71,026. Founded 1530 by Cortés, it is the center of an agricultural and stock-raising area. Famous for its baskets, Toluca also has textile and flour mills.

tomahawk, war hatchet of the North American Indian, used as a hand weapon or thrown as a missile. Those of Indian origin were of stone or horn, attached to wood handles; the whites later supplied the Indians with iron-headed tomahawks, including some combined with smoking pipes.

tomato, important herbaceous American plant (*Lycopersicon esculentum*) of the potato family. Introduced into Europe as an ornamental, known as the love apple, it was once thought poisonous. Its juicy fruit is now widely used, both raw and cooked. Tomatoes range in size from the small cherry types to the huge beefsteak varieties weighing a pound or more.

Graphic House
Tomato harvesting in New Jersey

Tombighee River, c.400 mi. long, formed by the junction of east and west forks in Mississippi. It flows into Alabama, where it joins the Alabama River to form the Mobile River.

Tombstone, city, SE Arizona; pop. 1283. Founded 1879, it became a mining boom town notorious for its lawlessness. Underground water had ruined the silver and copper mines by c.1900.

Tomsk, capital of Tomsk region, W central Siberia, on Tom River; pop. 249,000. It has light industries but is more important as the cultural center of W Siberia, with a university and technical and scientific schools. Boris Godunov founded it, 1604.

Tom Thumb, 1838-83, U.S. dwarf, b. Bridgeport, Conn.; real name Charles Sherwood Stratton. Discovered 1842 by P. T. Barnum, who named him General Tom Thumb, he was exhibited in the U.S. and Europe. He was at that time 25 in. tall and by the age of 17 had grown only 4 in. His success with Queen Victoria, Pres. Polk, and the crowned heads of Europe made him an even greater drawing-card. In 1863 he married Lavinia Warren, another dwarf. The name Tom Thumb comes from the 16th-cent. nursery tale, retold by Perrault.

tonality, in music, the adherence to a particular key or scale. Most western music prior to the 20th cent. follows tonal scheme. Modal music, until the 17th cent., remained within one of the twelve Greek modes for a single composition, and most later music was composed within one of the major or minor keys except when the key was changed in the middle of the work. This modulation, however, is a part of consistent formal structure, and the listener's awareness of one key in use at a time is preserved. **Atonality** is the 20th-cent. practice of composing without reference to any key, as used by Schönberg. **Polytonality,** the simultaneous use of many keys, and **microtonality,** are both negations of tonality.

Tone, Wolfe (Theobald Wolfe Tone), 1763-98, Irish patriot. Seeking the aid of the French Revolutionary government to liberate Ireland, he negotiated with the French envoy in Philadelphia, 1795, and with the authorities in Paris later. An expedition under Gen. Lazare Hoche, 1798, ended with his capture and suicide in prison.

tone poem—see *symphonic poem.*

Tonga or **Friendly Islands,** archipelago, S Pacific Ocean, S of Samoa; area 270 sq. mi.; pop. 62,000; capital Nukulofa (pop. 9202). The islands are divided into three groups: Tongatapu (seat of the capital), Ha'apai, and Vava'u. Though some are of coral formation, others are volcanic, and one (Niuafo'ou) had a violent eruption in 1946. The climate is mild and healthful. Copra and bananas are the chief products. Discovered 1616 by the Dutch, the islands were named the Friendly Islands by Capt. James Cook, who visited them, 1773. In 1900, the group, which is a constitutional monarchy with a Polynesian queen, was proclaimed a British protectorate. Government is by a legislative assembly composed of seven nobles, seven representatives of the people, and seven representatives of the crown. Britain administers the island group through the governor of Fiji and a local commissioner.

tongue, muscular organ attached to the mouth of most vertebrates. It can be moved and projected. The tongue is covered with a mucous membrane and at its base is in contact with the epiglottis and the pharynx. The upper surface of the tongue of mammals contains taste buds, which are the principal organs of taste. Aside from facilitating taste, the tongue functions in speech.

Tonkin or **Tongking,** former state, N Indo-China; now **North Viet Nam,** bounded N by China, W by Laos; area 44,670 sq. mi.; pop. c.11,000,000; capital Hanoi; other leading city Haiphong. Bordered N and W by high mountains, the region has a rich plain where rice, cotton, and other crops are grown. There are important coal fields. Inhabited mainly by Annamese, the region was the nucleus of the ancient state of Annam. It came under French rule, 1884, and was included in French Indo-China, 1887. Occupied by the Japanese, 1940-5, after the war Tonkin was incorporated in the independent state of Viet Nam (*q.v.*).

tonsils, two small masses of lymphoid tissue at the entrance to the throat. They are thought to serve as traps for germs passing into the throat. When they become chronically or repeatedly infected, especially in children, their removal (tonsillectomy) is often desirable. Inflammation of the tonsils (tonsillitis) may arise following a cold and is often accompanied by enlargement and pain in the glands of the neck. Streptococcal tonsillitis is at times associated with scarlet fever and may be followed by rheumatic fever; hence it should be treated promptly with chemotherapy.

Toombs, Robert, 1810-85, U.S. statesman, b. Wilkes co., Ga. He was U.S. Representative from Georgia, 1845-53, and Senator, 1853-61, resigning to become Secretary of State in the Confederacy, 1861, then brigadier general in the Confederate army. He fled to London after defeat of the South, 1865. After his return to Georgia, 1867, he never took the oath of allegiance to the Union which was necessary for restoration of his citizenship.

tooth, bonelike growth in the jaws designed for chewing. The main structure of the human tooth is a hard substance, dentine, chiefly calcium phosphate. The exposed part (crown) above the gum is covered with a hard, glossy material called enamel. The surface of the root is enveloped by the bonelike cementum, which in turn is enveloped by the peridontal membrane. Within the hollow central portion of the tooth lie the jellylike pulp, nerves, and blood vessels. In adult man there are 32 teeth arranged symmetrically, 8 on each side above and below. Each set has four incisors, two canines, four bicuspids, and six molars. Teeth develop in two sets: the milk teeth and the permanent. There are 20 milk teeth, 10 in each jaw, which drop out in the 6th, 7th, and 8th years. The first permanent tooth follows immediately, and others develop until the wisdom teeth manifest themselves about the 18th year or later; in some cases they never appear at all. Teething usually begins at the 6th month. Some babies become feverish with teething. Certain minerals (calcium, phosphorus, fluorine) and vitamins are essential for the healthy growth and upkeep of the teeth.

FIRST DENTITION
THE 20 DECIDUOUS OR BABY TEETH

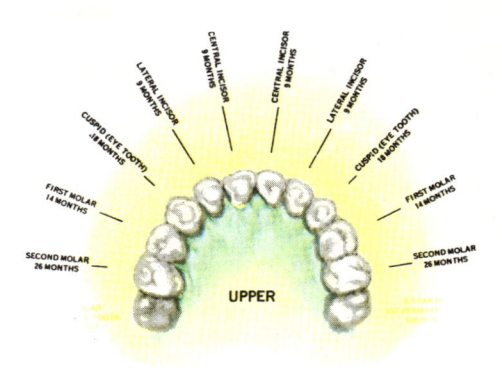

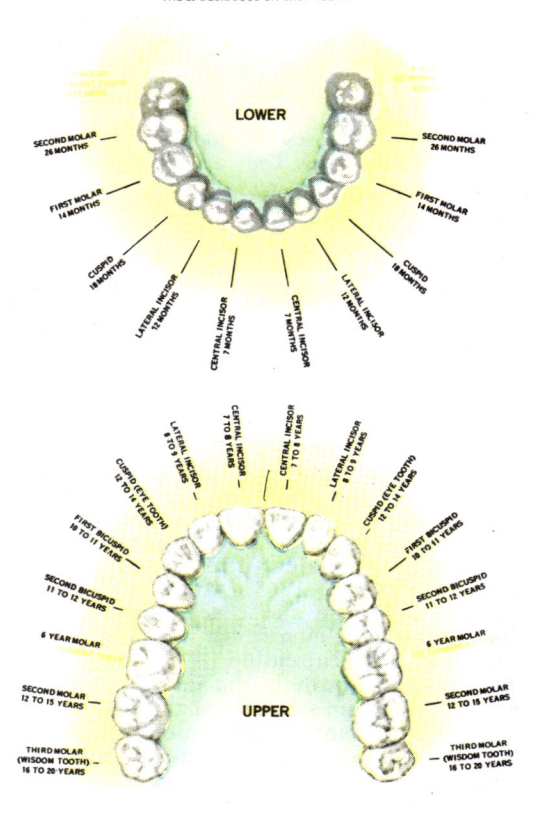

SECOND DENTITION
THE 32 PERMANENT TEETH

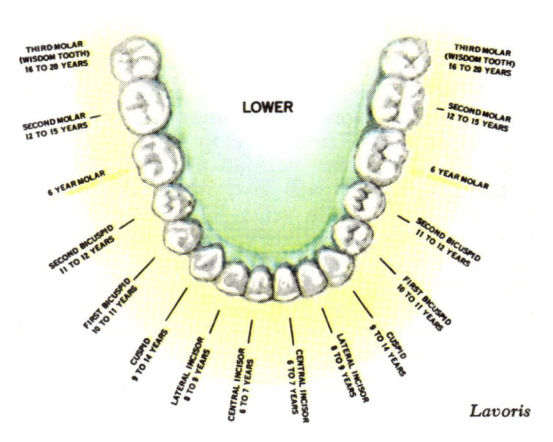

Lavoris

Sugar predisposes to decay (caries). The addition of minute amounts of fluoride to drinking water has been recommended, but not conclusively proved, as inhibiting tooth decay in children without unfavorable secondary effects. Toothache is usually a sign of decay, ulceration, or other trouble. See *dentistry*.

topaz, an aluminum fluosilicate; a valuable jewelry stone in its wine-yellow, brown and pink tints. Both brown quartz and citrine (yellow quartz) are often sold under the name of topaz, but since topaz has a hardness of eight while quartz only has a hardness of seven, topaz will scratch the quartz. Oriental topaz is also yellow, but it is a variety of corundum, which has a hardness of nine. Common topaz may be colorless, white, or pale blue. The finest of this last color were found in the Ural Mountains, U.S.S.R. Brazilian blue and brown topaz is also outstanding. The Brazilian brown topaz turns pink on heating; most pink jewelry topaz has been heated. Topaz is a favorite of mineral collectors because it is formed into beautiful, large, prismatic crystals. See *birthstones*.

Topeka, capital of Kansas, co. seat of Shawnee co., NE Kansas, on Kansas River; pop. 119,484. It is a trading and shipping center for an agricultural region. An insurance center, it also has large railway repair shops, flour mills, and meat-packing and printing plants. Topeka was settled 1854. In 1855 a Free State constitution was framed here; Topeka became the capital when Kansas was admitted to the Union, 1861. Building of the Atchison, Topeka, and Santa Fe RR helped the city's growth. Here is the Menninger Clinic for psychiatric research as well as a state mental hospital and Washburn College.

topography, physical features, natural and artificial, of the earth's surface, and the shape of bodies of land and water. It is a determining factor in rainfall, temperature, soil, and climate. Topographical maps, by various symbols, show contour and relation of physical features to each other.

Torah—see *Judaism*.

Torgau, town, Eastern Germany, on left bank of Elbe River; *c.*30 mi. NE of Leipzig; pop. 20,400. It has chemical, ceramics, and metal works. The town played a part in the Reformation (Torgau League of Protestants) and in the Thirty Years' War. It was the site of a victory, 1760, by Frederick the Great over the Austrians. Here, Apr. 27, 1945, during World War II, U.S. and Russian troops first established contact.

Torino—see *Turin*.

tornado, whirlwind in the center of which air spins at speeds of 60 m.p.h. or more. Traveling at speeds between 20 and 40 m.p.h. for distances of five to 300 miles, tornadoes may devastate the country as they go, uprooting trees, picking up and smashing buildings, and even moving heavy machinery. The tornado, seen as a funnel-shaped cloud, makes a peculiar roaring noise. At its center is an area of extreme low atmospheric pressure which exerts a sucking action sometimes of great destructive power. At sea it causes a waterspout, dangerous to small shipping. Tornadoes in the U.S. are most common in the basins of the Mississippi and Ohio Rivers, killing 50 to 400 people per year and causing damage up to $40 million annually. A U.S. Weather Bureau tornado detection service, developed in the late 1950s, has had considerable success in warning persons of the likelihood of tornadoes.

Toronto, capital of Ontario, co. seat of York co., S Ontario, on Lake Ontario; pop. 644,948. The 2nd-largest city of Canada, it is a lake port, with exports including lumber, farm products, and woolens, and a commercial, financial, and industrial center. In 1954, a new type of metropolitan government having almost full authority over all phases of public services and finances for the metropolitan area was set up in Toronto. The same system was later adopted by other large Canadian municipalities. Fort Rouillé, a French trading post, was here in the mid-18th cent.; the city, founded 1793, soon became the capital of Upper Canada. It was held twice by the U.S. in the War of 1812. In 1837 it was the center of the insurrection led by William Lyon Mackenzie. It is the seat of the Univ. of Toronto, York Univ. (est. 1959), the Royal Ontario Museum, and Roman Catholic and Anglican cathedrals.

Canadian Tourist Office
Downtown *Toronto* and its lake harbor

torpedo, in naval warfare, an explosive, self-propelled, cigar-shaped, underwater missile discharged against enemy vessels. The first self-propelled torpedo was invented by Robert Whitehead, an Englishman, 1864. Torpedoes are generally powered by steam compressed air, or electricity, and held on their course by a gyroscope; some are designed to be drawn into the enemy vessel's magnetic field before exploding. They travel under water, striking the target below the water-line, and some have a range of as much as eight mi. Modern torpedoes are c. two ft. in diameter and 24 ft. long and carry up to 600 lbs. of high explosives at a speed of c. 50 knots. "Homing torpedoes" are equipped with ultra-sensitive guidance systems which detect, at considerable distance, acoustic, magnetic or heat differentials set up in the surrounding water by any naval vessel. Once these torpedoes reach the general area of the enemy ship, their guidance system takes control and steers them into the target, correcting their course as necessary to counteract any evasive action which the enemy might take. Although torpedoes are the typical weapon of the submarine, other vessels such as destroyers and cruisers are also torpedo-equipped, as are the naval aircraft called torpedo bombers and various types of small, fast motorboats. See *warhead*.

torpedo boat—see *motor torpedo boat*.

Torquay, municipal borough, Devonshire, SW England, on Torbay; pop. 53,915. It is a popular winter resort and yachting center. Its small handicraft industry includes pottery making. Among other sites of historic interest is a ruined abbey.

torque, a personal ornament worn by certain ancient peoples, such as the Britons, the Gauls, and the Germans. It consisted of a stiff collar formed by a number of gold wires twisted together, and sometimes of a thin metal plate, also generally of gold. The torque was frequently worn around the neck as a symbol of rank and command.

torque, in physics, a concept which may be simply expressed as the effectiveness of a force in setting a body into rotation; or a moment (of forces).

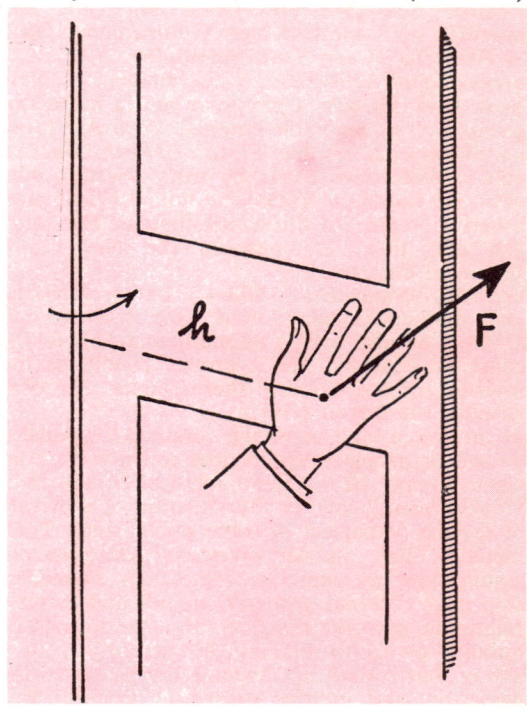

If the forces applied to a body (such as this door) do not all act upon a single point, the body will commence rotating; such movement is known in mechanics as *torque*.

For a single particle, the torque is the moment of the resultant force on the particle with respect to a particular origin. This is expressed by the vector relation $L = r \times F$, where L is the torque, r is the position vector with respect to the origin, and F is the resultant force. The torque is equal to the time rate of change of the moment of momentum. In engineering mechanics usage torque often refers to the torsional or twisting moment or couple which tends to twist a rigidly fixed object, such as a shaft, about an axis of rotation.

Torquemada, Tomás de, 1420?-98, head of the Spanish Inquisition. A Dominican monk, in 1483 he was empowered by Ferdinand and Isabella to organize the Inquisition in Spanish lands, and Pope Innocent VIII made him grand inquisitor in 1487. Under his ruthless administration at least 2000 persons were executed, and in

1492 he shared responsibility for expulsion of the Jews from Spain.

Torrance, city, California, S of Los Angeles; pop. 100,991. It was laid out in 1911 and incorporated in 1921. There are major petroleum, steel and metal products industries. The city's population quadrupled during the 1950s.

Torrens, Lake—see *Australia*.

Torreón, city, Coahuila state, N Mexico; pop. 159,358. Founded 1893, now an important rail center, it serves an irrigated agricultural area known as the Laguna District, chief crops of which are wheat and cotton. Important are the textile mills, foundries, a rubber factory, and a brewery.

Torres Strait, ocean channel, *c.*80 mi. wide, joining Arafura Sea (W) and Coral Sea (E), and bounded by S coast of New Guinea and NE tip of Australia (Cape York Peninsula).

Torrey, John, 1796-1873, U.S. botanist, b. New York City. He was a physician and a mineralogist as well as a notable botanist. With Asa Gray he collaborated on *The Flora of North America* and in collections made by early Western surveys. He was New York state botanist, and published a volume of illustrated flora of the state. His collections are now at the New York Botanical Garden.

Torricelli, Evangelista, 1608-47, Italian physicist and mathematician. For a time secretary to Galileo, he also served as mathematician to the court of Tuscany. He is known chiefly as the inventor of the mercury thermometer. He constructed the first in 1643.

tort, in law, a kind of wrong committed against a person or property which does not involve contract. It may be a direct invasion of the individual's legal rights, or the violation of a private obligation or neglect of some public duty. Torts include libel, slander, trespass, unauthorized assumption and exercise of the right of ownership over personal property, assault and battery, failure to perform the duty of a landowner or building owner to maintain his property in such a way that it does not become dangerous to the passer-by, and injuries caused by domesticated animals. An action for tort is a civil action for damages. The same act which gives rise to the civil suit in some instances may simultaneously be a crime, *e.g.,* theft.

tortoise, a land reptile of the order Testudinata, which also includes turtles and terrapins. Like these it has a boxlike armor beneath which head, limbs, and tail can be withdrawn for security. This "shell" consists of a bony dorsal carapace, formed from overgrown ribs and vertebrae, and a ventral plastron, which are overlaid with horny plates. Tortoises occur chiefly in warm regions. The several known species range in length from 6 in. to the 5 ft. sometimes reached by the Galápagos Islands giant tortoise. Some live over 100 years. The handsome mottled tortoise shell of commerce is obtained from one of the sea turtles (genus *Eretmochelys*). On heating it is easily molded and welded.

Tortola—see *Virgin Islands*.

Tortuga, island off N Haiti, *c.*25 mi. long. It was a favorite hideout of 17th-cent. pirates.

torture, practice of causing a person severe suffering, especially physical pain, to force him to do something against his will, such as making a confession or yielding information or money.

Diego Rivera's "Branding of the Indians" shows *torture* used during the conquest of Mexico by the Spanish in the 16th cent.

Torture was used as a judicial procedure to extort confessions during the Middle Ages, being legally endorsed by all European countries except England and Sweden. Applied in ancient Greece and the Roman republic only to slaves or enemies, it spread rapidly during the days of the Spanish Inquisition, when the most ingenious methods and instruments of torment were devised. France abolished torture at the time of the French Revolution, 1789, but in some countries it survived until the 19th cent. and was unofficially reintroduced by the police and security forces of totalitarian regimes of the 20th cent.

Tory, name of a former English political party. Originally an epithet applied to Irish Catholic outlaws, it was first used in England, 1679, to refer to those favoring the succession of James, duke of York, a professed Catholic. His conduct as James II united Tories and their Whig op-

Graphic House
The giant *tortoise*

ponents against him. The height of Tory power occurred in the last years of Anne's reign, 1710-4, but the Jacobite leanings of the Tory leader Henry St. John discredited his party for the first 50 years of Hanoverian rule. Under George III a faction of "king's friends" supported the royal prerogative against Parliament and became the nucleus for a new Tory Party. In the American colonies the term Tory was applied, as a synonym for loyalist, to all who supported the king against the colonies. The British defeat almost discredited the Tories in England, but the able leadership of the moderate William Pitt, with reaction against the excesses of the French Revolution, sustained them. In the reign of George IV, Peel courted the new industrial interests with his policy of moderate reform, but Wellington identified Toryism with reaction, and the party was decisively defeated in 1830. The right wing of British politics was reconstituted after 1832 as the Conservative Party, and the name Tory again became an epithet.

Toscana—see *Tuscany*.

Toscanini, Arturo, 1867-1957, Italian orchestra conductor. Hired as cellist for opera in Rio de Janeiro, 1886, at his first appearance there he replaced the regular conductor, who had been hissed off the podium, and took over for the rest of the season. He made his debut at La Scala, Milan, 1896. Gatti-Casazza, on becoming director of La Scala, engaged him as conductor, and the collaboration was extended at the Metropolitan Opera in New York, 1908-15. Toscanini was artistic director of La Scala, 1921-9, then turned from operatic to symphonic conducting and was regular conductor of the merged New York Philharmonic and Symphony orchestras, 1928-36. He toured with the orchestra, conducted at the Bayreuth and Salzburg Festivals, and in 1937 organized and conducted the NBC Symphony. He retired in 1954. Toscanini has been acclaimed as one of the greatest conductors of all time. He was a perfectionist, who demanded as much from himself as he did from the highly disciplined orchestras he directed. In his early years he introduced much new music to the public, but as he grew older he left that task to his juniors and relied on a traditional reportory. From the very outset of his career he conducted without scores. Bad eyesight forced him to develop his memory, which was possibly unequalled in musical history.

totalitarianism, modern form of government in which the state is controlled by a dictatorship (*q.v.*). Totalitarian governments have included Mussolini's in Italy, Hitler's in Germany, the Communist state in Russia, Franco's in Spain, Perón's in Argentina, Tito's in Yugoslavia, and Castro's in Cuba. Nationalism, militarism, governmental economic control, rigid censorship, an extensive propaganda machine, government control of education, and the use of secret police to stamp out opposition are characteristic of totalitarian states. See *corporate state*.

totalizator—see *horse racing*.

totemism, primitive belief in a mystic and intimate relationship with a species or type of object, especially an animal or plant, called the totem (a word of Algonkian origin). Totemism is an aspect of clan organization. Usually the clan believes it is descended from the totem; it bears the totem's name, refuses to kill or eat it, and as a group practices exogamy (marriage outside the group). Totemism was first intensively studied among the Australian aborigines by Sir James Frazer, who published his findings in *Totemism and Exogamy* (1910). It was widespread among North American Indians, but the so-called **totem poles** of the NW Pacific Coast tribes are not always typical of totemism. These poles, which contain intricate carvings of totems and other objects, show the indirect results of European influence, since apparently most, if not all, were made with imported tools later than 1830, and since they were made possible by affluence resulting from the trade in fur, and were built to demonstrate the wealth and prestige of the highly competitive chiefs. See *potlatch*.

toucan, bird of the family Rhamphastidae, of tropical South America. Allied to the barbets, toucans have large, vividly colored bills and brilliant plumage. Despite its size, the bill is light and thin-walled. The birds inhabit forest regions and feed on fruit, insects, and the eggs and young of other birds.

Toucans of South American rain forests

touch, that one of the five senses by which pressure or contact with the skin or a mucous membrane is perceived. From it the brain learns to distinguish the size, texture, nature of surface, and consistency, of objects touched. This sense is well-developed in the lips, tongue tip, fingertips, and palms of hands but touch sensation is present over most of the body surface. Deep tactile sensations from receptors in muscle give information as to the position of any part of the body and aid in performance of skilled movements. Pain sense and temperature sense are distinct from the sense of touch.

Toulon, city, S France, on Mediterranean c.30 mi. ESE of Marseilles; pop. 141,117. A seaport and naval base, it has shipbuilding and several manufactures, including machinery and chemicals. It exports wine and olive oil, and is a resort. Known to the Romans as Telo Martius, and frequently sacked in medieval times, it was developed as a naval base by Louis XIV. Here, 1744, an English fleet was defeated by a combined French-Spanish force. Following the fall of France, 1940, in World War II, the main part of the French fleet while moored in the harbor was scuttled to prevent its seizure by the Germans.

Toulouse, city, Languedoc, S France, capital of Haute-Garonne dept., on the Garonne and the Canal du Midi, c.180 mi. SW of Lyons; pop. 217,667. An important communication and educational center, in the productive Aquitaine basin, it has various industries, e.g., textiles, fertilizer, machinery, foodstuffs. The old university (founded 1230), academies, museums, and religous and trade schools are notable. The Romanesque church of St.-Sernin contains the tomb of Thomas Aquinas. Among architectural landmarks is the Gothic cathedral. The Tolosa of the Romans, Toulouse has often been the scene of religious and political strife. Taken by Visigoths, Franks, and Saracens, later it was capital of Aquitaine, 781-877. Here, Apr. 10, 1814, the British and Spanish under Wellington defeated the French under Soult.

Toulouse-Lautrec, Henri de, 1864-1901, French painter and lithographer. Though crippled, early in life he showed a brilliant talent. On moving to Paris he met Van Gogh and Degas, and from 1885 he lived in Montmartre, turning out endless sketches, posters, etchings, paintings, and lithographs of the life and personalities of the theater, cafés, cabarets, and brothels of Montmartre. His linear, summary technique and sparing dabs of color, influenced by Japanese prints, incisively suggest the characters and gestures of his subjects. He lived at a frenzied pace, and died insane at 37.

Touraine, historic region and former province of W central France. Tours was the capital. Touraine was ruled by the counts of Touraine, until joined with Anjou, 11th cent. When provinces were abolished during the Revolution, Touraine was divided between the departments of Indre-et-Loire and Indre. Crossed by the Loire River, the region is noted for its fertility and fine châteaux.

Touré, Sékou, 1922- , Guinean political leader, b. Faranah, French Guinea, son of a Moslem peasant family. He attended a technical college in Conakry and became a civil servant. He quickly joined the local labor movement and became a leader in the Confédération Général du Travail, a major union movement affiliated with the Communist-dominated World Federation of Trade Unions. He became president of the African branch of the CGT in 1956 and vice president of the WFTU. He had engaged in local politics since 1950, when he was elected to the legislative assembly of Guinea. He was chosen mayor of Conakry in 1955 and was elected to the French National Assembly in Paris in 1956. He formed and led his own party, the Democratic Party, from 1952, which he used as an instrument to conduct violent demonstrations against continued French rule of his country. On Oct. 2, 1958, Guinea became the first French African country to attain independence, breaking all its French ties, including (1960) its membership in the French franc area. Though Touré had denied since 1950 any Communist ties, he wooed the Communist bloc politically, seeking much aid from the U.S.S.R. and Communist China. At the same time he tried to get economic aid from the West.

tournament, originally, a mock combat between knights; now any contest in skill involving more than two teams or individuals—e.g., the National Collegiate Athletic Association basketball tourna-

Toulouse-Lautrec's "At the Moulin Rouge" was painted mainly within the café itself.

In jousting *tournaments* popular in medieval times, the combatant, clad in heavy armor, sought to unseat his opponent.

ment. Medieval tournaments were held as early as the 11th cent. in France and flourished in England and France until the mid-15th cent. Although combat was presumably friendly and Richard I established a court of honor to settle disputes, riots frequently concluded a day's jousting.

tourniquet—see *first aid*.

Tours, city, Touraine, W central Europe, capital of Indre-et-Loire dept., on the Loire, *c*.130 mi. SW of Paris; pop. 83,618. A railroad center, the city has an active trade in agricultural products, wool, wine, and spirits. It produces machinery, fertilizer, and pottery. Of pre-Roman origin, it flourished under Roman rule. Here St. Martin, apostle of the Gauls, was bishop, 4th cent. Later Tours became a monastic center, and Alcuin established here a famous philosophical and theological school. At the Battle of Tours (Battle of Tours and Poitiers), 732, Charles Martel defeated the Moors under Abd-ur-Rahman, checking their advance into W Europe. In the Franco-Prussian War, 1870, Tours was for several months the seat of the French government. Near the city are famous châteaux.

Toussaint L'Ouverture, François Dominique, *c*.1744-1803, Haitian revolutionist. Born a Negro slave, in 1791 he joined the successful revolt to free the slaves and in 1793 helped fight off the encroaching British, forcing them to withdraw, 1798. In 1801 he seized the Santo Domingo colony, lately ceded by Spain to France, and thus held the whole of Hispaniola. He was defeated, 1802, by a large French expedition under Gen. Leclerc. Seized by a ruse, he was sent to France and died in prison.

Tower of London, fortress, London, on Thames River. The massive central structure, the White Tower, was built under William I, shortly after the Conquest, on top of a Roman wall *c*.1000 years old. More than a dozen other towers were built in succeeding centuries and used as prisons. Many notable prisoners brought here were executed in the Tower or on nearby Tower Hill. The crown jewels are housed in Wakefield Tower, part of the fortress.

towhee, an American finch (genus *Pipilo*). The common towhee, also called the chewink, is found in eastern U.S. The male is black and rufous; the female, brown. The bird nests on the ground, and it scratches for food similarly to domestic fowl. Related species occur in the West.

town, center of population, often defined as one smaller than a city but larger than a village. During the Middle Ages towns developed as commercial centers and were distinct from cities, which were the seats of bishops. In the towns the public markets and the merchants' and craftsmen's guilds grew up. In colonial New England the town had special importance as a political unit; here most of the local residents participated in the town meeting, which framed local law and became a symbol of U.S. democracy. Town governments in the U.S. today vary greatly. See *commune; township*.

town planning, the physical organization of an urban community along lines beneficial to the population in general. A fairly recent development in human history, town planning as we know it today did not start until the days of the Roman Republic, at which time invading armies would set their camps in the shape of a square, intersected by two pathways which met in the square's center. Later, many of these camps became cities and retained their original shapes which continued to be useful from the standpoint of defense. Many British towns today, *e.g.*, Chichester, bear witness to this Roman style of planning. In the Middle Ages, towns were often defined by their city walls. However, many old cities in Europe are marked by street-patterns of concentric circles which reflect the outward growth of the town. Since the earliest towns were usually trading centers, the market place is very often found in the exact center of the original area. During the Renaissance, towns were able to expand greatly beyond their former borders; at this time, too, there was a greater interest in the construction of public buildings, so that their strong points would not be obscured by overcrowding, or the incongruity of differing structures built close together. The most cele-

The historic Tower of London   Pan American Airways

brated example of early town planning was the reorganization of the city of Paris undertaken by the idealistic leaders of the French Revolution; eye-catching new buildings were erected at the ends of broadened avenues, parks replaced shoddy sections of the town, and streets were built which led to the direct center of the city. This kind of planning was exported to the New World, where many cities could be planned before a single foundation was laid; the results can be seen in such cities as Detroit, Washington, D.C., and Indianapolis, where wide streets and avenues dissect the towns into quadrants and problems of new construction, sewage, and traffic congestion have thereby been kept at a minimal level. Older cities, though, on both sides of the Atlantic, were not so fortunate. Continuing on the lines of a pattern originating centuries before, they could not withstand the pressures of the Industrial Revolution. The results were crowded streets, an ugly and unaesthetic commingling of residential, business, and factory districts, and, of course, slums. It was not until the turn of the century that governments recognized the growing problems engendered by the rapidly expanding cities and took legislative measures to correct them. The most successful of these plans has been the "garden city," where tall buildings for dwelling and commercial activities utilize air space, leaving ample ground areas between structures for open spacing and attractive landscaping. This principle has been employed notably in New York City in urban renewal areas where it was necessary to provide housing for large numbers of people. In Pittsburgh, this concept was applied to office buildings in the city's newly redesigned "point" area. Aside from the slow rezoning and replanning of cities in sections, many visionary city-planners, and architects of the 20th cent. devised schemes for total cities. At mid-century, opportunities for application of these heretofore idealistic plans have come with the creation of the capital cities of Brasilia, in Brazil, and Chandigarh, in the Punjab (India). These were built on sites where no former towns existed; their design was unencumbered by old street plans. Opportunities such as these are rare, however, and the basic problem of the city-planner today remains that of revamping existing cities to fit modern requirements of traffic and increasing population. See *landscape architecture*.

Townsend plan, plan for old-age pensions fostered by Dr. Francis E. Townsend (1867-1960) of California. Annually $20 billion was to be raised by a federal tax and paid out in pensions of $200 monthly to each unemployed, law-abiding citizen 60 years of age or older. The plan had great publicity, 1933-4, claiming 5 million supporters, who asserted it would bring back prosperity by raising the purchasing power of the aged. The plan failed to make progress in Congress.

Townshend, name of an English family of statesmen and soldiers. **Charles Townshend,** 2d **Viscount Townshend,** 1674-1738, entered the House of Lords, 1697, as a Tory but turned Whig. Made secretary of state in the first cabinet under George I, 1714-6, he put down the Jacobite revolt and made defensive alliances with France, Holland, and the empire. He was also secretary of state, 1720-30, under Robert Walpole. His grandson **Charles Townshend,** 1725-67, was secretary of war, 1761-2, in the Bute cabinet and chancellor of the exchequer, 1766-7, in the ministry of the earl of Chatham (the elder William Pitt), taking control of the ministry on Chatham's death. To defray the costs of British administration in the American colonies, he sponsored the **Townshend Acts,** 1767, requiring merchants in the colonies to pay import duties on glass, lead, paints, paper, and tea. The colonists retaliated with boycotts and other forms of protest, and in 1770 Parliament repealed the duties except for tea.

township, in the U.S., any of various small political subdivisions of the county or parish. In New England, where the town antedated the county, the township is in most cases the equivalent of the town, being an important political unit. In the South the county or parish is the important political unit next to the state, the township ordinarily having little political importance. In the Northwest the township tends to be simply a geographical subdivision of the county.

toxemia (or eclampsia or eclamptogenic syndrome), a toxic state which occurs during pregnancy. In its mildest form, the patient has a moderate elevation in blood pressure and may have albumin in the urine with some peripheral edema. There may be headaches, and dizziness and the patient may see spots. The more severe form (eclampsia) is usually characterized by an accentuation of the above symptoms which produces a more toxic state at the time of delivery. Either toxemia or eclampsia may progress to the most severe form (eclamptogenic syndrome) which may threaten the victim's life by producing convulsions during delivery. The potential danger of toxemia is one of the major concerns of the obstetrician. Early diagnosis and careful preventive therapy may offset the development of the more severe complications.

Toynbee, Arnold Joseph, 1889-   , English scholar and historian. He studied and taught at Oxford, served the government as delegate to the peace conference following World War I, and taught Greek language and history at the Univ. of London, 1919-24. In World War II he directed research for the British foreign office, and he attended the Paris Peace Conference in 1946. His 10 vol. *Study of History* (1934-54; abridged eds. 1946 and 1957) elaborates his theory of the influence of nonmaterial factors on the rise and fall of cultures. *The World and the West* (1953) is a collection of broadcasts. *East to West,* a round-the-world travel chronicle, appeared in 1958 and *Hellenism* (1961). A one-volume *Study of History* (1961) reappraised many of his conclusions in his earlier 10-volume works.

Toynbee Hall—see *settlement house*.

Trabzon—see *Trebizond*.

Tracheophyta, a subkingdom of the plant kingdom including all those plants having well-developed vascular, *i.e.* conducting, tissue. The division takes in all higher plants from the club-mosses through the flowering plants.

tracheotomy, surgical opening of the trachea (see *throat*). Whenever there is a physical obstruction of the upper air passage (*i.e.* larynx and throat) by a foreign body or by edema and inflammation, as in croup, it may be necessary to do a tracheotomy which by-passes the obstruction and creates an artificial opening through which the patient may breathe. The incision is made in the neck, just below the Adam's apple. In an emergency the operation can be done safely without using precious time to insure sterile technique or administer anesthesia.

track and field athletics, contests of jumping, running, leaping over obstacles, and throwing weights. They have been known since antiquity, and today's meets parallel the ancient ones in some respects. The Olympic Games, first launched in 776 B.C., featured track and field athletics. The sport became popular in England c.1154; from 1800 to c.1868 in the U.S. it was generally on a professional basis. The first intercollegiate meet took place in England, 1864, between Oxford and Cambridge. The New York Athletic Club staged the first amateur meet in the U.S., 1868. The IC4A (Intercollegiate Association of Amateur Athletes of America) was formed, 1876, and the AAU (Amateur Athletic Union) 6 years later. Meets usually consist of events in sprints, middle and long distances, hurdles, broad and high jump, pole vault, shotput, discus, javelin, hammer throw, and relays. In the U.S. and the British empire distances are usually measured in yards, but in all other countries, and in the Olympics, metric measurements are the standard.

Track meets are popular throughout the world. The foot-races above were held in Germany; the meet below, in France.

Tractarians—see *Oxford movement*.
trade—see *balance of trade; exports and imports*.
trade acceptance—see *draft*.
trade association, organization of commercial or industrial firms that are in the same business. Its purpose is to promote common interests. Such associations—*e.g.,* the National Association of Manufacturers—occupy themselves with labor problems, market research, public relations, price policy, trade advertising, publications, and questions pertaining to credit, transportation, and production. Through lobbying they sometimes influence federal or state legislature.
trademark, distinctive mark placed upon goods to identify the manufacturer. It may be a device, label, ticket, heading, signature, word, letter, or numeral. If a word, it may not be one in general use as a name for that particular kind of product (thus *automobile* may not be a trademark for a motorcar) and not the name of a person (except a signature in facsimile) or place. It may not be morally objectionable or misrepresent the product. A trademark established in commerce is automatically protected at common law, but there are advantages in registering trademarks with the U.S. Patent Office under the Federal Trade-Mark (Lanham) Act of July 5, 1946. Many states also have trademark legislation.
trade schools—see *industrial education*.
trade union—see *union*.
trade winds, persistent winds blowing toward the equator. In the Northern Hemisphere they blow from the northeast, in the Southern Hemisphere from the southeast. In the days of sailing ships they were of the greatest importance to trade; hence the name. They are caused by the earth's rotation, which deflects air (in the Northern Hemisphere to the right, and in the Southern to the left) from the horse latitudes (about 30°N. and 30°S.), which have high barometric pressure, to the doldrums, which have low barometric pressure.
Trafalgar, cape of S Spain, on Atlantic Ocean, c.40 mi. W of Gibraltar. Here, Oct. 21, 1805, Nelson defeated the combined French and Spanish fleets under Villeneuve and saved England from the possibility of a French invasion. Nelson himself was killed in the hour of victory, his last order being "England expects every man this day to do his duty."
Trafalgar Square, open square in London that commemorates Nelson's victory, 1805, at Trafalgar. It has a column (completed 1867) 145 ft. high, surmounted by a statue of the hero, with four bronze lions at the base. The National Gallery faces the square, which is often the scene of political and other demonstrations.

tragedy, form of drama (*q.v.*) which developed in ancient Greece at the feasts of Dionysus. Tnespis (*q.v.*) is regarded as its founder. In the work of Aeschylus, Sophocles, and Euripides, tragedy rose to its peak. As defined by Aristotle in his *Poetics,* tragedy deals with an important theme in such fashion that the spectator is filled with terror and pity for the protagonist, who, however, although defeated in the course of the drama's conflict, achieves by his character an inward victory; and this in turn effects in the spectator a catharsis of the emotions and a final feeling of exaltation. The tragic character must be of noble proportions, with some flaw that leads to inevitable downfall, usually death. Thus, stated simply, tragedy is popularly distinguished from comedy by its unhappy ending. The tragic drama of the Renaissance was modeled largely on the works of the Roman Seneca, who had in turn used the Greek originals for his model. English tragedy began with *Gorboduc* (1562), by Thomas Sackville and Thomas Norton. The tragedies of Marlowe, and the greater ones of Shakespeare, disregarded the classical unities of time, place, and action and interjected the element of comic relief. The tragedies of Ben Jonson followed more closely the classical models, as did certainly the work of the 17th-cent. French playwrights Racine and Corneille, the unrelieved intensity of their tragedies strictly observing classical unity. Other great writers of tragedy include the 17th-cent. Spanish Lope de Vega Carpio and Calderón de la Barca, and the 18th-cent. Italian Alfieri and German Lessing, Goethe, and Schiller. Toward the end of the 19th cent. the importance of social drama was heightened by Ibsen's tragedies. The modern tragedy is represented by a French school (including Claudel and the *metteurs en scene*), and Irish school (including Synge, Yeats, and Beckett), and an American school. The American Maxwell Anderson wrote social tragedies in verse, using historical themes and contemporary events as the basis for his plays; Eugene O'Neill wrote tragedies examining individuals rather than society. Arthur Miller and Tennessee Williams are among America's more recent important writers of tragedy.

Trajan (Marcus Ulpius Trajanus), A.D. 53-117, Roman emperor, the first of non-Italian origin, b. Spain. Associated in the imperial office by Nerva, whom he succeeded, A.D. 99, Trajan continued his military career with the conquest of the Dacians, whose country he annexed as a Roman province, 107. This exploit, the first important expansion since Augustus, was commemorated by the Column of Trajan, still standing on the site of the forum he built. Trajan attempted further conquests, annexing the provinces of Arabia, Armenia, and Mesopotamia, but revolts among the Jews and in Britain and Africa forced his return home. He died en route and was succeeded by Hadrian.

trampoline, a gymnastic device developed during the 1930s. It consists normally of a steel tubular frame of about 9 ft. by 5 ft. in length and width and standing about 3 ft. high. Stretched across the frame is a canvas or webbing so attached as to give great elasticity. A person jumping on the canvas is sent to a considerable height and thus may perform gymnastic maneuvers in mid-air. The trampoline has long been used in school physical education training, but it did not become generally popular until about 1959 or 1960 when public trampoline establishments, where persons rented a trampoline for use on an hourly basis, suddenly became a fad in many parts of the U.S.

tranquilizers, drugs which calm, soothe, or pacify a patient. Since *c.*1950, there has been a tremendous increase in the use of tranquilizing drugs. These can be divided into three general groups. Those which are used for mild sedation and the reduction of chronic tension comprise the first group. Among these, Miltown or Equanil is the most widely used. Toxicity is almost unknown but it is common for the patient gradually to develop resistance to the drug which necessitates increasing doses to achieve the same effect. The second group includes the drugs derived from phenothiazine (*e.g.,* chlorpromazine or thorazine, and compazine). These drugs, more powerful and more amenable to routine psychotherapy, straint. They are effective in the treatment of mania or agitated depression. The use of these drugs has revolutionized the care of hospitalized mental patients by making them more tractable and more amenable to routine psychotherapy. The third group is comprised of the psychic energizers (*e.g.,* marsalid). Much less is known of the pharmacology (*q.v.*) of these drugs, and their toxic effects are more severe than the other two groups. They have been particularly effective in the treatment of depression but much more research remains to be done before they can be used safely.

Transcaucasia, district, S of Caucasus Mts. It was the scene in 1919 of prolonged fighting among the Tatars, Armenians, Georgians, and other peoples of the district. Eventually Armenia, Azerbaijan, and Georgia agreed to join the Union of Soviet Socialist Republics, and in 1922 the **Transcaucasian Soviet Federated Socialist Republic** was established, consisting of these three republics. Under the Soviet constitution of 1936 the three sections were separated again into constituent republics of the U.S.S.R.

transcendentalism, in philosophy, a mode of thought emphasizing the spiritual as against the material. Such was the doctrine defined in 19th-cent. New England by the literary **Transcendentalists** led by Ralph Waldo Emerson. In his book *Nature* (1836) and later writings, Emerson postulated a universe with the two aspects of power and form, pervaded by the divine presence which he called the Oversoul. Characteristic of his philosophy, related to Unitarianism and shared by Thoreau, William Ellery Channing, and other writers and preachers, was the spirit of optimistic self-reliance and belief that divine truth may be directly perceived by the individual. The Transcendentalists, influenced by the romantic movement generally and by German idealism, attempted to embody their theories in the short-lived Brook Farm. The term transcendental itself may be traced to Kant's transcendental philosophy, conceived as a science of "pure reason" but sometimes standing for the entire Kantian system. Schelling also gave that name to his philosophy of the mind, which declared the immanence and transcendence of the absolute.

transformer, electrical device that uses the principle of induction to increase (step up) or decrease (step down) the voltage of an alternating current. Transformers consist essentially of primary and secondary coils operating in the same magnetic field. When an alternating voltage passes through the primary coil, it induces a voltage in the secondary. The amplitude of the secondary voltage depends on the relative number of turns in the two coils. If there are twice as many secondary turns as primary turns, the secondary voltage will be twice the primary.

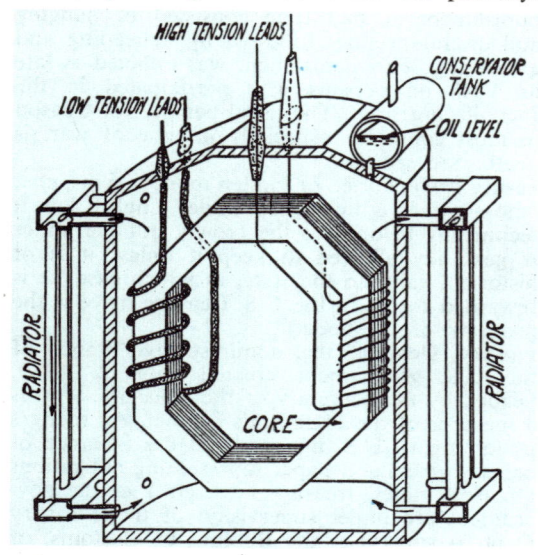

The ordinary single-phase *transformer* consists of a magnetic circuit, winding, leads, insulating bushings (solid dielectric, condenser, or oil-filled types), the insulating oil and its cooling system, a tank to contain the oil and support the other components.

Transformers make possible the widespread use of electric power. Power is transmitted for long distances with minimum loss by the use of voltages of 220,000 or more and is converted for low-voltage consumption in communities by local transformers. See *electric power transmission*.

transfusion—see *blood transfusion*.

transistor, electronic amplifying device based on the special properties of crystals of germanium (*q.v.*). In the transistor, developed 1947, a small piece of germanium is in contact with a flat base electrode. Two pointed electrodes. the emitter and the collector, closely spaced, are mounted on top of the crystal. A positive voltage is applied to the emitter, and a larger negative voltage to the collector. In these conditions a varying voltage applied between the emitter and the base will be amplified in the collector circuit. Transistors can replace vacuum tubes in many applications. They are strong and simple in construction and require a minimum of power to operate.

Trans-Jordan—see *Jordan*.

translocation, in plants, the movement of food and other metabolic products from one place or organ to another. Phloem tissue is most actively involved in large-scale translocation.

One type of *transistor* is the light-sensitive kind, or photodiode, which can operate a standard relay with no amplification. It is ten thousand times more powerful than an ordinary photo electric cell and can carry a hundred times as much electricity. Demonstrating its extreme sensitivity to light, a lighted match causes the transistor to close the relay and turn on an electric bulb. It can also amplify weak electric signals at high frequencies, and is thus useful in home television receivers.

Westinghouse Electric

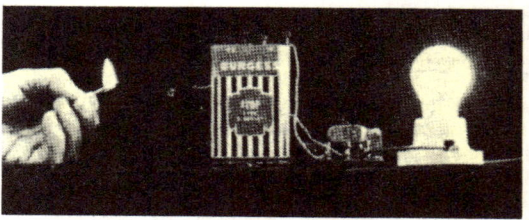

transmigration of souls—see *metempsychosis*.

transpiration, in plants, the loss of water in gaseous form from the aerial parts, chiefly the leaves. Most of the movement of water vapor out of a leaf takes place through the stomata (see *stoma*), pores which by opening and closing exercise some control over the rate of transpiration. As water is lost from the leaf cells, these in turn withdraw water from the xylem tissues of the veins, resulting in a transpirational pull on the columns of water in the veins, stems and roots. This pull is largely responsible for the rise of water in plants.

transportation, in law, conveyance of criminals to a penal settlement in a distant land. Banishment merely sends the offender out of the country, allowing him to go where he likes, whereas transportation sends him to a definite place for a definite period under supervision. From England prisoners were sent to work on the plantations in America until 1776; thereafter they were sent to Australia, until the practice ceased in 1853. In Russia, under the tsars and the Communists, prisoners were transported to Siberia.

Transvaal, province, Union of South Africa; area 110,450 sq. mi.; pop. 4,818,838, of which 3,612,126 are of non-European descent; capital Pretoria; largest city Johannesburg (pop. 1,052,600). Chief industry is mining. From the Witwatersrand region comes one of the world's largest yields of gold. Transvaal also leads the Union in production of coal, tin, and asbestos, and has important diamond and uranium deposits. Stock is raised on the veld; cotton, fruits, and grain also are grown. Industries include foundries, grain mills, breweries, pottery works, clothing factories, and tobacco, soap, and candle factories. Transvaal was first settled by Cape Boers fleeting from English control, and became

Transylvania, former province of central and N Rumania, sometimes called Ardeal (Hung. *Erdely;* Ger. *Siebenbürgen*), area 22,312 sq. mi.; pop. 3,420,859. It is a high plateau surrounded by a continuation of the Carpathians (E), the Transylvanian Alps (S), and the Bikor Mts. (W). The Someș and Mureș Rivers, tributaries of the Tisza, water the region. Chief city is Cluj. Other cities are Stalin (Brasov) and Sibiu, advanced industrial centers. The region is rich in minerals and thermal springs. Ethnically it is very complex. Under the Romans a part of Dacia, it was given up to Germanic invaders, A.D. 3d cent., and taken by Hungary, 1003. In 1526, after the Hungarian defeat by the Turks, it became independent. Transylvania welcomed the Reformation, and under George Rakoczy I, 1631-48, was leading champion of Protestantism in E Europe. Reduced to vassalage by the Turks, 1661, after the Turkish defeat at Vienna in 1683 Transylvania came under the Hapsburgs as part of Hungary. The privileged Saxon and Magyar communities now lost much of their supremacy, and the Rumanian peasantry rose until, in early 19th cent., a Magyar revival took place, the attempt at reunion with Hungary in 1848 leading to fighting between the Rumanian and Saxon and the Magyar factions. Transylvania was part of Hungary until 1918, when union with Rumania was proclaimed, Dec. 1. In World War II a large section was ceded, 1940, to Hungary, but returned to Rumania, 1945.

Trapani, seaport town in W Sicily; pop. 52,661; capital of Trapani province (968 sq. mi.; pop. 375,169). Lying 47 mi. WSW of Palermo, on a sickle-shaped peninsula, it is a fair-sized center of trade and industry, known for its production of Marsala wine, glass, soap, lumber, and building stones. The town, founded by Phoenician traders and originally known as Drepanum, fell to the Romans in 241 B.C. after the battle of the Aegates. A landmark for tourists, Trapani has many historic churches and cathedrals, dating from Gothic and Baroque times; palaces, a convent, and several important museums are also here.

Trappists, Roman Catholic monks of a reformed order of Cistercians, properly designated the Order of Reformed Cistercians since 1892. The reformation was carried out, 1664, by Abbot de Rancé (1626-1700) of the monastery of La Trappe, in Normandy. The rule is strict and ascetic, enjoining silence, frequent devotions, manual labor, and abstention from most foods.

treason, a serious offense against the state or its nominal head. Treason against the United States is specifically defined in the U.S. Constitution as consisting "only in levying war against them [the states] or in adhering to their enemies, giving aid and comfort to them." The constitutions of most states of the U.S. similarly define treason against the state. Formerly, in England, there were two kinds of treason: petty treason and high treason. Petty treason was an act of treachery of a vassal toward his lord; legal recognition of such treason was abolished in 1828. As defined by an Act of Parliament in 1848, high treason in England is any serious betrayal of the interests of the state. In Tudor times and earlier, many persons were put to death for treason; the punishment at that time consisted of hanging and disemboweling, followed by beheading and quartering. This punishment was inflicted as late as 1745 on persons who participated in the Jacobite uprisings. The usual penalty for treason in most countries, especially in time of war, is death. See *sedition.*

treasure trove, buried or hidden money, gems, etc., whose owner is unknown. Under English law it technically belongs to the crown, but the finder is generally allowed to keep it unless it is of historical value to the state, in which case he is rewarded for it. In the U.S. treasure trove is the property of the finder.

Treasury, Dept. of the, administrative branch of the U.S. government created Sept. 2, 1789, headed by the Secretary of the Treasury, who is a member of the President's cabinet. All matters pertaining to U.S. finances and the issuance of coins, money, and paper representing obligations (treasury notes, treasury bills, etc.) of the government are under supervision of the Treasury Dept. It supervises the Bureaus of Customs, of the Budget, and of Narcotics. In peacetime it has authority over the U.S. Secret Service and Coast Guard.

treaty, agreement made between two or more independent states. Treaties may formalize such matters as a peace settlement, a military alliance, or agreements concerning commercial activities. They are negotiated by diplomatic representatives of nations, sometimes by the foreign ministers. The national law of some nations provides that after a treaty is signed it must be ratified by national representative bodies; thus in the U.S. a treaty must be ratified by a two-thirds majority of the Senate, and in France and Britain the cabinets and parliaments must ratify. Occasionally a secret treaty is made, such as those promising Italy territory in return for her entry into World War I in 1915, and the secret agreements made by Pres. Roosevelt with the U.S.S.R. at the Yalta Conference, 1945. In countries which require ratification, secret treaties are not binding until ratified, but sometimes the arrangements made are virtually unalterable. Under the League of Nations, any member making a treaty was required to deposit it with the League; a similar ruling exists in the United Nations. Some nations voluntarily submit disputed interpretations of treaties to arbitration. Treaties generally have an expiration date, but many end simply by being broken.

treaty port, port opened to foreign trade by a treaty, usually one that is forced on the country owning the port. The term applies especially to certain sea and river ports of China, first created by the Treaty of Nanking, 1842, which followed the Opium War. The ports were Shanghai, Canton, Foochow, Amoy, Ninghsien. Other cities later were opened as treaty ports. European powers trading through treaty ports also gained concessions where they had rights of extraterritoriality (q.v.). Following Commodore Matthew Perry's successful expedition to Japan, 1854, several Japanese cities became treaty ports. Japanese ports lost this status in the late 19th cent., but Chinese treaty ports remained as an institution until the end of World War II.

Trebizond or **Trabzon,** city, NE Turkey, in Turkish Armenia; pop. 33,969. A port on the Black Sea, it was once of great importance as terminus of a European-Asiatic trade route. It was successively under the Roman and Byzantine empires and, 13th cent., became a center of the Greek empire of Trebizond. Captured by the Ottoman Turks, 1461, it gradually lost its eminence.

tree, perennial seedbearing plant with an upright woody trunk. Most trees produce a single trunk, although smaller trees, like shrubs, may sometimes develop more than one. The three major zones of a tree are the roots, trunk (stem), and crown (branches and leaves). The roots help support the tree, absorb water from the ground, and dissolve minerals for food; the trunk functions in support and in conduction of nutrients; and the leaves of the crown function in manufacturing food by means of chlorophyll. Most of the tree's bulk is in the trunk, which is composed mostly of wood, or xylem. Wood cells die as soon as formed, but are joined to form microscopic vessels, constituting the sapwood, which conduct dissolved minerals from the roots to the leaves. Only the outer layers of wood are functional in trees past the sapling stage; the inner, nonfunctioning core is the heartwood. Surrounding the wood is a layer of embryonic tissue called the cambium; a layer of downward-conducting tissue, called the phloem; and the nonliving, protective bark. Aside from the leaves, therefore, a tree may be visualized as a mostly dead cylinder, having a thin layer of living tissue surrounding a hard central core of wood. Cone-bearing trees are called conifers; they have narrow, often needlelike leaves, which in most conifers are shed a few at a time during the year as new ones grow in. A few conifers, *e.g.,* the larch and bald cypress, are not evergreens but deciduous; *i.e.* they shed their leaves in the fall and send out new ones in the spring. Conifers include the sequoias, which are the largest of all trees and the oldest living things on the earth. Most conifers are softwoods, whereas the other principal group of trees, called broadleafed trees, include a higher proportion of hardwoods. Most broadleafed trees, except for such as the liveoak, are deciduous. Conifers tend to be more characteristic of colder regions, broadleafed trees of temperate regions, but there is much overlapping.

Tree, Sir Herbert Beerbohm, 1853-1917, English actor-manager. In 1884 he was enormously successful as the curate in *Private Secretary*. He played melodrama for 10 years at the Haymarket Theatre and later, under his own management, presented Shakespeare with great success.

treehopper, any insect of the family Membracidae, order Homoptera. Treehoppers are generally of unusual shapes because of the often fantastic development of the thorax. They attack fruit and other trees, sucking the juices from leaves, twigs, and stems. While distributed throughout the world, they are most abundant and variegated in the American tropics, where they may resemble pieces of bark, dead leaves, or twigs. Their droll expression has earned them the name Brownie-bugs. Most are under ⅓ in. long.

tree toad, any of many widely distributed species of amphibians that live in trees and resemble toads and frogs, also called tree frogs. Most belong to the genus *Hyla*. The digits are furnished with adhesive pads adapted to tree climbing. Tree toads usually resort to water while breeding.

Treitschke, Heinrich von, 1834-96, German historian. His early liberalism became lost in enthusiasm for Prussian unification of Germany. After his election to the Reichstag, 1871, he supported Bismarck and advocated colonial expansion. He taught at various universities, including Berlin (from 1874). In his writings—among them his major work, *History of Germany in the 19th Century* (5 vols., 1879-95)—Pro-Russian sentiment and an imperial orientation are strong.

trench, in warfare, a long, narrow excavation in the earth used to protect soldiers from enemy fire. Trenches were first used extensively in military operations by Vauban (q.v.) to protect his attacking forces when laying seige to a fort. Trench warfare began in the U.S. Civil War at the siege of Petersburg. It was also used in the Russo-Japanese War (1904-5). Early in World War I, when the introduction of the machine gun on the western front made the massed infantry attacks of earlier wars prohibitively costly in terms of casualties, trenches were dug by the opposing forces, and in a short time lines of trenches extended from the Belgian coast to Switzerland. These were of various types, including advance, support, communication, and other elaborate constructions. Trench warfare lasted nearly four years. Trench raids were a feature of this period, and appropriate weapons and machines were developed, as a cutter for excavating trenches and a mortar for lobbing shells into them. In the more mobile mechanized warfare of World War II, trenches were little used, though soldiers often dug themselves into individual shelters called "foxholes."

trench mouth or **Vincent's angina,** contagious disease of the mouth which attacks gums and throat and sometimes leads to painful ulcerations. It is caused by a form of spirochete and by a spindle-shaped bacterium. The germ, generally spread by infected eating and drinking utensils, can be successfully combated with penicillin.

Trent (Ital.: *Trento;* Ger.: *Trient*), city, N Italy, capital of Trento province and of the autonomous Trentino-Alto Adige region (*compartimento*), on Adige River, *c.*45 mi. N of Verona on the route to the Brenner Pass; pop. 40,800. It is an archbishopric and has an old cathedral. The town is chiefly famous for the Council of Trent (see *ecumenical councils; Counter Refor-*

LEAVES OF NORTH AMERICAN TREES

HEMLOCK.

SHAGBARK HICKORY.

WITCH-HAZEL.

WHITE ASH.

WILD BLACK CHERRY.

AMERICAN ASPEN.

AMERICAN CHESTNUT.

BLACK SPRUCE.

SILVER MAPLE.

WHITE PINE.

MAGNOLIA.

AMERICAN HORNBEAM.

TREES OF THE UNITED STATES

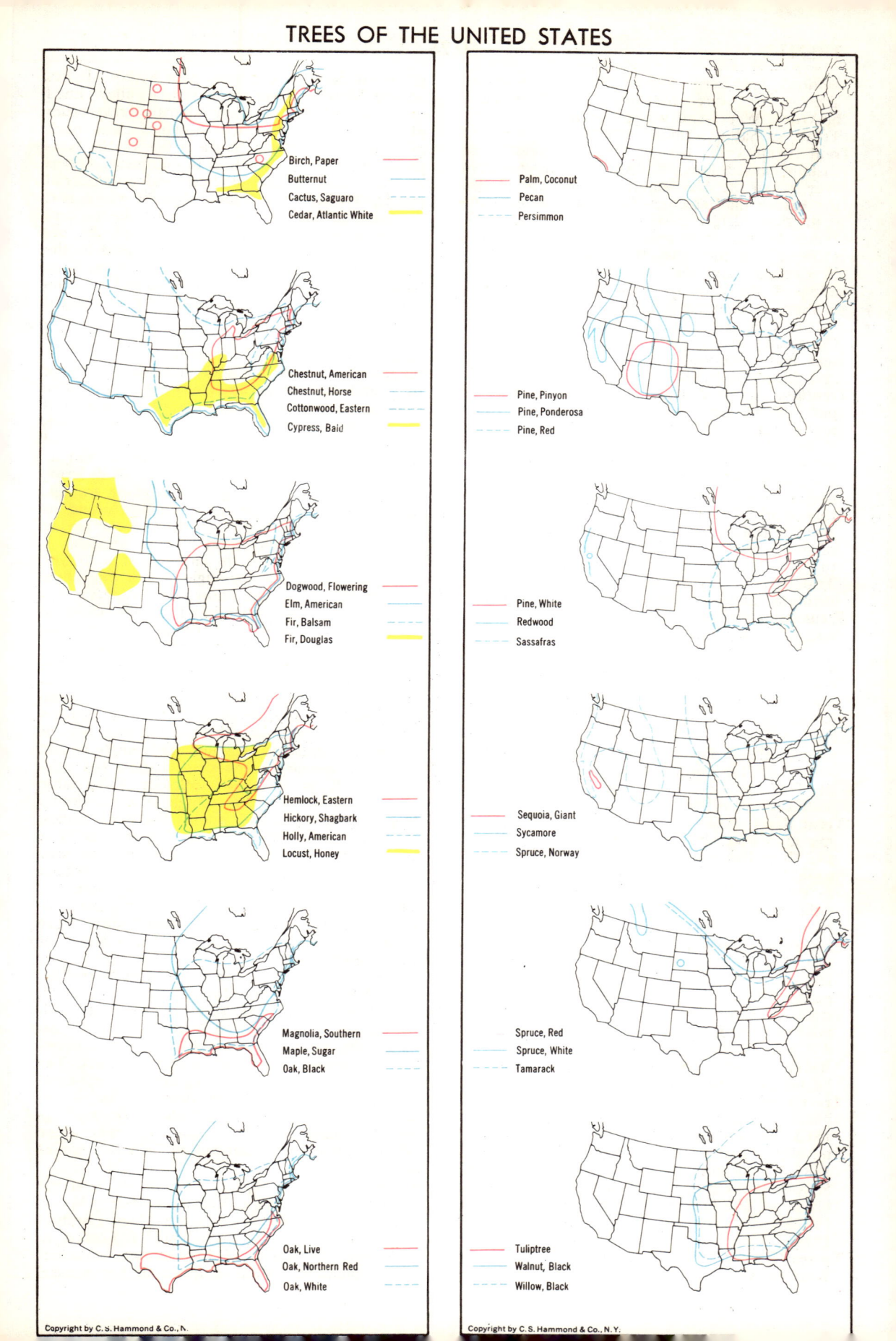

- Birch, Paper
- Butternut
- Cactus, Saguaro
- Cedar, Atlantic White

- Palm, Coconut
- Pecan
- Persimmon

- Chestnut, American
- Chestnut, Horse
- Cottonwood, Eastern
- Cypress, Bald

- Pine, Pinyon
- Pine, Ponderosa
- Pine, Red

- Dogwood, Flowering
- Elm, American
- Fir, Balsam
- Fir, Douglas

- Pine, White
- Redwood
- Sassafras

- Hemlock, Eastern
- Hickory, Shagbark
- Holly, American
- Locust, Honey

- Sequoia, Giant
- Sycamore
- Spruce, Norway

- Magnolia, Southern
- Maple, Sugar
- Oak, Black

- Spruce, Red
- Spruce, White
- Tamarack

- Oak, Live
- Oak, Northern Red
- Oak, White

- Tuliptree
- Walnut, Black
- Willow, Black

Copyright by C.S. Hammond & Co., N.Y.

mation), held here 1545-63. Formerly Austrian, Trent was captured by the Italians at the close of World War I and was ceded to them by the Treaty of Saint-Germain, 1919.

Trent Affair, crisis between the U.S. and Great Britain caused Nov. 8, 1861, during the Civil War, when the U.S. sloop *San Jacinto* stopped the British mail steamer *Trent* and seized from it the Confederate envoys to London and Paris, James M. Mason (1798-1871) and John Slidell (1793-1871). Sympathy for the South was strong in England, and war threatened. Tactful handling of the issue by U.S. Secretary of State William H. Seward and the British ambassador to the U.S., Lord Lyons, relieved the tension. Conceding that a principle of freedom of the seas had been violated, the U.S. freed Mason and Slidell, and they proceeded to England.

Trentino, Alpine district, S Tyrol, N Italy, now part of the autonomous **Trentino-Alto Adige** region (area 5256 sq. mi.; pop. 768,716) with Trent (Trento) as capital. It stands on both sides of the river Adige. Although Alto-Adige, with Bolzano as its chief city, is mainly German-speaking, Trentino is mainly Italian. Before World War I it was part of Austrian Tyrol, 400,000 Italians being under Austrian rule. Scene of heavy fighting in the war, it was later ceded to Italy. Trentino-Alto Adige was called Venezia Tridentina until 1947, when the new Italian constitution made it semi-autonomous.

Trenton, capital of New Jersey, co. seat of Mercer co., W New Jersey, on Delaware River; pop. 114,167. Its biggest industry is manufacture of wire rope and cables. It is a large pottery and cigar center, also, and makes airplane equipment and rubber goods. It is at the upstream limit of navigation on the Delaware. The vicinity was first settled by Quakers, 1679. Washington crossed the Delaware here to surprise the Hessians and capture c.900 in the famous Battle of Trenton, Dec. 26, 1776. The city became state capital, 1790.

Trent River, c.170 mi. long, central England, rising in Staffordshire, flowing NNE, and joining the Ouse River to form the Humber River. A canal links it with the Mersey. Third-largest river in England, it is navigable up to Gainsborough. Other towns along its course are Stoke-on-Trent, Newark, and Nottingham.

Trevelyan, George Macaulay, 1876-   , English historian, son of Sir George Otto Trevelyan. He was educated at Cambridge where he taught modern history, 1927-40. His works include a study of Garibaldi (1907-11), *History of England* (1926), *England under Queen Anne* (1930-4), and *English Social History* (1944). His *Autobiography* appeared in 1949, the same year he became Chancellor of Durham Univ.

Trevelyan, Sir George Otto, 1838-1928, English historian and statesman. Entering Parliament in 1865, he was successively secretary to the admiralty, 1880-2; chief secretary for Ireland, 1882-4; and secretary for Scotland, 1886, 1892-5. Among his many works are the biography of his uncle, *The Life and Letters of Lord Macaulay* (1876), and *The American Revolution* (1899-1914).

Trèves (Ger.: *Trier*), city, Rhineland-Palatinate, W Western Germany, near Luxembourg border c.180 mi. SSW of Cologne; pop. 86,700. It lies on the Moselle River, in a fertile valley, lined by vine-clad hills. It was the Augusta Treverorum of the Romans; its trade in wines dates back to antiquity. Its Porta Negra is one of the best-preserved Roman structures in Germany. Trèves also contains an amphitheater and an imperial palace. Through the Middle Ages it was a seat of monastic learning and had a university, and was a powerful prince-bishopric until the beginning of the 19th cent., when occupied by the French. Its archbishops were electors of the Holy Roman Empire. The city has a splendid cathedral. Many historic monuments were damaged in World War II.

trial—see *jury*.

triangle—see *percussion instruments*.

triangle, in geometry, a figure bounded by three lines and containing three angles. If the three lines or sides of a triangle are all straight, it is a *plane* or *rectilinear* triangle. If all three sides are equal, it is an *equilateral* triangle. If two of the sides only are equal, it is an *isosceles* triangle. A *scalene* triangle has three sides all differing in length. The three angles of a plane triangle are equal to two right angles or 180°, and its area is equal to half that of a rectangle or parallelogram of the same base or altitude. A triangle with each of its angles less than 90° is known as an *acute* triangle, but if one angle is over 90° it is then known as an *obtuse* triangle. A triangle containing a ninety-degree angle is known as a *right* triangle; in this case, the longest side (opposite the right angle) is known as the hypotenuse, whose square is equal to the squares of the sum of the other two sides (as stated by the Pythagorean Theorem). If the three sides of a triangle are all curves, the figure is said to be *curvilinear;* however, if only one or two of the sides are straight, the triangle is said to be *mixtilinear.* A *spherical* triangle has sides that are all arcs of great circles or of the same circle. The *altitude* of a triangle is a line drawn from the *vertex* of any one of the three angles, perpendicular to the opposite side or *base.* The geometrical equation for determining the area of a given triangle is ½ab (one half the product of an altitude, a, and its corresponding base, b). The triangle is considered the most basic geometric form, as any other many-sided figure (polygon) can be broken up into a series of three-sided shapes.

Trianon, two royal villas in the park of Versailles, near Paris. The Grand Trianon was built, 1687, for Louis XIV by J. H. Mansart, the great architect of the classical period of the French Renaissance. Its gateway with marble columns opens into a garden dotted with groves of trees. The Petit Trianon, a splendid example of 18th-cent. French architecture, was designed by J. A. Gabriel for Mme de Pompadour. In its English-style gardens is the miniature hamlet where Marie Antoinette pretended to lead the life of a farm woman.

Trianon, Treaty of, signed June 4, 1920, at the Grand Trianon palace, Versailles, ending World War I between Hungary and the Allies. (Neither Russia nor the U.S. participated.) Forced to cede over two-thirds of her former territories and population, including much of her natural wealth, to Czechoslovakia, Austria, Rumania, and the Kingdom of Serbs, Croats, and Slovenes (later Yugoslavia), Hungary signed the treaty under protest. Discontent with the treaty led to a Hungarian rapprochement with Italy and Germany and her participation in World War II, during which she regained many of her former territories. After the defeat of the Axis, Hungary lost these lands again by the Treaty of Paris, 1947.

Triassic Period—see *Mesozoic Era*.

trichinosis, disease caused by the parasitic roundworm trichina (*Trichinella spiralis*) and contracted in man by eating insufficiently cooked pork. The parasites mature in the intestine and produce embryos, which enter the blood stream and penetrate the host's muscles, often causing severe pain. After a while they become encapsulated and harmless. Some cases of the disease are fatal because the heart is affected. The course may be mild or marked by high fever, muscle pain, inflammation of the eyes, and an increase of white blood cells (particularly the eosinophiles). Trichinae are found in the muscles of humans, hogs, bears, and other animals. Heat (*c.*137°F) and cold (*c.*5°F) maintained for a sufficient period of time, will destroy the parasites. In many countries all pork legally sold has to be examined for trichinae. There is no specific preventative against the disease. Diagnosis is aided by a skin test.

Trier—see *Trèves*.

Trieste, seaport and resort city, at head of Adriatic Sea (Gulf of Trieste), at NW base of Istria peninsula, *c.*70 mi. ENE of Venice; pop. 283,842. It was capital of the **Free Territory of Trieste** (area 285 sq. mi.; pop. *c.*380,000) set up by the Italian peace treaty of 1947 under

Graphic House
Ruins of *Trieste*'s Roman amphitheater

nantly Italian-speaking, it was awarded to Italy by the Treaty of Saint-Germain, 1919, and became capital of Trieste province, a part of Venezia Giulia. In World War II, May 1945, Trieste was taken from the Germans by the Yugoslavs. Under the initial UN arrangement, Yugoslavia administered the larger rural Zone B in the south of the territory (area 200 sq. mi.; pop. *c.*70,000), largely inhabited by Slovenes, the chief town being Capodistria. Zone A (area 86 sq. mi.; pop. *c.*310,000), including the urban district of Trieste city, was ruled by an Anglo-American control board after World War II. An Allied decision, 1953, to put Zone A under Italian control aroused serious objections from Yugoslavia and attracted international interest.

Graphic House
The Castle Miramare in *Trieste*

authority of the Security Council of the United Nations. Wedged between NE Italy and NW Yugoslavia, both countries claimed parts or all of it. The city is a major shipping and manufacturing center, with large shipyards, petroleum refineries, iron and steel works, textile mills, and various consumer industries. It also ships petroleum products, timber, and iron and steel, and imports crude oil, cereals, flour, and coal. Headquarters of insurance companies, it maintains active trade fairs. There are Roman remains, a cathedral, a castle, a university, and notable museums. An ancient Roman colony, the town was under Austrian rule, 1382-1919. Predomi-

Graphic House
Governor's Palace in *Trieste*

Negotiations were begun that ended in Oct. 1954, with an agreement to give Zone B, plus about five additional sq. mi. to Yugoslavia. This area had a population of *c.*70,000 of which *c.*30,000 were Italians. Italy received the remaining territory, including the city of Trieste, with a total population of *c.*310,000, including *c.*65,000 Slovenes.

trigonometry, branch of mathematics based on the relations between the angles and the sides of a triangle. These relations (the trigonometric functions—sine, cosine, tangent, cotangent, secant, cosecant) depend only on the shape of the triangle, not on its size. Thus they are functions (*q.v.*) of the angles of a triangle. Triangle trigonometry, which involves determination of all parts of a triangle from measurements made on a few parts (*e.g.,* two sides and an angle), is the

TRILOBITE

fundamental tool of surveying, navigation, astronomy, and gunnery. It is called plane or spherical trigonometry, depending on the kind of surface on which the triangle lies. Analytic trigonometry, the study of identities between the triogonometric functions without regard to the value of the angle (*e.g.,* $\tan x = \sin x \div \cos x$ for any value of x), is a tool used extensively in the calculus and higher mathematics. Trigonometry appears to date from a set of books by Hipparchus of Nicaea (*c.*130 B.C.), but its development was left to the Hindus and Arabs until the time of Johann Muller (*c.*1460). Euler is responsible for the modern form of the rules and procedures of trigonometry.

trilobite, fossil marine crustacean of the Paleozoic Era, which evolved into a vast number of species. It was especially abundant in the Cambrian and Silurian periods. The oval, flattened body, up to 1 ft. long, covered by an exterior skeleton, had three lobes—head, thorax, and abdomen.

Trinidad and Tobago, British colony, West Indies; part of the West Indies federation, area 1980 sq. mi.; pop. 825,700; capital Port of Spain on Trinidad. It is composed of the islands of Trinidad (1864 sq. mi.) and Tobago (116 sq. mi.). Trinidad was discovered, 1498, by Columbus, settled by the Spanish, attacked by the Dutch, British, and French intermittently in the 17th cent., and awarded to Great Britain, 1802. Exports include petroleum, asphalt (from Pitch Lake), sugar, cocoa, and rum. Tobago, first settled by the English, changed hands more than any other West Indian island and came to Great Britain finally in 1814. It exports hardwoods, copra, and cocoa. The two islands were united administratively, 1899, and in 1958 with other islands of the British West Indies, joined the British Caribbean Federation. Port of Spain was named the federation's provisional capital. U.S. naval and air bases have been maintained on Trinidad since World War II. An agreement was reached in Dec. 1960, to extend U.S. control of these bases for 17 more years.

trinitrophenol, yellow, explosive, crystalline substance, also called picric acid, formed by action of strong nitric acid upon phenol. It acts as a strong acid, forming highly unstable salts used in explosives. It is sparingly soluble in water, and, in solution has been used in medicine as an application for burns. It is used as a dye and enters into the composition of high explosives.

trinitrotoluene (T.N.T.), powerful explosive, also called trinitrotoluol. It is a compound of oxygen, nitrogen, hydrogen, and carbon, and forms in pale yellow to reddish-brown crystals. Mild shocks do not set it off; a detonator is used. It was widely employed in World War I and thereafter as a high explosive in shells and bombs.

Trinity, in Christian theology, the threefold being of God: God the Father, God the Son or Word (*Logos*), and God the Paraclete or Holy Ghost. Each of these persons is coequal and coeternal according to the Athanasian Creed. Disputes on this point occupied church councils until all other views were declared heretical. Traces of the doctrine appear in the New Testament (Matt. xxviii:19); the term was first used by Tertullian. A basic Roman Catholic doctrine, it is accepted, with varying interpretation of the Holy Ghost, by the Eastern Orthodox Churches and, sometimes with modification, by most Protestant churches, although rejected by the Unitarians.

At left is *Trinidad's* scenic Savannah Park. The boats above are harbored at Maracas Bay in Trinidad. Below, natives harvest coconuts in a Trinidad "orchard."

Alcoa Steamship Co.

Dürer's "The Adoration of the *Trinity*" (1511)

Trinity Sunday—see *festivals, religious.*
triode—see *electronics.*
Triple Alliance, established, 1882, between Italy, Germany, and Austria-Hungary. Italy, resentful at French occupation of Tunis, joined the secret Dual Alliance between Germany and Austria-Hungary aimed against France and Russia. Since Italian territorial ambitions conflicted with the interests of Austria-Hungary, Italy's adherence to the alliance was weak. In 1915, after the outbreak of World War I between Germany and Austria-Hungary and their allies and the powers of the Triple Entente, Italy joined the latter, formally renouncing the Triple Alliance.
Triple Alliance, War of the, 1865-70, between Paraguay and the allies Brazil, Argentina, and Uruguay. Expansionist ambitions of the Paraguayan dictator Francisco Solana López and the intervention of Brazil in Uruguayan affairs led Paraguay to declare war on Brazil. Argentina, refusing to let Paraguayan troops cross its territory, joined Brazil, and Uruguay then allied itself with Argentina and Brazil. The war, disastrous for Paraguay, left her population reduced from $c.1,337,000$ to only $c.220,000$, including $c.200,000$ women.
Triple Entente, informal defensive alignment of France, Russia, and Great Britain against Germany before World War I. After development of the Triple Alliance between the Central European powers, France and Russia formed a military alliance, 1894. Great Britain, fearing growth of German power and expansion in the Near East, formed closer diplomatic ties with France and Russia, resolving her colonial differences with France in the Entente Cordiale of 1904 and with Russia in the entente of 1907. At informal meetings of British and French military staffs, plans were drawn up to repel a possible German attack on France. In World War I, 1914-8, the Triple Entente powers fought against Germany, Austria-Hungary, and their allies.
triplets—see *multiple birth.*
Tripoli, capital of Libya; pop. 172,200. Situated on a promontory of the Mediterranean, it is at the intersection of three caravan routes. Products include fish, sponges, tobacco, and carpets. Its ancient occupation by Romans and Arabs is attested by the arch of Marcus Aurelius and many mosques. It was occupied also by Turks, 1551-1911, and in much of this period was a base for Barbary pirates. There Stephen Decatur recaptured and burned the frigate *Philadelphia* during the war against the Barbary States, 1801-5. Taken by Italy, 1911, Tripoli was made capital of Libya. It was an Axis base in World War II and was taken by the Allies, 1943.
Tripoli, city, Lebanon, capital of North Lebanon province, 40 mi. NNE of Beirut; pop. 115,000. A Mediterranean seaport and a railroad center, it is also the terminus of the oil pipe-line from Kirkuk, Iraq.
Tripolitania or **Tarabulus,** region, W Libya, on Mediterranean Sea; area $c.135,000$ sq. mi.; pop. 738,338. Its coast, dotted with fertile oases, stretches to the Sahara. Tripoli is the chief city. The region was colonized by Phoenicians, 7th cent. B.C., was occupied by Rome, and suffered invasions by Vandals, 5th cent., and Arabs, 7th cent. Later it was under the influence of the Knights Hospitalers. Taken by Turkey, 1553, it was noted for the activities of its Barbary pirates. The region was occupied by Italy, 1911, and annexed, 1912. It was the scene of much fighting in World War II. Tripolitania was administered by the British until 1951, when it became, upon United Nations decision, part of the independent kingdom of Libya. Rich petroleum deposits were found here in the late 1950s.
Tristan—see *Tristram.*
Tristán de Cunha, island group, S Atlantic Ocean; main island area 75 sq. mi.; pop. (until 1961) 292. Only inhabited island of the volcanic group was Tristán da Cunha (40 sq. mi.), which rises to $c.8000$ ft. and was important for its meteorological and radio station. Fishing was the main source of income. Principal communication was with South Africa. Tristán da Cunha was discovered by the Portuguese early 16th cent. The group became British territory, 1816, and was included, 1938, as a dependency in the crown colony of St. Helena, $c.1600$ mi. away. In Oct. 1961, a volcanic eruption forced the evacuation of the population to St. Helena. It was feared that the island would long remain uninhabitable.
Tristram or **Tristan,** hero of medieval legend. While escorting Isolde of Ireland to Cornwall, where she was to marry his uncle King Mark, Tristram and the maiden drank a potion that caused them to fall hopelessly in love. Isolde married Mark, but her illicit affair continued until Tristram fled to Brittany, where he married another Isolde. Wounded in battle, he sent for the first Isolde, who alone could cure him. Isolde of Ireland came, but the Breton Isolde concealed her coming from Tristram, who died. This tale, related

to the Arthurian cycle inasmuch as Tristram was described as a knight of the Round Table, first appeared in literature in the 12th cent., and has since been the theme of numerous stories, poems, and operas, *e.g.* Wagner's *Tristan und Isolde* (1865).

tritium, in chemistry, the super-heavy isotope of the element hydrogen, having an atomic mass three times that of ordinary hydrogen. This isotope of hydrogen is produced artificially, has the same electrical charge of 1 unit negative that ordinary hydrogen nucleus (proton) has, and is radioactive. The high mass of the tritium nucleus makes it very effective as an atomic projectile in cyclotrons and other nuclear accelerators.

Triumvirate—see *Augustus; Caesar.*

Troilus, in medieval legend, a Trojan hero, in love with the maiden Cressida. Troilus, in the Greek legend of the Trojan War, was a son of Priam killed by Achilles, but the tale of his love for the daughter of the priest Calchas was developed in the Middle Ages. Cressida's uncle, Pandarus, from whose name the word "pander" is derived, brought the two together, but Cressida was exchanged for a Trojan prisoner in Greek hands, and proved faithless despite her vows. The tale is the theme of Chaucer's poem *Troilus and Criseyde* and Shakespeare's play *Troilus and Cressida.*

Trois Rivières or **Three Rivers,** city, S Quebec, on St. Lawrence River at mouth of the St. Maurice; pop. 50,483. It is an industrial city, working largely with lumber, pulp, and iron. Founded, 1634, by Champlain, it became an important French trading post, through which passed many explorers, trappers, and missionaries. In the mid-1950s its importance increased as the main port for the shipping of iron ore from the rich Ungava ore fields to the north.

Trojan War, in Greek legend, a 10-year war between the Greeks under Agamemnon and the Trojans. The Greek kings, resolved to recover Helen after her abduction by Paris, assembled over 1000 ships at Aulis. The sacrifice of Iphigenia won a fair wind, and the host reached Troy, which they besieged. Homer's *Iliad,* best source of the legend, begins in the last year, with Achilles' withdrawal, and recounts the stirring duels between Menelaus and Paris, Patroclus and Hector, and finally between Achilles and Hector, as well as the plagues, intrigues, and constant intercession of the gods on each side. Troy finally fell through Odysseus' stratagem of the Trojan horse, a wooden model in which the Greeks hid a contingent after apparently abandoning the siege. The Trojans dragged the horse within the walls (see *Laocoön*), after which the Greeks emerged, opened the gates to the main host, and sacked the city. The legend is apparently based on an actual war, 12th cent. B.C.

Trollope, Anthony, 1815-82, English novelist. In his long career, 1834-67, in the postal service he rose to inspector. Official travels to Ireland, the West Indies, Egypt, the U.S., Australia, and South Africa gave him material for travel books. By adhering to a systematic work schedule he produced more than 50 novels and much nonfiction. His novels include the Barchester series, describing life in an imaginary cathedral town and including his best-known novels, *Barchester Towers* (1857) and *The Last Chronicle of Barset* (1867); and the Parliamentary series, dealing with politics and including *Phineas Finn* (1869) and *The Prime Minister* (1876). *Orley Farm* (1862), outside these categories, also is popular. Trollope fully exploited his gift for creating character and incident, avoiding unfamiliar milieus. His mother, **Frances Trollope,** 1780-1863, who had lived in Cincinnati, Ohio, 1827-31, began a successful literary career in England by writing the controversial *The Domestic Manners of the Americans* (1832).

trombone, brass wind instrument with a cylindrical bore, a bell-shaped end, and a cup-shaped mouthpiece. By means of a sliding mechanism the effective length of the instrument is increased; the seven available positions make possible the production of tones throughout the chromatic scale for three more octaves by adjusting the lip pressure. While there are four different sizes of trombone (alto, tenor, bass, contrabass), the symphony orchestra commonly has a complement of three tenor and one bass. The trombone developed from the large trumpet, to which a slide was added in the 14th cent.; it was called sackbut from French words meaning "pull-push" (*saquer, bouter*). It was common in ceremonial and church bands, and Gabrieli's *Sacrae symphoniae* (c.1600) called for trombones. Beethoven first introduced them into the symphony and Berlioz and Wagner made them permanent members of the orchestra.

Graphic House

The tenor *trombone*

Trondheim (formerly Trondhjem), city and Atlantic seaport of W Norway; capital of Sör-Tröndelag county, on Trondheim Fjord, c.250

mi. N of Oslo; pop. 58,915. An active trading, shipbuilding, and fishing center, it has a technical college and a noted old cathedral. Since 1818 kings of Norway have been crowned here. Founded 996, Tronheim was capital till 1380, then declined. In 1930 it briefly changed its name to the old name Nidaros. The town was taken Apr. 1940 by the Germans in World War II.

tropics, region between the two parallels of latitude 23½°N and 23½°S (respectively the Tropics of Cancer and Capricorn) which lie on either side of the equator. The tropics are known also as the tropical, or torrid, zone. The sun's rays are perpendicular to every point in this area at least once during the year. The summer solstice occurs when the sun's rays are perpendicular at the Tropic of Cancer (so called because it is traced by the constellation Cancer) on or about June 22, and the winter solstice when the sun reaches the Tropic of Capricorn (traced by the constellation Capricornus) on or about Dec. 22. There is little seasonal temperature variation in the tropics, and local climate is largely determined by such factors as elevation, exposure, and location with respect to large bodies of water.

tropism, growth movements of plants in response to certain external stimuli, such as light. Most such responses seem to be controlled by plant hormones called auxins (*q.v.*). Among the common tropisms are **phototropism,** the response to light; **geotropism,** the response to gravity; and **thigmotropism,** response to contact or pressure.

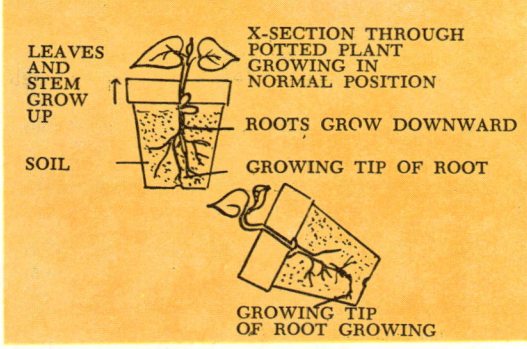

Above, a plant reacts to the sunlight with a positive photo*tropism*, also known as heliotropism. Below, a plant displays geotropism, in that its root grows toward the earth's center of gravity (positive geotropism), while the rest of the plant—stem, leaves, etc.—grows upward (negative geotropism).

A response that causes the plant to grow toward the source of the stimulus, *e.g.*, the response of a shoot in bending toward light, is called a **positive tropism.** Growth away from the source of the stimulus, as a shoot growing upward (away from the earth) is a **negative tropism.**

Tromp, Maarten Harpertszoon, 1597-1653, Dutch admiral. In the 17th-cent. struggle for sea supremacy between the Dutch, Spanish, and English, he was victorious in many encounters. However, in the last major action of the first of the Dutch Wars, the battle of 1653 off the Holland coast, the Dutch lost 30 vessels, and although the blockade of the Dutch coast was broken, Tromp was killed. His son **Cornelis Tromp** (1629-91) was a prominent Dutch admiral in the second and third of the Dutch Wars.

Trossachs, valley, Perthshire, central Scotland, between Lochs Katrine and Achray. In a mountainous and scenic area, the valley has become famous through Scott's descriptions in *Lady of the Lake* and *Rob Roy*.

Trotsky, Leon Davidovich, 1879-1940, Russian Communist leader. Born Lev Davidovich Bronstein, of middle-class parents, after an excellent education he joined the revolutionaries and was exiled to Siberia, 1898. Escaping to England, 1902, with a passport belonging to a soldier named Trotsky, he took that name. He became close to Lenin, but after the split, 1903, between the Bolshevik and Menshevik wings of the Social Democratic Party he attempted to found his own group midway between them. Arrested after his return to Russia during the revolution of 1905, he escaped again. During World War I he was active in pacifist circles in Europe and the U.S. He returned to Russia following the Mar. 1917 revolution, until July refused to join Lenin's Bolshevik Party, but played a major role in the Bolshevik revolution in Nov. As commissar for foreign affairs, he agreed to German demands and secured peace at Brest-Litovsk. Thereafter, becoming commissar for war, 1918, he built the Red Army by conscription and defended the revolution from both Russian antirevolutionaries and Allied armies. He accepted Lenin's New Economic Policy (*q.v.*), but their relations cooled, and after Lenin's death, 1924, the triumvirate of Stalin, Kamenev, and Zinoviev shunted Trotsky to minor posts. Disagreements within the triumvirate brought him support from Kamenev and Zinoviev, but his proposals for departure from the New Economic Policy, 1926, and for resumption of effort toward world revolution were rejected, and he was expelled from the party, 1927, and exiled from Russia, 1929. From Turkey, France, Norway, and Mexico he denounced Stalin as uneducated, as un-European, as betrayer of the revolution. In the party purges of 1936-8, Zinoviev, Kamenev, Bukharin, Rykov, and other leaders were accused of complicity with Trotsky in attempting to overthrow Stalin, and were executed. Trotsky was murdered by a Russian agent, 1940, in Mexico. A brilliant orator and writer, Trotsky wrote much, including the long *History of the Russian Revolution* (1932). He also wrote *My Life* (1930) and *Stalin* (1940).

troubadours and trouvères, poets and musicians of 12th-13th cent. France. Rejecting Latin as the language for their poetry, the troubadours of Provence and S France used the vernacular *langue d'oc* of that region, the trouvères of N France singing in the prevailing language of the north, the *langue d'oïl.* Most of each group were of noble birth, singing their own compositions at court on themes of war, religion, and especially love, in complex meters and rhyme schemes, although the troubadours later used traveling singers, *jongleurs,* to perform their compositions. The great *chansons de geste (q.v.)* were composed by trouvères, who derived their inspiration from the slightly earlier troubadours and preferred longer narratives to the lyrics popular in the south.

Performing *troubadors* from an illustration in an early 14th-cent. manuscript.

trout, any of various fresh-water stream and lake fishes belonging to the same family as salmon (Salmonidae). The principal genus is the European *Salmo;* American species belong to *Salve-*

Rainbow *trout*

linus and *Cristivomer.* The brook trout, called also speckled trout (*Salvelinus fontinalis*), has fine, irregular bars and small, round red spots. Somewhat differently marked trout may be of the same species; distinctions are difficult. Trout generally are smaller than salmon. Given to fighting when hooked, they are prized by sportsmen, as well as epicures. Weights vary from ½ to 20 lb., the largest species being the lake trout (*C. namaycush*). The common European species (*Salmo fario*), introduced into the U.S., is the brown trout. The name "sea trout" is applied to various marine fishes, including the salmon (a large species of trout) and weakfish.

trouvères—see *troubadours and trouvères.*

Troy, city, co. seat of Rensselaer co., E New York, on Hudson River; pop. 67,492. It is the E terminus of the New York State Barge Canal, opposite the mouth of the Mohawk River, and is at the head of tidewater navigation of the Hudson. It manufactures collars, shirts, and other clothing, machinery, and engineering instruments. It is a big distributing point. Troy was part of the large patroonship granted Kiliaen Van Rensselaer by the Dutch West India Co. Rensselaer Polytechnic Institute and Russell Sage College are here.

Troy or **Ilium,** ancient city, NW Asia Minor, near the Hellespont. The present site is a hill, Hissarlik. Before its excavation by Schliemann and Dörpfeld, 1870-94, the Homeric tales of Troy were considered legend, but these and later archeologists found at Hissarlik nine communities, one above the other. The oldest five were prehistoric, the most impressive being Troy II, *c.*2000 B.C., contemporary with the arrival of the Hittites. The Homeric city was Troy VII A, destroyed *c.*1200 B.C. in a conflict reflected in the Trojan War story, probably an Achaean expedition against an Asiatic alliance centered at Troy, contemporary with the "sea raids" against Egypt. Later communities, except the Greco-Roman Ilium, Troy IX, were insignificant.

Troyes, city, NE France, capital of Aube dept., on Seine *c.*85 mi. ESE of Paris; pop. 58,819. A textile center, it flourished particularly in the Middle Ages, when it was the site of large fairs. Troy weight was named for the town. Today Troyes has various manufactures. Of great antiquity, it was the Augustobona Tricassium of the Romans. In the 11th cent. it became capital of the Champagne. Later it achieved renown as a center of the arts. Many of the town's fine medieval and Renaissance buildings were damaged in World War II.

true bug, any insect of the orders Hemiptera and Homoptera. True bugs vary extremely in size and shape but all suck plant juices; few are predaceous or parasitic on animals. In the Hemiptera the wings are thickened in the basal half and lie flat over the back; Homoptera wings have no such thickening, and the wings are held "rooflike." The metamorphosis is incomplete, and the young more or less resemble the adults. Many Hemiptera, as the giant water bugs, water boatmen, and water striders, are aquatic; no Homoptera are. The latter include such well-known forms as the cicadas, leafhoppers, treehoppers, plant lice, and scale insects. Many Homoptera are parthenogenic; some (aphids) have a complicated life history.

Trujillo Molina, Rafael, 1891-1961, president of the Dominican Republic (1930-8, 1940-52). As head of the army Trujillo overthrew Pres. Horacio Vásquez, 1930. He instituted reforms, *e.g.* the building of roads and redistribution of land, but was known for his brutality toward political opponents and friction with Caribbean neighbors. Succeeded 1952 by his brother, Gen. Hector Trujillo Molina, he became representative to the United Nations, while retaining real power in his own hands. Accused of sponsoring revolts in other Caribbean countries, his own regime was threatened by internal dissatisfaction and by the revolutionary government of Cuba, 1959. However, his assassination in 1961 was carried out by local dissidents. His son Ramfis temporarily took over the government but strong pressures forced the Trujillo family to leave the country in late 1961.

Truk, island group, Eastern Caroline Islands, W Pacific Ocean; area 37.5 sq. mi.; pop. 14,084. It comprises *c.*55 volcanic islands and islets forming a large atoll. The main produce is copra. The Japanese established a naval base here which they used in World War II. U.S. forces neutralized it through repeated bombings and bypassed its garrison. Truk now forms part of the U.S. Pacific Islands Trust Territory.

Truman, Harry S., 1884-   , 33d U.S. President (1945-53), b. Lamar, Mo. From the family farm he entered the U.S. Army in World War I, became a captain of field artillery, served in France, and was discharged as major. Unsuccessful in the haberdashery business, he entered local politics under Democratic "Boss" Pendergast and became a county judge, meanwhile studying law in Kansas City. He was U.S. Senator, 1935-44, distinguishing himself as head of a committee which investigated and helped to streamline the national defense program. Chosen Democratic nominee for Vice President to run with F. D. Roosevelt in the Presidential election of 1944, Truman succeeded to the Presidency on Roosevelt's death, Apr. 12, 1945. With Stalin, Churchill, and Attlee he held in July 1945 the Potsdam Conference, which determined the demilitarization and control of Germany and issued an ultimatum to Japan demanding unconditional surrender. It was he who made the decision to use the atomic bomb against Japan. In the postwar rivalry between the Western allies and Russia, Truman promulgated the Truman Doctrine (*q.v.*) to help countries imperiled by Communism, and also promoted the European Recovery Program or Marshall Plan (for Secretary of State Marshall), to stabilize and rehabilitate European democracies with U.S. money and goods. At home Truman's "Fair Deal" attempted to extend housing and health insurance, maintain price controls, and raise minimum wages, but a conservative Congress defeated many of his efforts. Because of his attempt to extend the civil rights of Negroes, a group of white Southerners in the 1948 Presidential campaign left the party and, as "Dixiecrats," nominated J. S. Thurmond as their Presidential candidate. Henry A. Wallace, former Secretary of Commerce, ran for President on the Progressive Party ticket. Despite these defections, Truman defeated his major opponent, Republican Thomas E. Dewey, winning 303 electoral votes to Dewey's 189. Truman's second administration initiated a vast defense program,

Missouri Resources and Development Commission
In the Harry S. *Truman* Library, Independence, Missouri, the ex-President stands before a mural by U.S. artist Thomas Hart Benton.

implemented the North Atlantic Pact as a defensive alliance against Communism, and prosecuted the Korean conflict of 1950-3. Truman did not seek the Democratic Presidential nomination against Republican candidate Dwght D. Eisenhower in 1952. In 1955 and 1956 two volumes of Truman's memoirs were published. The Harry S. Truman Library, Independence, Mo., a permanent place for the study of the presidency, was opened in 1957.

Truman Doctrine, statement by U.S. Pres. Harry S. Truman, Mar. 12, 1947, that the U.S. would resist Soviet Russian aggression in Europe, overt or subversive, by giving economic and military aid to the threatened nations. Accordingly U.S. military and economic aid was given to Greece and Turkey, 1948. The later European Recovery Program and North Atlantic Treaty Organization were, in effect, economic and military extensions of the Truman Doctrine.

Trumbull, John, 1756-1843, U.S. painter, b. Lebanon, Conn. Son of Jonathan Trumbull (1710-85), he served in the American Revolution and studied under West in London. There, 1784, he began the famous series of historical pictures that occupied his lifetime, *Signing of the Declaration of Independence, Surrender of Burgoyne at Saratoga, Surrender of Cornwallis at Yorktown,* and *Resignation of Washington,* which were commissioned by Congress for the rotunda of the Capitol at Washington, D.C. Best of Trumbull's work are his small oil paintings, many of which were studies for larger works. In 1831 Trumbull turned over his collection of paintings to Yale, thereby founding the Trumbull Gallery, one of the first museums in the U.S.

Trumbull, Jonathan, 1710-85, American colonial statesman, b. Lebanon, Conn. Governor, 1769-84, of Connecticut during the American Revolution, he was prominent in organizing supply for the Continental armies and was a close adviser to George Washington. He was the father of John Trumbull (*q.v.*) and of **Jonathan Trumbull,** 1740-1809, who was governor of Connecticut, 1797-1809, after service on Washington's staff, 1781-3, and in the U.S. House of Representatives, 1789-95, and Senate, 1795-6. Another son was **Joseph Trumbull,** 1737-78, commissary general of the Continental army, 1775-7.

trumpet, brass wind instrument with a long cylindrical bore, usually coiled, a bell-shaped end, and a cup-shaped mouthpiece. It has a brilliant, penetrating tone. Trumpets date back to ancient times. The early natural trumpet, limited to one key, was the ancestor of both trombone and modern trumpet. In the 17th cent. crooks, lengthening the tubing, were added to increase range.

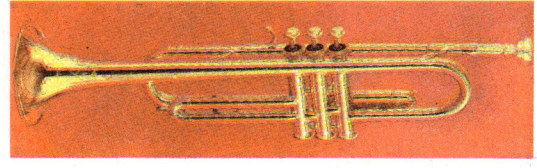

Graphic House

Other devices, including slides and keys, were used at various times, but with the invention of valves (early 19th cent.) the modern trumpet evolved. Two or three trumpets have been regularly used in orchestras since the 18th cent. See *wind instruments.*

Truro, municipal borough and city, Cornwall, SW England, on Truro River near Falmouth; pop. 13,328. It is a market town for a wide area in S Cornwall, and also a port and resort. There is a modern cathedral.

trust, in business, a combination of corporations whose stockholders transfer their voting power to a board of trustees. The term "trust" also means any combination of several corporations for monopolistic purposes, *e.g.,* to pool capital resources, simplify production, fix prices, eliminate competition, or control distribution. Trusts tend to reduce the competitive factor in capitalism and also may take advantage of the con-

An 1882 political cartoon depicts the early struggle in the U.S. against the power of the large *trusts* and holding corporations.

sumer. In the U.S. legislation was early introduced to outlaw trusts or curtail their undesirable practices. First such measure was the Sherman (Anti-Trust) Act of 1890, by which any industrial or commercial combination in restraint of trade was declared illegal. Though it lent itself to curbing labor-union activities, the act was ineffectually enforced against trusts until the trust-busting campaigns of Pres. Theodore Roosevelt's administration. The Clayton (Anti-Trust) Act of 1914 undertook to reinforce inadequate earlier legislation. The Federal Trade Commission, established 1914, was authorized to look into abuses such as unfair competition and proceed against them. The Robinson-Patman Act of 1936 prohibits discriminatory pricing practices. (See *cartel; holding company; monopoly*). The term trust also refers to various arrangements for investing a private individual's capital, or the capital of a family group. A trust fund, usually administered by a trust company, a bank, or private individuals serving as trustees, is a common device to assure the beneficiaries experienced investment management. Such funds are often set up for children or widows who are not financially competent. Unless the trust indenture specifies particular investment procedures, state regulations usually apply, setting limits trustees must respect to assure the beneficiaries of reasonable safety of the capital. Trustees are usually remunerated with a percentage of yearly trust income. Periodic accountings of trusts are legally required. An investment trust (*q.v.*) serves the same essential purpose as a trust fund, since it furnishes the financially untrained with professional investment services. The essential difference is that an investment trust, such as the mutual fund, invests the pooled capital of many individuals, permitting extensive diversification in holdings, rather than investing the capital of a family group or individual as an independent portfolio, A share in an investment trust represents a fractional interest in the fund's total holdings. Here again there are legal limits on the investment program.

trust company, in the U.S., a bank organized to administer estates or trusts and to handle transactions between corporations and stockholders, apart from regular banking activities. Under state laws such a bank is permitted to act as banker and trustee but cannot issue bank notes. Some banks have special trust divisions. National banks may exercise trust powers to the extent permitted by the National Bank Act.

trusteeship, control of a non-self governing territory by an individual nation under authority of Chapters XII and XIII of the United Nations Charter. Control is exercised under supervision of the UN Trusteeship Council, according to a system corresponding to the mandate (*q.v.*) system set up by the League of Nations after World War I. Areas under trusteeship include those detached from the control of Germany, Italy, and Japan after World War II. The trusteeship system aims to promote the economic, social, and educational advancement of the inhabitants with a view to their eventual self-government or independence; to encourage respect for human rights without discrimination because of race, sex, language, or religion; and to encourage equal treatment for all member nations and their nationals in such territories. The 1950s and early 1960s saw most of the UN trust territories gain full independence, *e.g.,* Libya, Togo, Cameroun, Somalia, Tanganyika, British Cameroons, and Western Samoa. Only South-West Africa (actually still a mandated territory) and parts of New Guinea remained as large trust territories. Freedom for Ruanda-Urundi, a likely prospect, would reduce the remaining trust territories to Northeast New Guinea, Nauru, administered by Australia, and the U.S. trust territory of the Pacific covering former Japanese islands (Marianas, Marshalls, Carolines) in the Central Pacific.

Tsaldaris, Panyoti, 1868-1936, Greek statesman. He was leader of the Populist Party which, though royalist, had accepted the republic. While he was premier, 1932-3, 1933-5, royalist sentiment grew. In 1935, after republicans under Venizelos had revolted against the Tsaldaris government and had been suppressed by Gen. Kondylis, Tsaldaris announced a plebiscite on restoration of the monarchy. Kondylis, preferring force, by a *coup d'état* overthrew Tsaldaris, ousted republicans from the government, and recalled King George II to the throne. **Constantine Tsaldaris,** 1884-   , cousin of Panyoti and also a leader of the Populist Party, became premier, 1946, and arranged the recall of George II after World War II. He served also as foreign minister (1947-50) and as parliamentary deputy.

tsar, or **czar,** an alternative to the title of Emperor as applied to the hereditary rulers of Russia before the revolution. First adapted by Ivan the Terrible in 1547, the term is most probably a slavic corruption of the Roman "Caesar." At the same time, the wife of the czar was called *czarina* or *czaritza;* the heir-apparent and his wife were known respectively as the *czarowitz* (*cesarevitch*) and *czarevna* (*cezarevna*). As the term is used in colloquial English today, any individual who exercises extreme and autocratic power may be referred to as a tsar or czar.

Tsaritsyn—see *Volgograd.*

Tsarskoye Selo—see *Pushkin.*

Tschaikovsky, Peter Ilyich—see *Tchaikovsky.*

Tse Hsi—see *Tz'u Hsi.*

tsetse fly, any of various bloodsucking dipterous flies of the family Glossinidae, native to tropical Africa. They inhabit low-lying bush or forest regions near water, and by their bites transmit the parasites of sleeping sickness and the cattle disease nagana.

Tshombe, Moïse, 1919-   , Congolese political leader, b. Musumba, Belgian Congo. He was educated at mission schools and traveled in Europe. Married to the daughter of a tribal chieftain, he became a successful businessman and then head of the Conakat Party agitating for Congolese independence on a basis of continued close economic relations with Belgium. When the Congo became independent in mid-1960, he assumed the governorship of Katanga Province, center of the principal mineral wealth of the country. Almost immediately he broke with the central government at Léopoldville, declaring his province independent. He received useful backing from Belgian business interests and employed European military officers. For a time he maintained peaceful relations with Léopoldville in late 1960 and early 1961; during this period, deposed Premier Lumumba was entrusted to his care and was probably murdered by his orders. But he again broke with the central government, which asked UN forces to attempt to quell his rebellion. UN Secretary-General Dag Hammarskjöld died in a plane crash while flying to meet Tshombe to discuss a cease-fire, which was achieved shortly thereafter, only to be broken again by Tshombe's own orders. Late in 1961 Tshombe was taken prisoner by the Central Congolese government and during this time promised a truce once he was released. However, upon his return to Katanga, he broke his promise.

Tsinan, capital of Shantung province, on the lower Yellow River, NE China; pop. 862,000. A rail junction, it manufactures much silk textiles, food products, paper, and ceramics. Cheloo Univ. is here. An ancient city, containing an old walled town, Tsinan was not opened to foreign trade until 1906.

Tsinghai, Chinghai or **Koko Nor,** province W China, N of Tibet, capital Sining; area c.320,000 sq. mi.; pop. 2,050,000. The population and economy are concentrated in the NE part of the province. Outside of this area, Tsinghai is largely inhabited by Tibetan herders. The main products are wool, hides, and salt; the major occupations are agriculture and animal husbandry. Gold and coal are mined. The Yellow, Yangtze, and Mekong rivers all have their sources here.

Tsingtao or **Chingtao,** seaport, Shantung province, NE China, on Yellow Sea; pop. 1,121,000. Long a fishing village, it became important, 1891, when a naval station was established here. It is one of China's best ports and, connected to the interior of Shantung province by railroad, is a maritime outlet for the province's products. There are various textile and food industries. As capital, 1898-1914, of the former German territory of Kiaochow, the city was modernized. In World War I Tsingtao was occupied by the Japanese; in 1924, restored to China. The Japanese again held it, 1937-45. It was a U.S. naval base, 1945-9.

Tsu Hsi—see *Tz'u Hsi*.

Tsushima, two islands, Korea Strait, belonging to Japan (Nagasaki prefecture); area 274 sq. mi.; pop. 69,556; chief town Izuhara. Fishing is the main occupation. The decisive naval battle, 1905, of the Russo-Japanese War, in which the Russian fleet under Rozhdestvenski was virtually annihilated by the Japanese fleet under Togo, was fought near here.

Tuamotu Islands or **Low Archipelago,** coral group, S of the Marquesas and belonging to French Polynesia; area 345 sq. mi.; pop. 7615. They include 80 atolls; most important is Fakarava. Pearl shell and copra are main products. The group was annexed, 1881, by the French.

tautara—see *sphenodon*.

tuba, name for a group of bass-pitched brass instruments other than trombones. They usually have a wide conical bore, cup-shaped mouthpiece, and three to five valves, and are played in a vertical position. There are tenor, bass, and double-bass tubas. The Wagner tubas, which he designed for the *Ring*, have a narrower bore and a funnel-shaped mouthpiece, giving them the agility of the cornet with the timbre of the tuba. Bass and double-bass saxhorns are called tubas, as is the so-called sousaphone, the tuba of dance orchestras. In symphony orchestras the scores usually call for no more than one tuba. See *wind instruments*.

tuber, an enlarged, usually underground stem, modified for storage of reserve food. The most familiar example of a tuber is the white potato.

tuberculin test—see *Mantoux test*.

tuberculosis, infectious disease caused by the tubercle bacillus, discovered by Robert Koch, 1882. It may attack almost any tissue. Infection of humans is usually by contact with other human beings or through milk from cows suffering from the disease. The latter type of infection, which attacks mostly young children, has been greatly reduced in the U.S. by pasteurization. Tuberculosis generalized throughout the body is called miliary tuberculosis. Usually the disease localizes in one or more organs, sometimes following direct infection from outside the body, sometimes after a generalized spread through the blood stream. Pulmonary (lung) tuberculosis, the commonest type, constitutes the main problem, but kidney, laryngeal, gastrointestinal, bone, and meningeal tuberculosis are not rare. Symptoms of pulmonary tuberculosis include loss of energy, weight, and appetite, as well as fever and cough. The disease is infectious only when the cough contains tubercle bacilli. Diagnosis of pulmonary tuberculosis is by X ray, sputum examination, and tuberculin skin test. Treatment consists of rest, supplemented when indicated by surgery, pneumothorax (lung collapse by putting air in the chest), and drug therapy. At present streptomycin and para-aminosalicylic acid form the cornerstones of medical treatment, but recently derivatives of isonicotinic acid have shown promise. Tuberculosis has diminished as a public-health problem due to milk pasteurization, more effective case-finding methods (*e.g.,* X-raying large masses of people), careful study of contacts, and isolation of infectious cases. The effectiveness of immunization by vaccination is still under investigation.

Tübingen, city, Baden-Württemberg, S Western Germany, on Neckar River, c.20 mi. S of Stuttgart; pop. 46,200. It manufactures clothing, machinery, cement, and precision instruments. The city dates back to the 11th cent. The university, with which Melanchthon and other leaders of the Reformation were associated, was founded 1477. Tübingen retains its medieval and German Renaissance character. Among noted buildings are St. George Church, the old castle, and the town hall.

Tubman, William Vacanarat Shadrach, 1895- , Liberian political leader, b. Harper, Lib., descendant of Negro freedmen from Georgia who came to Liberia in 1834 and 1872. He attended

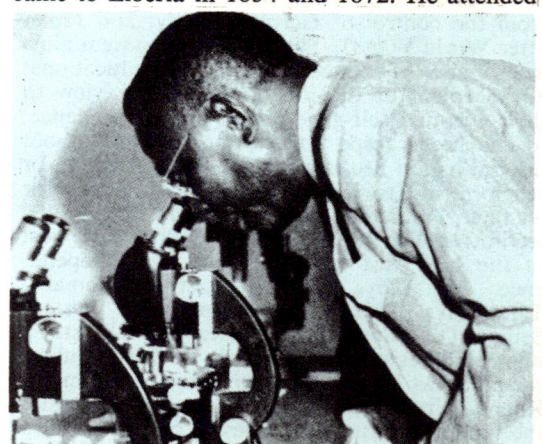

President *Tubman* of Liberia looks through a microscope in a newly decorated library of the Liberian Institute.

college in Liberia and became a lawyer and civil servant. He was elected to the Liberian Senate in 1923 and re-elected in 1929. After a government scandal in 1931 in which he was implicated, he resigned from the Senate but returned again in 1934. In 1937 he was named associate justice of the Supreme Court and in 1943 was elected president of Liberia for an eight-year term. During his first term he undertook various projects to develop the economically backward country, including construction of the Port of Monrovia. He secured an amendment to the constitution that permitted him to succeed himself for a four-year term and he was re-elected president in 1951, 1955, and 1959.

Tubuai or **Austral Islands,** volcanic group, S Pacific Ocean, S of the Society Islands and belonging to French Polynesia; area, including Rapa and other islets as an administrative area, 115 sq. mi.; pop. 3600. Tubuai is the largest of the five inhabited islands (area 19 sq. mi.; pop. 1088). Productive islands yield coffee, copra, arrowroot, timber, and livestock. The group was discovered, 1777, and annexed by France, 1880. The natives are of Polynesian stock.

Tucson, co. seat of Pima co., Arizona, on Santa Cruz River, c.100 mi. SE of Phoenix; pop. 212,892. "The Old Pueblo" grew up around one of the oldest Spanish settlements in the U.S., founded as the Mission of San Xavier del Bac by Father Kino, 1700. It was a military post of

Dexter Press

Tucson's Mission San Xavier del Bac, built in 1772, the oldest church in the U.S.

New Spain, then of Mexico, and was acquired by the U.S. as part of the Gadsden Purchase, 1853. The 2nd largest city in the state, Tucson is now the center of an agricultural, livestock, and mining region, has railroad shops and other industries, and is a health and winter resort. The Univ. of Arizona and several museums and libraries are here. The city annexed c.36 sq. mi. of adjacent territory in 1959 and another 25 sq. mi. in 1960. Its population more than quadrupled in the decade 1950-60.

Tucumán, capital of Tucumán province, NW Argentina; pop. 194,166. It is the center of a sugar-growing region. Founded 1565, it was the scene of Argentina's declaration of independence from Spain, 1816.

Tudor, dynasty of English monarchs. The family was of Welsh origin; the first known, Owen, married Catharine, widow of Henry V, c.1429, and died in battle during the Wars of the Roses. His son Edmund, earl of Richmond, married Margaret Beaufort, great-granddaughter of John of Gaunt, duke of Lancaster, 1455; their son Henry became head of the house of Lancaster on the death of Henry VI, led the Lancastrian forces in the last phase of the Wars of the Roses, and became the first Tudor monarch as Henry VII, 1485-1509. His marriage to Elizabeth of York united the warring houses. Among their children were Margaret, from whose marriage to James IV of Scotland the Stuarts derived their claim to the English throne; and Henry VIII. The succeeding and last Tudor monarchs were Henry's children, Edward VI, Mary, and Elizabeth I; all died without issue, and the Tudor dynasty was succeeded, 1603, by that of the Stuarts.

Tudor style, in English architecture, a style that lasted from the end of the 15th to the mid-16th cent. Sometimes identified with the last phase of the Perpendicular Gothic architecture, it also marks the beginning of the transition—displayed to a greater degree in the subsequent Elizabethan style—to Renaissance architecture. Gothic in character, it nevertheless used some incongruous Renaissance ornament. During the period many manor houses were built, in which, although they retained the great hall as a main feature, other rooms were smaller and were furnished for comfortable family living. Mullioned and bay windows, huge chimneys, peaked gables, and a combination of wood and brick characterized the exteriors. See *English architecture.*

Tu Fu, 713-70, Chinese poet. Ranked with Li Po as the greatest of Chinese lyric poets, he was slow to gain recognition at court, because of his unorthodox views. Except for brief periods when he held minor government posts he lived an unsettled life in hardship with his family. His best poems, notable for fantastic imagery, were written out of abject poverty in his last years.

Tuileries, former palace, Paris, begun 1564 for Catherine de' Medici by Philibert Delorme and much modified later. It stood between the Louvre and the Place de la Concorde. During the French Revolution Louis XVI and his family were virtually imprisoned here, 1789-92. In the days of the Paris Commune, 1871, a mob burned the edifice. The Tuileries gardens, formal in design and containing many sculptures, are renowned for their beauty.

Tukhachevski or **Toukhachevski, Mikhail Nikolayevich,** 1893-1937, Russian soldier. A former tsarist officer, he was captured by the Germans (Feb. 1915), but escaped (1917) and returned to lead armies of the Russian Bolshevik forces, rising to command of the entire Western front. In 1928, made a commander of the Leningrad military district, he was later marshal and a member of the Union Central Committee. Accused as a Trotskyite, he was tried for treason and executed.

Tula, capital of Tula region, central European Russia; pop. 345,000. It manufactures metal goods, notably firearms, and has sugar refineries, tanneries, and flour mills. Established 12th cent., it was a fort against the Tatars, who with the Lithuanians frequently stormed it, 14th-15th cent.

tulip, genus (*Tulipa*) of hardy, spring-blooming, bulbous plants of the lily family, native to Asia and the E Mediterranean. They were introduced into Holland, 16th cent., and have since been widely established as garden favorites. Owing to crossing and selection, there are now an enormous number of varieties in a wide range of color. Holland is still the tulip capital of the world, though bulbs are now grown extensively in the U.S. and elsewhere.

tulip tree, North American large-flowered timber tree (*Liriodendron tulipifera*) of the magnolia family. Mainly abundant in the South, there it is commonly called poplar. This tall (sometimes 180 ft.), straight-trunked tree ranges as far north as Massachusetts. The wood, valuable as lumber and for furniture, is known as whitewood or yellow poplar.

Tulsa, city, co. seat of Tulsa co., NE Oklahoma, on Arkansas River; pop. 261,685. The 2nd-largest city of the state, it is the oil capital of the world and has large oil refineries as well as headquarters for many oil companies and factories making petroleum equipment. It is also the commercial center for a rich farming and grazing area. Manufactures include glass, cotton textiles, chemicals, and furniture. There is also a large aircraft factory. Settled 1882 as a railroad stop on Creek-owned land, the town boomed in 1901 with discovery of oil. Here is the Univ. of Tulsa.

tumblebug—see *dung beetle.*

tumor, abnormal tissue growth (literally, a swelling), which may occur in any part of the body. Tumors are either malignant or benign, although some are not easily classifiable. Malignant tumors (see *cancer*) spread locally and to distant parts of the body via the blood stream and the lymphatic system. Unless treated in time, they are usually fatal. In most cases benign tumors lie in a well-defined capsule and do not spread beyond it. They are not dangerous unless they mechanically obstruct or impair an organ. Tumors are classified according to the kind of tissue they resemble or develop from: *e.g.* carcinoma from epithelial cells, sarcoma and fibroma from connective tissue, and adenoma from gland tissue. The causes of tumors are unknown. Irritation, viruses, and heredity have been suggested, but none explains all cases. Although many malignant tumors are fatal, many are curable if diagnosed and treated early. Simple removal cures most benign tumors.

tuna—see *tunny.*

Tunbridge Wells, municipal borough, Kent, SE England; pop. 22,141. Famous as a spa, 17th-18th cent., it is now a fashionable residential center.

tundra, cold desert area, as in N Russia and Siberia. It lies behind the arctic coasts of that region and during the long winter is covered with ice and snow. In summer only the surface becomes thawed, the temperature being even then only about 48°-50°F. It is a treeless plain, sparsely bearing lichen, mosses, and low shrubs. The fauna include caribou and reindeer. Tundra occurs also in Greenland, Iceland, Canada, and Alaska.

tung oil, varnish base extracted from the seeds of the **tung tree** (*Aleurites fordii*), native to E Asia and Pacific islands. Black tung oil is made by roasting, powdering, and pressing the seeds; white tung oil is made by cold-pressing the seeds. Tung trees are now raised on the Gulf Coast of the U.S., which is now the second largest producer of tung oil. The oil is used for waterproofing and other purposes.

tungsten, element no. 74 (sym. *W*; at. wt. 183.92; m.p. 6100°F; sp. gr. 18.6), a dull white, somewhat malleable metal occurring in minerals scheelite and wolframite. It was discovered by the D'Elhujar brothers, 1783. Added to steel, it increases hardness and cutting qualities. Because of its high melting point (highest of all metals) it is used in electric-light and vacuum-tube filaments. Its compounds are used in ceramic glazes, dyes, and fireproofing. Its name was officially changed to wolfram, 1949.

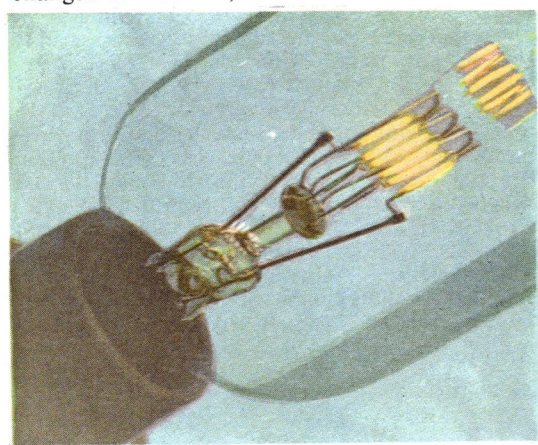

Tungsten **filament of an electric bulb**

Tungting Lake, N Hunan province, China, depth varies by season; area *c.*1450 sq. ft. It serves as a natural floor reservoir for the Yangtze River to which it is joined by several channels. The lake receives four main rivers, which all connect with major trade centers and are navigable for junks. The Tungting basin is in the "rice bowl" of China.

Tunguska, name of three rivers in Siberia. Each is a tributary of the Yenisei River: Nizhnyaya (Lower) Tunguska, *c.*2000 mi. long; Podkamennaya (Stony) Tunguska, *c.*1000 mi. long; and Verkhnyaya (Upper) Tunguska, identical with the Angara River in its lower course.

Tunis, capital of Tunisia, on Lake of Tunis; pop. 695,000. Connected by canal with the Mediterranean through the Gulf of Tunis, it is accessible to ocean-going vessels and has always been an important center of trade. It was capital of a

The Place Bab Sujka in the center of the old Moslem quarter of *Tunis.*

TUNISIA

Berber dynasty, 12th-16th cent., and became a center of trade and piracy. In World War II it was used by the Axis in their last desperate stand in North Africa, 1942-3. The ancient city has many fine examples of Arab architecture, chiefly mosques. Nearby are the ruins of Carthage.

Tunisia, republic, N Africa; area 48,332 sq. mi.; pop. 3,783,169 (incl. 255,324 Europeans); capital Tunis. Bounded N and E by the Mediterranean. Tunisia has excellent fisheries and harbors. Agriculture is the chief occupation, cereals being grown in the valleys of the Atlas Mts., and citrus fruits in the northeast. In central Tunisia stock are raised, and in the oases of the Sahara, dates. Olives, olive oil, and wine are exported.

The flag of *Tunisia*

From the mountains come mineral resources, particularly phosphates, iron ore, and lead. Settled by Phoenicians and Carthaginians, Tunisia later became part of the Roman empire and, 7th cent., was invaded by Arabs, who converted the population to Islam. From the 13th to the 16th cent., when it was taken by Turks, Tunisia was ruled by a Berber dynasty. By the 18th cent., although still nominally under Turkey, it was virtually independent. It was part of the notorious Barbary Coast, and piracy flourished along its shores. The country was occupied by France, 1881, and made a protectorate despite protests of the Italians, who long continued to claim it. In this region in World War II the German army, pinned between Allied forces from the east and from the west, made its last stand in Africa, 1942-3. After World War II Tunisia experienced increasing demands for independence. Considerable self-government was instituted in 1951, but disorders continued. In 1954, France offered Tunisia full domestic autonomy which was instituted in 1955. Nationalist leader Habib Bourguiba was freed. In 1956, France gave the country its complete independence and Bourguiba became the first premier. Tunis gave asylum to the leaders of the Algerian nationalists. In 1961, fighting broke out between Tunisian troops and French troops at the naval base at Bizerte. France agreed to negotiate toward the eventual relinquishment of this base.

Graphic House

Upper left: the harbor at Sfax, *Tunisia*.

Lower left: Tunis as seen from old Carthage.

Upper right: rooftop in Tunis' Moslem quarter.

Lower right: narrow street in Moslem quarter.

tunnel, artificial subterranean or underwater passage for water, gas, pipe, or traffic. The longest and some of the earliest tunnels were constructed to carry water, drainage, or sewage. Such a tunnel, built by the Romans to drain Lake Fucinus, completed A.D. 52, was over 3 mi. long and required the labor of 30,000 men for 11 years. Of tunnels built under watercourses, the oldest known was built by the Babylonians under the Euphrates. The river was diverted from its channel; the bed was then excavated and fitted with a brick passage which was covered with earth before the river was allowed to resume its former course. Modern underwater tunnels are begun from each shore; shields are used to prevent seepage until an adequate permanent barrier is built. Among the most notable such tunnels are the Severn Tunnel, between England and Wales (4½ mi., completed 1886); the St. Clair Tunnel from Huron, Mich., to Ontario (6000 ft., 1891); the Liverpool-Birkenhead Tunnel under the Mersey (over 2 mi., 1934); those under the Hudson and East Rivers at New York, particularly the Brooklyn-Battery Tunnel (9117 ft., 1950); and the Baltimore Harbor tunnel (7650 ft., 1958).

Traffic tunnels bored through mountains are mostly modern and result from the need to avoid steep gradients in railroad and superhighway construction. A slight gradient is required for drainage; except for passages through solid rock, a waterfast and erosion-proof sheath must surround the tube through which the roadbed is laid, and ventilation must be provided by shafts or forced draft. Among the earliest and best-known tunnels are those bored through the Alps, made possible by the invention of the compressed-air drill, first used on the Mont Cenis Tunnel (8 mi., 1871); then at St. Gotthard (over 9 mi., 1882); and at Simplon, longest in the world (12½ mi., 1905), with a second tunnel (1921). The earliest railroad tunnel in the U.S. was through Hoosac Mountain, Mass. (4½ mi., built 1856-73); the longest in the U.S. is through the Cascade Mts. of Washington (7¾ mi., opened 1929). Tunnels through the Appalachians are features of the Pennsylvania Turnpike. Another type of tunnel is that constructed for rapid transit railways in urban areas (see *subway*).

Tunney, Gene (James Joseph Tunney), 1898-   , U.S. prize fighter. After winning the light heavyweight title from Harry Greb, Tunney won the world heavyweight championship from Jack Dempsey by a 10-round decision, 1926, in Philadelphia. In 1927 he successfully defended his crown against Dempsey in Chicago, surviving by reason of the famous "long count." He retired undefeated, 1928, and never attempted a comeback but went into private business.

tunny or **tuna,** large marine fish of the mackerel family, known also as the "horse mackerel." The great tunny (*Thunnus thynnus*), abundant in warm seas, is widely distributed. It may attain 8 to 10 ft. and 1500 lbs. Valued for food, it is extensively caught in the Mediterranean. *T. saliens* is a popular game fish of the Pacific Coast of North America; an Atlantic Coast species is *T. secundodorsalis*. Tunny flesh, extremely oily, is often canned, especially for use in salads.

tupelo, trees of the genus *Nyssa*. *N. sylvatica,* also known as blackgum, sourgum, or pepperidge, is a useful timber tree widespread in the eastern U.S. Because of its attractive glossy foliage, becoming brilliant in the fall, the tupelo is frequently planted as a shade tree. In swamps of the deep South another species, *N. aquatica,* is called water tupelo.

Tupper, Sir Charles, 1821-1915, Canadian political leader and physician. As premier of Nova Scotia, from 1864, he strongly supported the movement for uniting it with the Dominion of Canada. While in the cabinet under Macdonald he achieved completion of the Canadian Pacific Ry. As Conservative prime minister of Canada, 1869, he vainly promoted a preferential tariff arrangement with the empire.

Tura, Cosmé (Cosimo), (bef. 1431-95), Italian artist, famous for his frescoes, the first great painter of the Ferrarese school. From 1451 he was court painter to Borso d'Este and Ercole d'Este, but much of his production has been lost. His style, influenced by Mantegna (*q.v.*), is characterized by vigorous draughtsmanship and modeling, austerity of feeling, clashing colors, and a consistent hard and metallic sense of form. Important examples of his work are the organ panels, *Annunciation* and *St. George Slaying the Dragon* in the Cathedral at Ferrara; a *Portrait of a Man* in the National Gallery, Washington; and the *St. Jerome* in the National Gallery, London.

turbine, rotary motor employing water, gas, or steam to rotate it directly in its bearings. In its simplest form it consists of a wheel with vanes moved by the pressure of water. In the steam turbine, steam is the motive power. Turbines are

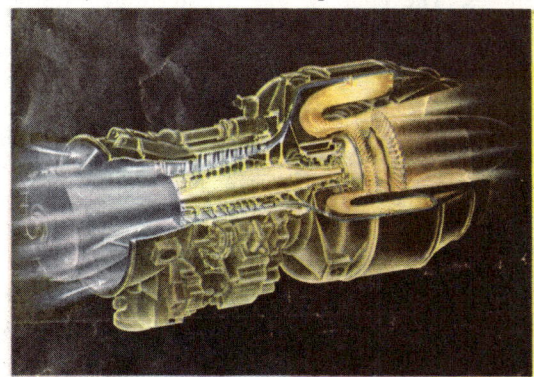

Avco Corp.

Air is being blown through this modern *turbine* engine, an economical machine which can operate under diverse climactic conditions.

used where high speeds and continuous operation are required, as in electric generating stations. The first reaction engine was that of Hero of Alexandria (2d cent. B.C.). The modern turbine was invented by Charles Parsons, an Englishman, 1884.

turbot, flatfish (*Psetta maxima*) found in European waters, popular as a food fish. It weighs up to 40 lbs. In California the halibut (*Hypsopsetta guttulata*) is known as the turbot. Those of the W Atlantic are small and of little commercial importance. See *flatfish*.

Turenne, Henri de La Tour d'Auvergne, vicomte de, 1611-75, marshal of France. Though raised as a Protestant, he was entrusted by Richelieu, 1641, with supreme command of French troops engaged in the Thirty Years' War. With his friend Condé he gained notable victories. During the civil wars of the Fronde, 1648-53, Turenne led royal troops against Condé. In the third of the Dutch Wars, 1672-8, he conquered parts of the Spanish Netherlands, ravaged Alsace and the Palatinate, advanced into Germany, but was killed at Salzbach.

Turgenev, Ivan Sergeyevich, 1818-83, Russian author. Of aristocratic family, he knew well the life on late 19th-cent. Russian estates, but also spent much time in Europe. A foe of serfdom, he described its evils tellingly.

Turgot, Anne Robert Jacques, baron de l'Aulne, 1727-81, French statesman and economist. Son of a Paris merchant, he studied briefly for the church, then became intimate with Voltaire and the *philosophes* and with the leading economic reformers, the Physiocrats. Applying physiocratic principles while intendant of Limoges, 1761-74, he reformed taxation and encouraged agriculture, industry, and road building. His reforms and his writings on economics (including *Réflexions sur la formation et la distribution des richesses,* 1766-70, arguing for free trade) caused his appointment as minister of marine in the national government and then as comptroller general of finances, 1774. His efforts against administrative extravagance and sinecures were initially successful, but his establishment of freedom of grain trade in France, 1774, was unpopular and had to be rescinded because, as a result of poor harvests, it led to rising prices and bread riots. The court disliked him increasingly, and his actions against privileged trading corporations and efforts to win tolerance for Protestants alienated merchants and clergy. Through lack of tact he finally lost also the support of the king, Louis XVI, from whom alone he could win acceptance of reforms necessary to avert national bankruptcy. He then retired, 1776, to devote himself to writing. The subsequent bankruptcy of France was one of the factors leading to the French Revolution, 1789.

Turin (Ital.: *Torino*), city, NW Italy, capital of Piedmont and Torino province, on upper Po River, c.75 mi. WSW of Milan; pop. 889,249. One of Italy's leading industrial cities, 4th in size, it produces automobiles, machinery, rolling stock, metal goods, silk, chemicals, and foodstuffs. Hydroelectric stations in nearby Alpine foothills provide power. Turin is also an important trade and communication hub. The many cultural institutions include a university (founded 1405), an academy of science, and several museums. Notable are the Cathedral of St. John the Baptist, the Church of San Filippo, the Palazzo Madama, and the Palazzo Reale. The old capital of the Taurini, Turin was the Augusta Taurinorum of the Romans, later the center of a Lombard duchy. The house of Savoy gained it, 11th cent., and in the 16th cent. it was held by the French, then returned to the dukes of Savoy, under whose rule it became, 1720, capital of the kingdom of Sardinia. When Italy was united, Turin was its first capital, 1861-4. Repeatedly bombed during World War II, the city suffered considerable damage.

Turkestan—see *Turkistan.*

Turkey, republic, SE Europe and SW Asia (Asia Minor), consisting of Turkey-in-Europe and the much larger Turkey-in-Asia; area 301,380 sq. mi.; pop. 27,802,224; capital Ankara. The European section comprises Eastern Thrace, bounded by the Black Sea (E), Bulgaria (N), and Greece, along the Maritsa River (W). It is separated from Turkey-in-Asia by the Dardanelles, the Sea of Marmara, and the Bosporus, which link the Black Sea with the Aegean. These strategic waters are often referred to as The Straits. On the Bosporus lies the country's largest city and former capital, Istanbul (Constantinople). Asiatic Turkey embraces the vast Anatolian highland (average altitude above 2000 ft.), rimmed by escarpments (Taurus, Antitaurus, Pontic Mts.) and narrow fertile lowlands along the Black Sea (N), Aegean Sea (W), and the Mediterranean proper (SW). In the E regions, which include parts of Armenia and Kurdistan, Anatolia rises to its greatest heights, culminating in Mt. Ararat (16,945 ft.). Here E Turkey borders on the Georgian and Armenian Soviet Socialist Republics and Iran. In the SE it is adjoined by Syria and Iraq. The Euphrates and Tigris Rivers both rise in the Anatolian plateau. Largest river entirely in Turkey is the Kizil, which drains into the Black Sea, while the Büyük Menderes (the Maeander of antiquity) flows to the Aegean coast. The climate

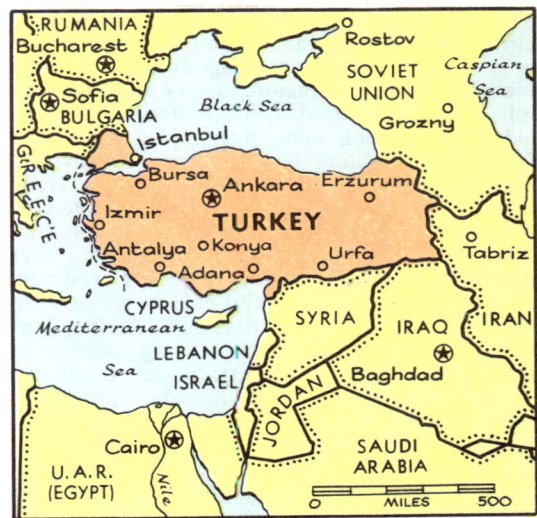

The flag of *Turkey*

varies greatly, being mild and equable on the Mediterranean but harsh and extreme on the plateau, where the summers are dry and hot,

TURKEY

Ankara's National Bank of *Turkey*

Ankara's Grand National Assembly Building

and the winters cold. The Armenian Black Sea coast is the most humid section, with semi-tropical conditions. Turkey is primarily agricultural and pastoral, and about two-thirds of the people are peasants. Though methods are still antiquated, all kinds of crops thrive. Tobacco, Turkey's leading export, is chiefly grown in Thrace and along the Black Sea. Cereals, soybeans, fruit, sugar beets, and sunflowers are raised for local consumption, though some wheat is now shipped. The Aegean and Mediterranean lowlands yield citrus fruit, grapes, raisins, and olives, while tea is grown in the NE. Other agricultural products include opium, flax, hemp, canary seed, licorice, nuts, almonds, dried fruit, cotton, silk, skin, hides, furs, wool, and gums. Industries, apart from textile milling (notably carpet weaving), are predominantly of the processing type. However, since the inauguration of the 1934 five-year plan, mining and the manufacturing of iron and steel, paper, glass, sugar, cement, etc., have made great strides. Today there are iron and steel works at Karabük, and coal mines at Zonguldak. The mineral wealth is considerable. Turkey is one of the world's leading sources of chromium, emery, and meerschaum. Other important natural resources include manganese, zinc, copper, antimony, mercury, asbestos, silver, sulphur, and petroleum. Except for Ankara, all the major cities are in the lowlands, among them Istanbul, Izmir (Smyrna), Adana, Bursa, Iskenderun (Alexandretta), Trabzon (Trebizond). Interior towns of importance are Eskişehir, Gaziantep, Konya, Kayseri, and Erzurum. There are four universities: one at Ankara, two at Istanbul, and a new (1956) Aegean University at Izmir. Two additional universities are being built at Erzurum and Trabzon, with U.S. assistance. Robert College, the oldest American college outside the U.S., was founded in 1863 at Istanbul. The population is now fairly homogeneous, including nearly 90% Turks, whose religion (separated from the state) is Sunnite Mohammedanism. Kurds, Armenians, Circassians, Lazis and Jews form minorities. The republic of Turkey was organized as of 1921. A constitution provides for election by universal suffrage, every 4 years, of the national assembly, which elects a president for a coextensive term, to exercise, with his appointed council of ministers, executive power subject to assembly control.

The Modern Turks enter European history as a central-Asiatic tribe migrating long after the Seljuk Turks to Anatolia and establishing themselves here, 13th cent., under Osman, founder of the Ottoman empire. Thenceforth the Turks advanced into the Balkans, making Adrianople their capital and defeating the Serbians at Kosovo, 1389, and the Hungarians and Poles at Nikopol, 1396. Thus they gained control of most of the Balkan Peninsula, sealed by the destruction of the Byzantine empire through the fall of Constantinople, 1453. Under Suleiman I, the Magnificent, the Turks took Belgrade and won part of Hungary at Mohács, 1526. They reached the gates of Vienna, swept to the Crimea, and expanded into North Africa, Arabia, and Mesopotamia. Cairo and Algiers were taken 1517. The Turks suffered their first severe setback at the naval Battle of Lepanto, 1571. In the early

Atatürk Boulevard in Ankara, named for Kemal Atatürk, the founder of modern *Turkey*.

The President's House at Ankara

TURKEY

The ruins of the Valens Aqueduct in Istanbul, Turkey, built by the Romans in 368 A.D.

Turkish village in the Taurus mountains

19th cent. they lost Greece. Beginning 18th cent., Russia waged many wars against the Ottoman empire, appearing as champion of Christians suffering under Turkish rule, and gradually pushing the Turkish border in Europe southward. The Crimean War, 1853-6, saw England and France united in protecting the sultan's empire against Nicholas I. In 1875 uprisings among subject peoples of the Ottoman empire were mercilessly suppressed, and Europe rang with reports of atrocities. Again in the war of 1877 and the resultant Congress of Berlin, 1878, it was foreign interference which saved the "sick man of Europe" from Russian domination. The Young Turk Reform Party was ruthlessly suppressed, 1901, but drove Abdul Hamid from his throne, 1908. In World War I the Turks stayed the Allied attempts to force the Dardanelles, 1915. Turkey lost, however, all her Arab lands. A nationalist revolution, 1919, resulted in establishment at Ankara of a separate government ignoring the humiliating Treaty of Sèvres, 1920. A war with Greece ended in Turkey's favor, 1922, the Greeks being expelled from Asia Minor. On Nov. 1, 1922, the sultanate was abolished and on Oct. 29, 1923, Turkey was declared a republic with Mustapha Kemal, called Atatürk, as President. He was re-elected, 1927. The Treaty of Lausanne, 1923, recognized the present boundaries of Turkey, apart from the Sanjak of Alexandretta (Hatay), ceded by France, 1939. The Straits were demilitarized, but this provision was revoked by the Montreux Convention, 1936, which was, however, disputed by the U.S.S.R. after World War II. Turkey's insistence on the creation of a purely national state caused the repatriation of large ethnic minorities after the Treaty of Lausanne. Some 2 million Greeks and 500,000 Turks were exchanged over a six-year period (1923-9) under the direction of the League of Nations. Radical changes, intended to bring Turkey up to European cultural and economic levels were introduced by Atatürk. Industry and agriculture were advanced, the position of women raised to European status, and European methods adopted generally. In World War II Turkey first maintained a neutral though friendly attitude toward the Axis. After German defeats in Russia, it shifted sympathies to the Allies, eventually declaring war on Germany and Japan, Feb. 1945. Turkey was included in the Truman Doctrine (*q.v.*) in 1947, and thereafter was the recipient of large U.S. military and economic assistance. It was one of the original signatories of the Baghdad Pact. Its traditional alignment with the West against Russia was re-emphasized by its inclusion in the North Atlantic Treaty Organization (1952), and by its treaties of friendship with Greece and Yugoslavia in 1953 (see *Balkan Pact*). However, growing official corruption and suppression of all political opposition by the government of Pres. Celal Bayar and Premier Adnan Menderes led to a revolt in 1960. It was instigated by students and carried out by army groups led by Gen. Amal Gürsel, who became acting chief of state. The military regime tried and hanged Bayar, Menderes, and other political leaders in 1961. Elections in Oct. 1961 left control in the hands of a coalition led by Gürsel as president.

This craft is plying the Bosphorus River toward the harbor at Istanbul, Turkey.

The towers of Yedikule, part of the ancient city walls surrounding Istanbul, Turkey.

Graphic House

turkey, large bird of the genus *Meleagris*. A native of North America, it has two species. The common domesticated birds are derived from the wild turkey, a number of varieties having been evolved by breeders. The male, which may weigh up to 30 or more lbs., often struts and gobbles with spread tail and puffed-out feathers. The bird is extensively bred for the table.

Farmers, on a typical *turkey* farm, prepare the birds for shipping and marketing.

Graphic House

turkey vulture, large, blackish-brown bird of North and South America, with a naked red head. It is 26 to 32 in. long. Like other vultures (*q.v.*) it lives on dead animals and offal. Protected by law in the U.S., it soars gracefully and tirelessly in search of food.

Turkic languages, a sub-family of the Ural-Altaic languages (*q.v.*), spoken in a vast area extending from SE Europe (Balkan states), across Asia Minor (Turkey) and through central Asia as far E as the Mongolian People's Republic. It includes the many languages and dialects of Azerbaijan SSR, Turkmen SSR, Uzbek SSR, Kazakh SSR, Tajik SSR, Kirghiz SSR, and a number of the bordering autonomous oblasts of the USSR, as well as parts of N Iran, N Afghanistan and W China (Sinkiang Province). The best known of the Turkic languages is Turkish. The main characteristic of the Turkic languages is vowel harmony. This phenomenon occurs with such regularity in Turkish that it seems almost artificial. Vowels are classed as either front (e, i, ö, ü) or back (a, o, u, ı). Front ö and ü are pronounced as in German; back ı (undotted i) is roughly the equivalent of the unstressed vowel sound in Eng. *Cyril;* the others are pronounced as in Italian. The principle of vowel harmony is simply that front or back vowels only may be used in a given word, not in combination; the pattern is established by the vowel of the root word. Thus, we have:

ev, "house" and: *at,* "horse"
evler, "houses" but: *atlar,* "horses"
evlerim, "my houses" but: *atlarım,* "my horses"
evlerime, "to my houses" but: *atlarıma,* "to my horses"

It will be noted that Turkish is an agglutinative language, *i.e.,* individual words are built into meaningful phrases by means of suffixes and infixes. In the above examples, *ev* and *at* are the root words; the front/back variants *ler/lar* indicate plurality; *im/ım* show possession by the first person singular; *e/a* signify "direction toward" (dative case); etc. The Arabic script was used almost universally for all Turkic languages until 1924-39, when a latinized alphabet —or, where Russian influence was dominant, a modified Cyrillic alphabet—was substituted. This change took place in Turkey, for instance, by official decree in 1928, and is one of the outstanding examples in the history of the world where an entire literature was rendered obsolete (except in transliteration), virtually overnight. This seemingly drastic move, however, has increased literacy appreciably in that country. See *language.*

Turkish languages—see *Turkic languages.*

Turkish music—see *Oriental music and dance.*

Turkistan or **Turkestan,** region, central Asia, including parts of Russia, China, and Afghanistan. Russian Turkistan, sometimes called Western Turkistan, includes several Soviet Socialist Republics: Turkmen, Uzbek, Tadzhik, Kirghiz, and Kazakh. Chinese Turkistan, or Eastern Turkistan, is now included in the Chinese province of Sinkiang. A section in NE Afghanistan is sometimes called Afghan Turkistan. There are deserts in W Turkistan. In the east are the Pamir region and the fertile Fergana Valley. Most inhabitants of Turkistan speak Turkic languages; many belong to nomadic tribes. In early history the region was possessed successively by Persians, Greeks, Chinese, Huns, and Mongols.

Turkmen Soviet Socialist Republic or **Turkmenistan,** constituent republic, U.S.S.R., central Asia; area 188,417 sq. mi.; pop. 1,520,000; capital Ashkhabad. It is bounded W by the Caspian Sea, S by Iran and Afghanistan, NE by Uzbekistan, and NW by Kazakhstan. Most of the region is desert. Sheep and goats are raised, and in the oases and river valleys cotton, silk, dates, figs, vegetables, and grains are produced. Oil wells and fisheries are found along the Caspian Sea. Almost three-quarters of the population is Moslem. The Russians conquered the region late 19th cent.; then it became part of the Transcaspian region of Russian Turkistan. It became a constituent republic of the U.S.S.R., 1925.

Turks and Caicos Islands, British colony, group of islands, West Indies; area 169 sq. mi.; pop. 5716; chief town, Grand Turk. A dependency of Jamaica, they are geographically a SE extension of the Bahama Islands. The chief products are salt, sponges, and sisal hemp.

Turku (Swed.: *Abo*), manufacturing city and Baltic seaport, SW Finland, *c.*145 mi. W of Helsinki; pop. 120,095. The country's 3d-largest city and its capital until 1812, it has two universities and a 13th-cent. cathedral. Among the many industries are shipbuilding, lumbering, flourmilling, sugar refining, and distilling. The Treaty of Abo, signed here, 1743, awarded Vyborg (Viipuri) dept. to Russia.

Turner, Joseph Mallord William, 1775-1851, English landscape painter, b. London. Turner studied at the Royal Academy and made topographical drawings for several magazines. He first exhibited at the Academy, 1793, and later became a member. In 1802 he made the first of many trips to the Continent. His early work is characterized by browns and muted golds, but

Joseph *Turner*'s "Fighting Téméraire"

in later efforts he shows a love of rich coloring inspired by the Italians. His handling of atmosphere and broken patches of pure color in such romantically inspired works as *The Slave Ship, The Fighting Téméraire,* and *Approach to Venice* later influenced the impressionists. His *Liber Studiorum* (1806-19), a book of etched landscape drawings produced as a challenge to Claude Lorrain's *Liber Veritatis,* influenced a whole school of English engravers and raised the standards of this art in England to a hitherto unparalleled level. Also of great beauty were his water colors. Through his life increasingly eccentric, he finally became a virtual recluse. He left his work to the English nation.

Turner, Frederick Jackson, 1861-1932, U.S. historian, b. Portage, Wis. He taught history at the Univ. of Wisconsin, 1885-1910, and Harvard, 1910-24. His address, "The Significance of the Frontier in American History" (1893), emphasizing the frontier influence in the development of the national character and institutions, strongly affected later U.S. historical writing. The address appeared in his book of historical essays *The Frontier in American History* (1920). Turner's *The Significance of Sections in American History* (1932) was awarded the Pulitzer Prize for American history.

Turner, Nat, 1800-31, U.S. slave leader, b. Southampton co., Va. A preacher claiming divine inspiration, he led a rebellion (Nat Turner's Insurrection) of Negro slaves, Aug. 13-23, 1831, in his native county. With about 60 followers he murdered his owner's family and about 50 other whites. In the ensuing manhunt scores of Negroes were killed. Turner and 19 others were captured, tried, convicted, and hanged.

turnip, Old World biennial herb (*Brassica rapa*) having a large, white-fleshed root used as food for man and cattle. The leaves are frequently used as greens. Turnips are less important in the U.S. than in Europe.

turpentine, volatile oil obtained by distillation of the oleoresin from certain trees, particularly the pine. It is separated from the rosin by distillation with steam, and may be prepared by distillation from wood itself (wood turpentine). The properties vary somewhat according to the trees used. Turpentine is used as a drying oil for paints and varnishes, in manufacture of linoleum, soap, ink, and in various medicines.

turnpike—see *highway.*

turquoise, a hydrous, basic, aluminum phosphate plus copper; a gem, usually found in thin veins in alumina-rich rocks of desert regions. Its color varies from green to blue, but the blue is considered the most desirable. While most of the fine turquoise has come from Iran and Tibet, localities in Arizona, New Mexico, Nevada, Colorado and California have become very important. There is an iron-stained fossil bone known as odontolite, or bone turquoise, which has often been mistaken for and used in the same ways as true turquoise, but it can be distinguished by testing for copper. The Navajo Indians make fine, symbolic jewelry from turquoise and silver. See *birthstones.*

Some *turquoise* gems: 1 and 2. polished Persian turquoise; 3. uncut turquoise from the mines at Los Cerillos, N.M.

turtle, a reptile of the order Testudinata, especially a marine form. Sea turtles have paddle-like limbs and lay their eggs on sandy shores. The hawksbill turtle (*Eretmochelys*) yields tortoise shell. The green turtle (*Chelonia*) is used for turtle soup. The common snapper (genus *Chelydra*), an American fresh-water turtle, seizes its prey by snapping its jaws together firmly; it reaches a length of 3 ft. and ranges from eastern U.S. to Ecuador. The larger alligator snapper (*Macroclemmys*) occurs in southeastern U.S. Most fresh-water turtles of the Northern Hemi-

TURTLEDOVE

sphere are better called terrapins. They are usually smaller than snappers, with narrower heads and shorter tails. Most turtles are carnivorous, eating a wide variety of animal food, while the true tortoises are chiefly herbivorous. Some turtles have been known to live more than 100 years. The skeleton of turtles and tortoises, largely external, forms a kind of shell into which they can draw themselves when attacked. Both the under part (plastron) and the upper part (carapace) are made up of many bony plates nicely fitted together and overlaid with horny scutes. Some have a covering so jointed that they can shut it up after drawing in head, legs, and tail. See *reptile*.

turtledove, name applied to various European and Asian small, wild doves of gentle aspect. Sometimes the name is shortened to turtle, as in the references to the "voice of the turtle" in the Bible. The name is sometimes used for the mourning dove.

Tuscaloosa, city, co. seat of Tuscaloosa co., W central Alabama, on Black Warrior River; pop. 63,670. An industrial city lying in a coal-mining region, it produces iron, clay, paper, rubber, and wood products. Univ. of Alabama is here. The city was state capital 1826-46. Union forces captured it 1865.

Tuscan order—see *Doric order*.

Tuscany (Ital.: *Toscana*), region (*compartimento*), N central Italy, along Tyrrhenian Sea and crossed by the Apennines; area 8876 sq. mi.; pop. 3,262,048; capital Florence. Bordered by Liguria (NW), Emilia-Romagna (N and NE), The Marches (E), Umbria and Latium (SE), it encompasses 9 provinces, named for the principal cities: Arezzo, Massa e Carrara (formerly Apuania), Firenze (Florence), Grosseto, Livorno (Leghorn), Lucca, Pisa, Pistoia, Siena. Tuscany is watered by the Arno, whose fertile valley is one of the peninsula's chief agricultural districts south of the Po Valley. In the mountains iron, copper, mercury, manganese, and lignite are mined. Carrara furnishes celebrated marble. Ancient Tuscany was the main part of Etruria, a great civilization when conquered by Rome, 3d cent. B.C. In the Middle Ages it became a Lombard duchy, then broke up into city republics. In the Renaissance it was a great center of art. From 1530 to 1737 ruled by the Medici, upon their extinction it was given to the dukes of Lorraine, one of whom, Leopold I (later Emperor Leopold II), carried out extensive reforms. During the French Revolutionary Wars Tuscany was overrun, and in 1801, by the Peace of Lunéville, was given to Spain, only to be ceded to Napoleon, 1807. Under grand Duke Leopold II a constitution was granted, 1848, but revolution broke out, and in 1859 Leopold was driven out by the Florentines. In 1860 Tuscany voted for annexation to Sardinia, and thus became part of the Italian kingdom, 1861.

Tuscarora, American Indian tribe of the eastern woodlands, speaking an Iroquoian language. See *Indians, American*.

Tuskegee Institute, just outside Tuskegee, Macon co., Alabama, 38 mi. E of Montgomery. A coeducational normal and industrial school and one of the oldest and most important centers of Negro education in the U.S., it was founded,

An algebra class in the early days of the Tuskegee Institute, when most students were past the age of today's high school pupils.

1881, and directed by Booker T. Washington until his death, 1915. George Washington Carver, noted Negro scientist, worked and taught here. In 1958, the town of Tuskegee removed the area containing the institute from the incorporated area of the town so as to prevent the Negro residents of the area from voting in local elections.

Dexter Press

The George Washington Carver Museum at Alabama's Turkegee Institute displays many of the products which the great scientist derived from sweet potatoes and peanuts.

Tussaud, Marie, 1760-1850, English effigist, b. Switzerland. She established Madame Tussaud's Exhibition in London, 1802, gradually building up the famous waxwork show which is still in existence. These life-sized wax figures of famous people, living and dead, are realistically modeled and dressed.

Tutankhamen, *fl.* after 1358 B.C., pharaoh of Egypt. Son-in-law of the great pharaoh Amenhotep IV, he ruled after the latter's death, *c.*1358 B.C. He apparently retained for a time the cult of Aton instituted by Amenhotep. No details of Tutankhamen's reign are known, but the life of his court may be reconstructed from the abundance of art works discovered in his tomb in 1922 by the archeologists Howard Carter and the earl of Carnarvon. The tomb, unlike other burial sites of the pharaohs, had never been

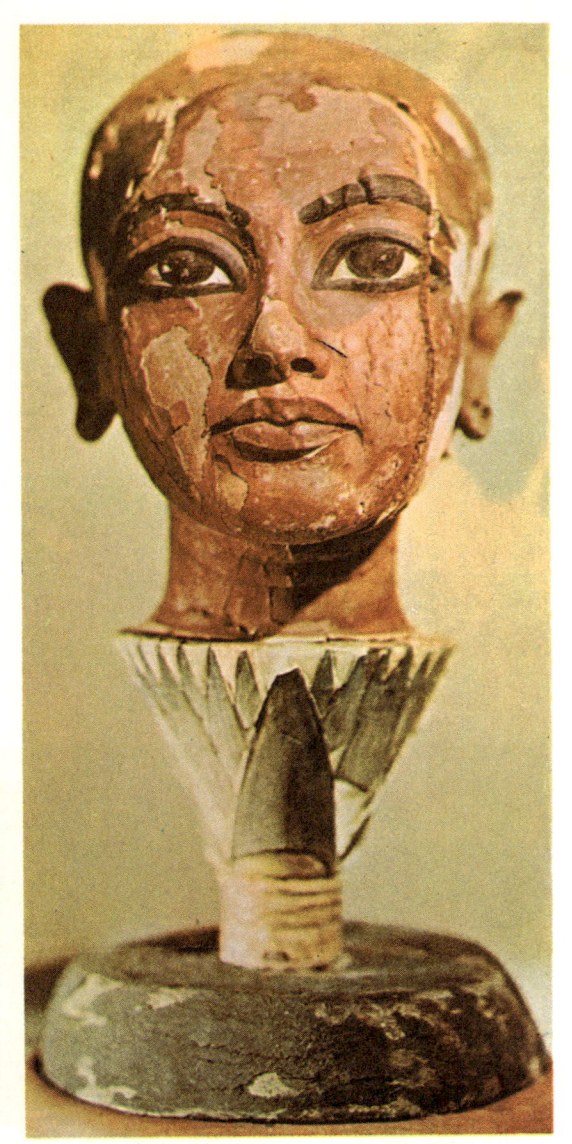

A portrait of the Pharaoh *Tutankhamen*, c.1350 B.C., now in the Cairo Museum, Egypt.

pillaged, and yielded treasures of inestimable value and great beauty.

Tutuila—see *Samoa*.

Tuva Autonomous Region (formerly Tannu Tuva or Uriankhai), division of Soviet Russia in Asia, on NW border of Outer Mongolia between Sayan and Tannu Ola Mts. of S Siberia; area c.64,000 sq. mi.; pop. 172,000; capital Kyzyl. It is mountainous, watered by the Yenisei, with good pasture for varied livestock. Most inhabitants are Tuvinians, a Turkic group, with some Russians, Chinese, and Mongols. As Uriankhai, it was part of Outer Mongolia until 1911; then it came under Russian influence and, 1921, was declared the Tannu-Tuva People's Republic. It became part of the U.S.S.R., 1944.

TVA—see *Tennessee Valley Authority*.

Tver—see *Kalinin*.

Twain, Mark, pen name of **Samuel Langhorne Clemens,** 1835-1910, U.S. author, b. Florida, Mo. He was brought up in Hannibal, Mo., background of his novels *Tom Sawyer* and *Huckleberry Finn*. After experience as a journeyman printer in Hannibal and Eastern cities, 1847-55, he was a Mississippi River pilot, 1857-61, then went to Nevada, 1862, and after failing as a mining prospector began writing for the Virginia City *Enterprise,* using the pseudonym "Mark Twain" (the Mississippi River boat leadsman's call for 2 fathoms). Immediate fame came with his amusing frontier story "The Celebrated Jumping Frog of Calaveras County," published 1865 in the New York *Saturday Press*. Sent by the Sacramento (Calif.) *Union* to the Sandwich (Hawaiian) Islands, on his return, 1866, he lectured widely, delighting audiences with his wit. An account of his journey to Europe and the Holy Land, *Innocents Abroad; or, The New Pilgrims' Progress* (1869), was equally popular. In 1870 he married Olivia Langdon, then settled in Hartford, where, with Charles Dudley Warner, he wrote the satirical *Gilded Age: A Tale of Today* (1873). There he also wrote the autobiographical narrative *Life on the Mississippi* (1883) and the novels built on his boyhood, *The Adventures of Tom Sawyer* (1876) and the classic *Adventures of Huckleberry Finn* (1884). Notable also were the historical novels *The Prince and the Pauper* (1882), *A Connecticut Yankee in King Arthur's Court* (1889), and *Personal Recollections of Joan of Arc* (1896). Failure in 1896 of the publishing firm of Charles L. Webster, of which Clemens was a partner, left him bankrupt, and to pay his debts he embarked on a world lecture tour, writing of his experiences in *Following the Equator*

A long-established tradition in California is the yearly Angels Camp celebration of *Mark Twain's* famous story of the old gold mining town, "The Jumping Frog of Calaveras County," which was published in 1865.

Bank of America

(1897). The last years of his life, darkened by the death of his wife and of two daughters, were marked by growing bitterness, expressed notably in *The Mysterious Stranger* (posthumously published, 1916). He is remembered more for the sharp but genial social satire and local color of his earlier works, which established him in the front rank of U.S. writers.

Tweed, William Marcy, 1823-78, U.S. politician, b. New York City. New York City alderman, 1852-6, and U.S. Representative from New York, 1853-5, he became a leader of Tammany Hall (*q.v.*) and built his system of graft and vote-buying. The **Tweed Ring**—Tweed and Mayor A. Oakey Hall, City Chamberlain Peter B. Sweeny, and Comptroller Richard B. Connolly—defrauded the city of $75 to $250 million on municipal contracts. Tweed dictated nominations and controlled elections for mayor and governor of New York, and dominated the state legislature by bribery. After exposures through the cartoons of Thomas Nast in *Harper's Weekly,* 1869-71, and by the New York *Times,* 1871, Samuel J. Tilden led other Democratic political leaders in smashing the ring. Tweed was convicted Nov. 1872 and sentenced to 12 years in jail. He escaped, fled to Spain, was extradited 1876, and died in jail.

Tweed River, *c.*95 mi. long, SE Scotland and NE England, rising in Peeblesshire and flowing to the North Sea at Berwick. It forms part of the boundary between Scotland and England. The river yields salmon.

Twelve Tables—see *Roman law*.

twelve-tone system—see *scale; tonality*.

Twenty-one Demands, Japanese demands presented to China, Jan. 18, 1915, which would virtually have reduced China to a Japanese protectorate. Japan was to obtain, by negotiation, Germany's former rights in Shantung and, in addition, would have been permitted to build a railroad in the province and open several new treaty ports. Japan also demanded more influence in Manchuria and that China employ Japanese advisers in political, commercial, and military affairs. China assented, with modifications, to the demands concerning Shantung and Manchuria; but she refused, or postponed for further consideration, the more oppressive ones.

twilight, the period of slightly more than an hour following sunset, characterized by gradually diminishing light. Twilight is due to the existence of the earth's atmosphere, which reflects and scatters sunlight after the sun has passed below the horizon. If there were no atmosphere, darkness would come abruptly after sunset. The term twilight is applied also to the comparable period preceding sunrise.

Twin Falls, city, co. seat of Twin Falls co., S Idaho; pop. 20,126. On land irrigated by the Snake River, which also supplies power, its farms produce fruit, vegetables, wheat, and sugar beets. Processing and other industries have been set up. The city was founded 1903.

twins—see *multiple birth*.

Two Sicilies, kingdom of the—see *Naples; Sicily*.

Tyburn Gallows, in London, where executions were held until 1783. The gallows stood near the Marble Arch in Hyde Park, and derived its name from the Tyburn River, now underground, which was once a tributary of the Thames.

Tyler, city, E Texas, co. seat of Smith co.; pop. 51,230. Founded in 1846, the town grew in importance after an oil boom in the region in the 1920s. Refineries were established here. The town is also noted for its rose nurseries. Tyler Junior College and two colleges for Negroes are here.

Tyler, John, 1790-1862, 10th U.S. President (1841-5), b. Greenway, Va., son of John Tyler (1747-1813), jurist and governor of Virginia, 1808-11. After graduation from William and Mary Col-

Twilight at Rundhögen, Sweden, shows above the pine forest through altocumulus clouds.

lege, 1807, he studied law, served in the Virginia legislature, 1811-6, and was U.S. Representative, 1817-21. A states'-rights Democrat, he was governor of Virginia, 1825-7, and U.S. Senator, 1827-36. In 1840 the Whigs chose him as candidate for Vice President to run with Gen. W. H. Harrison. On Pres. Harrison's death, Apr. 4, 1841, a month after inauguration, Tyler succeeded him. His administration was troubled by much party strife and controversy with Congress, but achieved the Webster-Ashburton Treaty, which settled the U.S.-Canadian boundary in the northeast, and the annexation of Texas. Retiring after 1845, in Feb. 1861 Tyler presided over an assembly for peace in Washington which tried to avert strife between North and South. When Virginia seceded, he was elected to the Confederate Congress, but he died before it met.

Tyler, Wat, d. 1381, English peasant leader. He led a revolt, 1381, caused by imposition of a poll tax at a time of extreme social unrest. Peasants and artisans, estimated at about 100,000, seized Canterbury and marched on London, pillaging and burning. They demanded and won an audience with Richard II, then 14, who granted all their demands, including the abolition of serfdom and pardon for their crimes. The next day Tyler was killed in a scuffle, and the king easily led his followers, with false promises, out of London. Richard then revoked his concessions and put the remaining rebel leaders to death.

Tyl Eulenspiegel—see *Eulenspiegel, Till.*

tympani—see *percussion instruments.*

Tyndale or **Tindal, William,** *c.*1492-1536, English translator. He lived in exile from 1524, and his noted translation of most of the Bible was prepared in Germany, 1525-30. Although at first vigorously opposed by English church authorities, his work was largely incorporated in the editions of Miles Coverdale. Tyndale was charged with heresy at Antwerp, and strangled and burned at the stake.

Tynemouth, co. borough, Northumberland, N England, on mouth of Tyne River at the North Sea; pop. 70,112. It is a fishing port and seaside resort, with a shipbuilding industry. It exports coal. Among notable buildings are early medieval priories and a 12th-cent. church.

Tyne River, 30 mi. long, Northumberland, N England. It is formed by the confluence of the North Tyne (rising in the Cheviot Hills) and South Tyne, and flows past Newcastle and Jarrow, to the North Sea at Tynemouth.

type, the cast or cut piece of metal or wood used to print a letter, numeral, or other sign. The letter is cut in reverse on the type so that, when inked, it will make a proper impression of the

Along with Luther, men of many lands translated the Scriptures into their native tongues; William *Tyndale* translated them into English.

Before new *type* is made, the characters of the alphabet must be designed, outlined, and inked in, as these craftsmen are doing.

American Type Founders

TYPE   2650

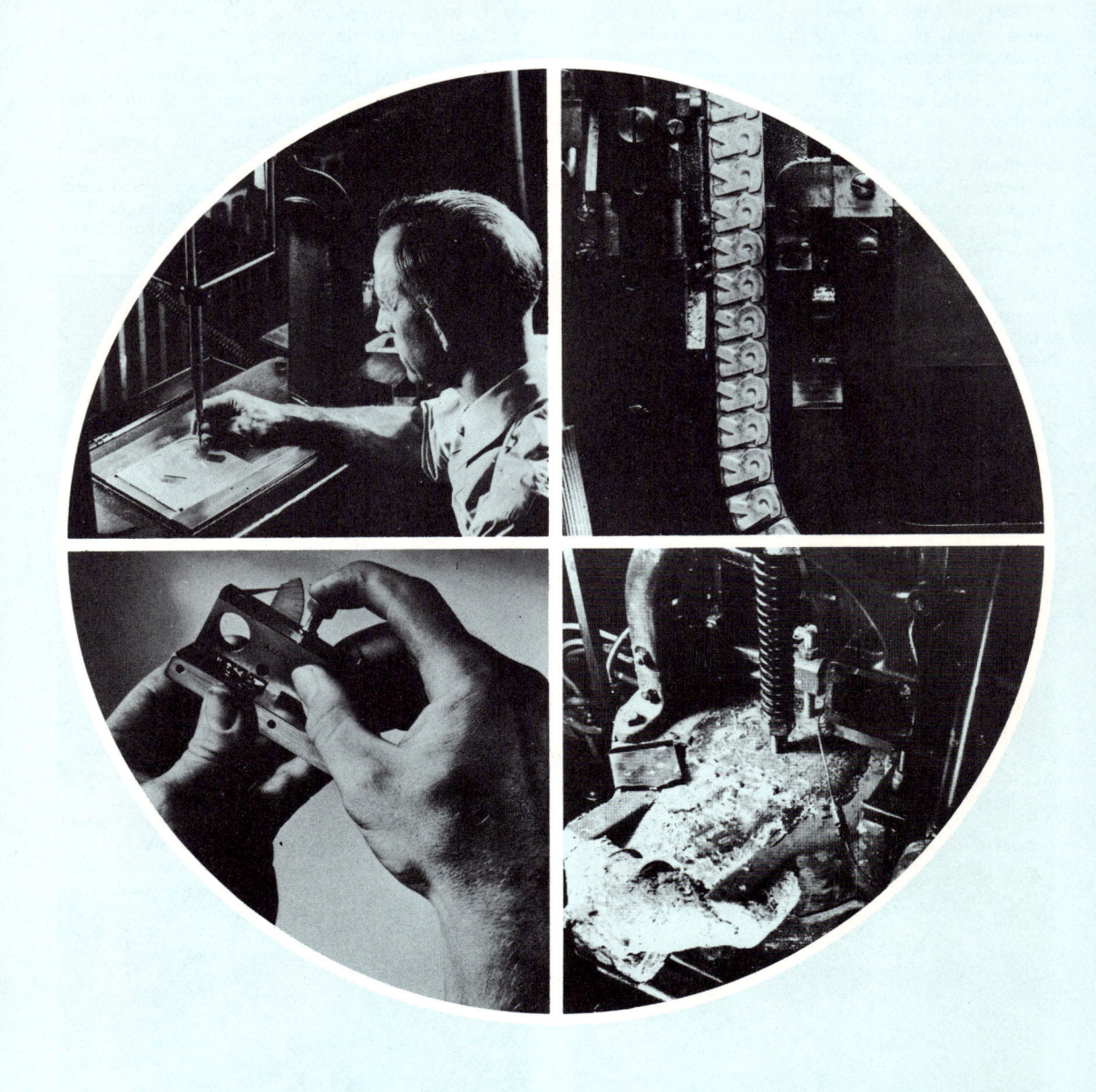

American Type Founders

Upper left, letters of a newly designed *type* "face" are engraved on a metal plate. The various sizes of the type are merely reductions or enlargements of the basic pattern. Lower left, .918 inches is a vital typographic standard. A plus or minus variation of .001 of an inch can measure the difference between a good and a bad reproduction or affect the amount of time a printer must spend in preparation for his job. Lower right, in metal pots of the type-casting machine, thermostatically controlled electrodes provide high, even temperatures for melting lead. Great pressure forces the molten metal into water-cooled molds which can be used for but one size of type. Upper right, type is ejected from its mold and is carried past a series of knives which groove its ends and smooth its edges so that it may fit evenly into the printer's locks and frames.

letter on paper. Formerly, a type was cut by hand from hard wood. Later, matrices were made for casting type from metal. Today almost all type is cast in type metal, an alloy of lead, tin, and antimony, to a standard height (0.918 in.) so that it can be fitted together (set) into lines, paragraphs, etc., for locking in a frame (chase) to be placed on a press and printed (see *printing*). For many years all type was set by hand, letter by letter being picked out from cases (the *upper case* containing capital letters and the *lower case* small letters). Then came typecasting machines, supplanting hand casting, and afterward type-setting machines,

American Type Founders
Above, a mono*type* casting machine runner takes the newly molded letters from the casts. Below, the new type is gauged for uniform height by specially designed calipers

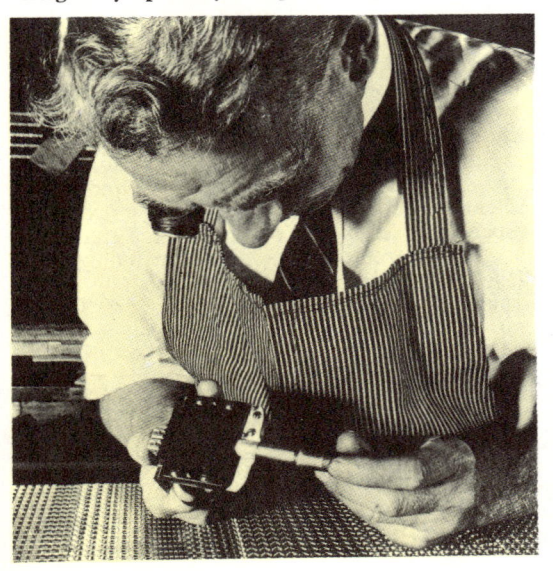

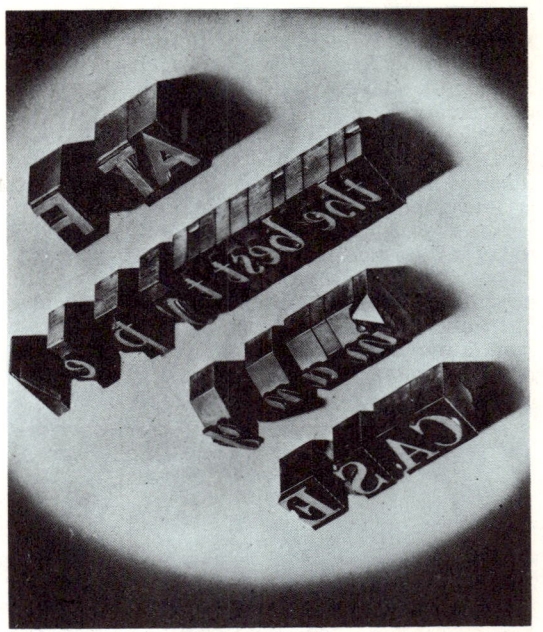

American Type Founders
The products of the process of *type*founding are finished casts of *type* faces.

supplanting hand setting. The new Foto setter, much like a Linotype (*q.v.*), and Photon, more like a Monotype (*q.v.*) but using an electric relay instead of paper tape, both are complete photographic typesetting machines.

The first movable type was clay, then wood, used in China, 1041. Cast bronze types were used in Korea, 1403. The independent invention of movable type in Europe is credited to Gutenberg (*q.v.*).

Type was soon made in various sizes which were known by names such as pica (12 point). The point system of designating sizes (72 points to 1 in.) was developed and is now universal in the U.S., although some of the older names are occasionally used. In each size of type there are many different faces or styles, named sometimes for the designers or typefounders who first cut them, and sometimes known by arbitrary names such as Century, Gothic, etc. A font of type normally has roman (with capitals, small capitals, and lower-case letters) and italic (with capitals and lower-case letters); for example:
CAPITALS, ROMAN and *ITALIC*
lower case roman and *italic and* SMALL CAPITALS.
It may have **boldface roman** in **CAPITALS** and **lower case,** and might be used with *BOLD italics* and even BOLD SMALL CAPITALS. The boldface may be of the same or a contrasting face. Type sizes run up to 144 point and larger. Type designing, encompassing the choice of size, style, and arrangement on a page, is called typography.

typewriter, manually operated device for mechanically imprinting, by operation of a keyboard, letters or symbols more clearly and rapidly than by writing. An English patent for a crude typing machine was recorded as early as 1714. The next century and a half witnessed the invention of numerous experimental models, many for the

TYPHOID

use of the blind. The forerunner of all modern typewriters was produced in France, 1883, but not until the Remington Co. undertook manufacture of an American machine in the 1870s did practical, rapid typing become possible. Knowledge of touch typing, common by 1900, greatly furthered the use of typewriters and influenced their development. Electric typewriters and teletyping machines, in which electric impulses cause the keys to strike, are widely used today, as are noiseless and portable manual machines. In 1961, a new electric typewriter was introduced in which the carriage does not move but rather letters are struck by electric impulse from a moving, rotating cartridge. This development increased the possible speed of typing by about 10%.

A modern electric typewriter

typhoid fever, infectious disease caused by the typhoid bacillus and conveyed by contaminated water supply, milk, or food. Contamination may result from flies, sewage pollution of water supplies, and food handling by typhoid carriers (*i.e.* healthy persons who harbor typhoid bacilli in their stools). The average incubation period is 10 to 14 days; then comes a gradually rising temperature with chilly sensations, aching, and slow pulse. A rose-colored rash (rose spots) appears early in the second week. There may be diarrhea, constipation, bronchitis, and nosebleed. Temperature finally starts to fall in the third week. Complications include intestinal hemorrhage and perforation, inflammation of the bones

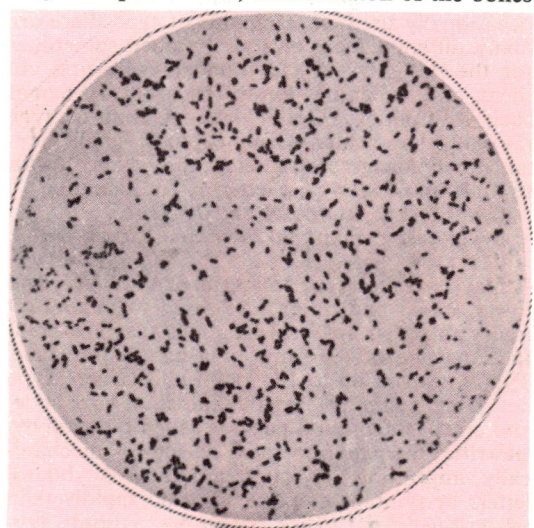

The cause of typhoid fever is Typhosis bacillus, a microbe which has only on rare occasions been successfully isolated.

and gall bladder, pneumonia, and thrombosis. Diagnosis is chiefly by blood, stool, and urine cultures. The antibiotic chloromycetin has been found to be specific against typhoid. Careful sanitation and immunization with dead typhoid germs have greatly reduced typhoid as a scourge of armies. Paratyphoid fever is a similar, usually less severe disease due to a paratyphoid organism. Treatment and prevention are less satisfactory than in typhoid.

typhoon, cyclonic hurricane, especially a violent type of hurricane occurring in the China Sea from July to Nov., and having its origin in the southern waters under calm conditions and extreme heat. Apart from the danger to shipping, the immense waves associated with the typhoon often cause destruction along the coasts. There is no basic difference between a typhoon and a hurricane (*q.v.*) except that the former occurs in the Pacific and the latter in the Atlantic. The word "typhoon" is an anglicization of the Chinese *Tai fung* (great wind).

typhus, infectious disease caused by the germ rickettsia and transmitted by lice. It occurs in epidemic form in crowded areas (*e.g.,* Central Europe, Russia, China), particularly in armies and slum districts. Sporadic (murine) typhus, transmitted by the rat flea, still occurs in Southern U.S. The incubation period is 8 to 12 days. In most cases typhus is severe, with general prostration, headache, high temperature lasting almost 2 weeks, and a dark red spotted eruption. Until recent years mortality was high. Diagnosis is by blood test. Vaccination and sanitation, particularly delousing with D.D.T., have considerably reduced frequency of the disease. Few cases occurred in the U.S. armed forces in World War II, thanks to immunization. Treatment with certain antibiotics is effective.

typography—see *type.*

Tyrannosaurus, a genus of dinosaur (*q.v.*) that roamed what is now Montana and Wyoming in the Upper Cretaceous Period. The only known species (*T. rex*), up to 18 ft. high and 38 ft. long, was the largest of the carnivorous dinosaurs.

tyrant, any of the absolute rulers of ancient Greece (*q.v.*) during the 7th and 6th cent. B.C., known as the Age of Tyrants. Some of these rulers, governing without limitations on their authority, were benevolent. Because other absolute rulers in history have often exercised their power oppressively, the term "tyrant" has popularly acquired the meaning of oppressor.

Tyre, ancient port of Phoenicia, called Sur by the Phoenicians, Zor by the Hebrews. Founded 2nd millennium B.C., it was noted for its industry (especially the dyeing of cloths in Tyrian purple), commerce, and colonies, including Carthage. King Hiram of Tyre was an ally of the Israelite King Solomon. The history of Tyre is that of Phoenicia, of which it was one of the two major cities, and the only one to resist Nebuchadnezzar II, who besieged it vainly, 585-573 B.C. It later fell to Alexander the Great, 332 B.C. Conquered from the Byzantines by the Moslems, A.D. 7th cent., it has since been mostly in Arab hands.

Tyrol or **Tirol,** province, W Austria, bounded W by Switzerland and Liechtenstein, N by Bavaria, Germany, E by Salzburg province, and S by

Wiesberg Castle, nestled in the *Tyrolean* Alps

Trentino-Alto Adige, semi-autonomous Italian region, historically a part of Tyrol, with which it was united 1919; area 4883 sq. mi.; pop. 441,200; capital Innsbruck. Dividing Tyrol from Trentino-Alto Adige are the Otztal Alps. The famous Brenner Pass on the Italian border links the two regions. Both have well-known resorts, *e.g.,* Kitzbühel in Austria and Merano in Italy. With the tourist trade, fruit growing and stock raising provide the population with a livelihood. Salt, silver, and lead are mined, and there is some textile milling.

The original Tyrolese were Celts, followed by the Rhaetians, who were subdued by the Romans, 15 B.C. Later the region was invaded by Germanic tribes. Some southern sections came to be ruled by bishops. The north part belonged to the Hapsburg domains after 1363, and in 1801 Austria gained all the Tyrol, which was, however, awarded by Napoleon to Bavaria, 1805. In 1809 Andreas Hofer led the Tyrolese in an unsuccessful revolt against the French and Bavarians. Austria recovered all the Tyrol, 1815. The Treaty of Saint-Germain, 1919, ceded the southern part to Italy, which granted it autonomous rights, 1947. Italian jurisdiction over S Tyrol has caused considerable discontent among its German-speaking inhabitants which has been the cause of strained relations between Austria and Italy. Petitions to review the Treaty of Saint-Germain were presented to the UN by Austria in the late 1950s and 1960s.

Tyrone, county, W central Northern Ireland; area 1218 sq. mi.; pop. 133,000; co. town Omagh. The county, rugged in terrain, is important chiefly for stock raising and agriculture (potatoes, cereals, flax). Textiles and whisky are made on a small scale. Some coal is mined. The stronghold of the O'Neills through the 16th cent., Tyrone was the chief part of the old province of Ulster (*q.v.*).

Tyrrhenian Sea, part of the Mediterranean Sea, between Sicily on the S, Sardinia and Corsica on the W, and the Italian coast on the NE and E. It was named after the ancient Etruscans (Gr. *Tyrrheni*).

Tz'u Hsi, Tsu Hsi, or **Tse Hsi,** 1834-1908, dowager empress of China, known as the "Old Buddha." A consort of the Ch'ing emperor Hsien Feng (d. 1861), she was the mother of his successor, T'ung Chih, and after the latter's death, 1875, she put her nephew Kwang Hsü on the throne,

Disapproving of his reform policies, in 1898 she imprisoned the emperor and took the throne herself. Opposing Western influences in China, she supported the Boxer Rebellion (1899-1900), and when it failed, fled temporarily to Siam. The empress dowager finally agreed, 1907, to constitutional reform, but it never materialized. She died one day after the imprisoned emperor; Henry Pu Yi (*q.v.*) was her successor.

U, the twenty-first letter and the fifth vowel of the English alphabet. The Phoenician alphabet had no such sign, but ended with *t*. A sign for the *u*-sound was added by the Greeks and was written indifferently as either *V* or *Y* (*qq.v.*), but the latter finally established itself as the accepted form, while the former became customary in the derived Italian alphabets; later, the Romans were able to import *y* as a separate character. The primary sound of *u*, however, was the same as in most languages in modern Europe, *e.g.* the sound of *oo* as in *cool*. In chemistry, *U* is the symbol of the element uranium (*q.v.*).

Ubangi-Shari—see *Central African Republic; French Equatorial Africa.*

U-boat, German submarine, so called from the German name *Unterseeboot,* used in the two World Wars. These "undersea boats" were marked with the letter U and a number. See *submarine.*

Above, the engine room of a German *U-boat*. Right, a snorkel used for changing the air.

Ucayali River, *c.*1000 mi. long, formed by the junction of the Apurimac and Urubamba Rivers, E Peru. It flows north to the Marañón River, with which it forms the Amazon above Iquitos.

Uccello, Paolo, 1397?-1475, Florentine painter; real name Paolo di Dono. Influenced by Ghiberti and his friend Donatello, he made valuable contributions to Italian painting in his experiments with linear perspective and foreshortening, which made for realism. Well known are his series of pieces showing the Battle of San Romano. He also designed mosaics and stained-glass windows.

Udall, Stewart Lee, 1920- , U.S. political leader, b. St. Johns, Ariz. Educated as a lawyer, he formed a law firm in Tucson, Ariz., with his brother after World War II service in the Air Force. He was first elected to Congress from Arizona in 1954, where he became quickly noted for his liberal views. In 1961, Pres. Kennedy named him Secretary of the Interior in his first cabinet. As a cabinet member, he became recognized as one of Kennedy's chief political lieutenants.

Udmurt Autonomous Soviet Socialist Republic, in W foothills of Ural Mts., E European Russia; area *c.*15,000 sq. mi.; pop. 1,333,000; capital Izhevsk. It is an agricultural, stock-rasing, and lumbering area, producing flax, grains, and potatoes. More than half the population are Udmurts, once called Votyaks, a Finno-Ugrian people. Settled by Russians, 16th cent., it became an autonomous republic, 1936.

Ufa, capital of Bashkir Republic, E European Russia, on Belaya and Ufa Rivers, near S Ural Mts.; pop. 546,000. An industrial center, with rich oil fields nearby, it produces mining machinery, airplanes, and textiles, and ships lumber and grain. Ufa, founded 1574, was on an old trade route to Siberia. It became capital of the Bashkir Republic, 1919.

Uffizi, palace in Florence, Italy. Built 16th cent. by Giorgio Vasari, it now houses the Italian National Library and the famous **Uffizi Gallery,** which contains a rich collection of European art, notably masterpieces of all Italian schools.

Uganda, British protectorate, E Africa; bounded N by Sudan, E by Kenya, S by Tanganyika, Lake Victoria, and Ruanda-Urundi, W by the Congo; area 93,918 sq. mi. (of which 13,689 sq. mi. are water); pop. 6,538,031, including 10,866 Europeans; administrative headquarters, Entebbe (pop. 8500). Kampala (46,714) is the main commercial center. Within Uganda are Lakes George Kyoga, and Salisbury, and parts of Lakes Victoria, Edward, and Albert. Mountains form the Kenya border (highest point, Mt. Elgon, 14,176 ft.); the highest point of the Ruwenzori group on the W is Mt. Margherita (16,791 ft.). There are dense forests in the W, a plateau region in the SW, and marsh areas around Lake Kyoga and the N shore of Victoria. The original native kingdom of Buganda came under control of the British East Africa Co. in 1890; in 1894 the kingdom and adjoining territory were proclaimed a protectorate of the Crown. The protectorate is divided into four administrative provinces; Buganda is the main native province (area 25,390; pop. 1,881,149). Most of the Africans speak Bantu languages. Coffee and cotton are the most important agricultural products; others are tea, tobacco, sugar, and maize. Hides and skins are also exported. Since the opening of the Kilembe mine in 1956, copper has become the major mineral export, followed by tin, gold, and lead. The Owen Falls hydroelectric project on the Victoria Nile near Kampala is one of the major power sources for East Africa; a power line to Nairobi, Kenya, was opened in 1958. Since 1927 Uganda has been united with Kenya and Tanganyika in a customs union which virtually makes the three a single trade unit. The University College of East Africa was founded at Kampala, 1939. In 1960 the province of Buganda agitated for independence separately from the rest of Uganda. When a petition to the Queen asking this was denied, the native government voted to secede. The British suppressed this movement but promised to work for independence in the near future.

Ugric languages—see *Finno-Ugric languages*.

Uighurs, Turkish tribe. From the mid-8th to the mid-9th cents., the Uighurs dominated most of Mongolia and were on terms of equality with China. They used a variation of the Syriac alphabet which became the written language of the Mongols, and they adopted Manichaeism as their religion. Though their real power ended in the 9th cent., for the next five centuries, scattered among the Turkish tribes of the N, they transmitted the culture which they had previously absorbed from the Arabs and the Chinese.

Uinta Mountains, range extending from NE Utah to SW Wyoming, part of the Rocky Mts. Their largest peak is King's Peak (13,498 ft.), highest point in Utah.

Ukraine (officially, Ukrainian Soviet Socialist Republic, constituent republic of the U.S.S.R., extending N from the Black Sea and Sea of Azov to Byelorussia, and bordered W by Czechoslovakia and Poland and E by Russian Soviet Federated Socialist Republic; area 232,046 sq. mi.; pop. 41,893,000 (2nd among the Soviet republics); capital Kiev; other large cities Kharkov, Odessa, Dnepropetrovsk, Stalino, and Nikolayev. The Dnieper, Bug, and Donets are its main rivers; the Dniester flows along its SW border. Its black steppe land is one of the great wheat-growing areas of the world. Many heavy industries are located here. Great coal deposits exist in the Donbas region, iron in the Krivoi Rog area, and manganese around Nikopol. Dneprostroi furnishes electric power. About 80% of the people are Ukrainian, a Slav group with their own language.

Scythian and Sarmatian inhabitants in ancient times were succeeded by Goths and Huns. In the 7th cent. the Khazars, Turkish nomads, dominated. The dukes of Kiev extended their power to the Ukraine, 9th-10th cent.; the Golden Horde conquered it, 13th cent., and the dukes of Lithuania, 14th cent. Turks ruled part of Ukraine, 15th cent., but Ivan III, grand duke of Muscovy, reconquered part late in that century. Cossacks revolted, 17th cent., against Polish rule of NE Ukraine, and it was ceded to Russia, 1667, the rest of the Polish Ukraine being ac-

Kampala, above, the leading industrial and commercial center of *Uganda*, is seen here from neighboring Nakasero Hill. Buganda Province, Uganda, has been governed by one dynasty since the 19th cent. Below, a recent king is crowned by his mother.

British Information Services

UKRAINIAN

The Lzura-Kiev Pechersky Museum and cloisters contain Ukranian relics and works of art.

An old stone bridge in the gardens of the Municipal Park of Kiev, Ukrainian capital.

Modern paintings and sculpture are shown at the Ukrainian Art Museum at Kiev.

quired by Russia in the partition of Poland, 1793. The Germans seized the region, 1918, but had to withdraw; it was then overrun by Gen. Denikin's counterrevolutionaries and by the Polish and Red armies. The Ukrainian Soviet Socialist Republic was proclaimed, 1917, finally established, 1920. In 1922 it formed, with the Russian, Byelorussian, and Transcaucasian Soviet Republics, the new U.S.S.R. In 1940 parts of Bukovina and Bessarabia were joined to the Ukrainian Soviet Socialist Republic after their cession by Rumania. In World War II the Ukraine was a battleground, occupied 1941-4 by Axis armies. Many Ukrainians, anti-Russian in sentiment, deserted to the Germans. As a result, thousands were executed or sent to slave labor camps after the war. In 1945 the Carpatho-Ukraine, formerly part of Czechoslovakia, was ceded to the Ukraine. The Ukraine, along with Byelorussia, became a charter member of the United Nations, 1945.

Ukrainian language—see *Slavic languages*.

ukulele, Hawaiian instrument of the guitar family. It has four strings and a long fingerboard usually fretted, and is played by strumming with the fingers. It is derived from the Portuguese guitar, machete, and became popular among amateurs in the 1920s in the U.S.

Ulan Bator (formerly Urga), capital of Mongolian People's Republic (Outer Mongolia); pop. 170,000. Linked by railroad, motor, and canal route with Siberia, it is an important center for cattle, camels, horses, and sheep. It is a center of Buddhism and has a university.

Ulan-Ude—see *Buryat-Mongol Autonomous Soviet Socialist Republic*.

ulcer, open sore characterized by localized loss of skin or mucous membrane. It may be chronic or acute; it may result from injury, poor circulation, wound infection, or cancer. Stomach and duodenal (upper intestinal) ulcers are thought to be due partly to increased acid secretion resulting from emotional disturbances. Treatment is usually by medication, occasionally by surgery.

ulcerative colitis—see *colon*.

Ulfilas, c.311-381, Gothic churchman. He was made bishop, 341, and preached the Arian version of Christianity (see *Arianism*) among his people. He is chiefly remembered for his translation of the Bible into Gothic. The extant fragments of this work are the oldest known writings in any Germanic language.

Ullswater, 2nd-largest lake (7½ mi. long) of England, in the Lake District, noted for its beauty.

Ulm, city and river port, Baden-Württemberg, S Western Germany, on upper Danube, c.45 mi. SE of Stuttgart; pop. 89,800. Ulm is at the head of Danube navigation. It has metal, textile, and food industries. An old imperial city, it is noted for its Gothic cathedral, considered one of the largest in existence. This escaped damage during World War II. Other parts of the city were severely hit. Ulm fell within the U.S. occupation zone, 1945.

Ulster, northernmost of the old provinces of Ireland; area c.8330 sq. mi. The area is now occupied by the counties of Cavan, Donegal, and Monaghan (area 3123 sq. mi.; pop. 235,863) in the republic of Ireland, and the major parts of the counties of Antrim, Armagh, Down, Fermanagh, Londonderry, and Tyrone in Northern Ireland. The old province was a stronghold of the O'Neills. During the long Anglo-Irish struggle many English and Scottish colonists were brought here. The republic of Ireland continues to claim the major northern British and predominantly Protestant section, often referred to as Ulster.

ultramontanism, Roman Catholic doctrine that the pope is supreme in ecclesiastical matters. In the Middle Ages controversies arose between the popes and lay rulers over such questions as appointments to benefices and investiture of appointees. The rise of nationalism and the theory of the divine right of kings resulted, especially in France after the 13th cent., in the rejection of papal interference in national church administration. The doctrine of those supporting the king was known as Gallicanism, because it favored the administrative autonomy of the Gallican, or French, church; its opponents were called ultramontanists, as partisans of the authority *ultra montes,* "beyond the mountains," i.e. the Alps.

ultraviolet rays or **ultraviolet light,** invisible rays of light that are beyond the violet end of the visible spectrum, and are at the opposite end of the spectrum from infrared. They are present in sunlight and are necessary to life processes. With proper intensity and duration they are fatal to most bacteria, are conducive to formation of vitamin D, and although invisible can be registered on a photographic plate. They are produced artificially by the carbon arc and mercury lamp and are thus available as a substitute for sunlight. Ultraviolet rays cause sunburn and in too large doses are dangerous for the skin. See *electromagnetic radiation.*

Ulysses or **Odysseus,** in Greek legend, king of Ithaca, and craftiest of the Greeks. He leagued the kings to recover Helen of Troy (*q.v.*) but tried to evade participation in the Trojan War by feigning madness. During the war his counsel was so valued that, on Achilles' death, he was awarded the hero's armor. The successful stratagem of the Trojan horse was his idea. In the *Odyssey* Homer recounts his adventures in the 10 years after the war, before he reached home. After his men were rescued from the tempting land of the Lotus-eaters, they fell afoul of Polyphemus the Cyclops. Then they opened the bag of contrary winds entrusted them by Aeolus and were blown to the land of the Laestrygonians, who ate all save one crew. These landed on Circe's island, where Odysseus saved them from transformation into beasts. After a visit to Hades, where Tiresias advised him on his homeward course, Odysseus sailed his ship past the Sirens' isle and Scylla and Charybdis, only to have the ship destroyed at Thrinacia because his men slew Apollo's cattle. Odysseus was saved, but lingered 7 years on Calypso's isle while, back home, his wife Penelope staved off insolent suitors and their son Telemachus searched for him. Finally arriving at Ithaca, he slew the suitors with the bow he alone could stretch and regained his wife and kingdom. The Greek spelling *Odysseus* is now preferred to the more familiar *Ulysses,* a modern adaptation of the Latin *Ulixes.*

Umbria, region (*compartimento*), including provinces of Perugia and Terni, central Italy, surrounded by The Marches (E), Latium (S and SW), Tuscany (NW); area 8265 sq. mi.; pop. 820,568; capital Perugia. This landlocked region lies in the Apennines and is crossed by the Tiber River. Agriculture is the mainstay (fruit, wine, cereals, olives, tobacco); hydroelectric power is produced also. The name is derived from the Umbri, one of the chief Italian tribes before the Etruscan and Roman conquests. In the Middle Ages the region was divided into independent cities and duchies, then gradually passed under the temporal control of the Papacy and formed one of the Papal States until the unification of Italy, late 19th cent. Umbria is noted for its contribution to Renaissance painting, centered at Perugia.

UN—see *United Nations.*

Unalaska, one of the Aleutian Islands, off W Alaska; area 1074 sq. mi.; pop. 218. Dutch Harbor, a village on Amaknak Island in Unalaska Bay, with one of the few good harbors in the Aleutians, is the site of U.S. naval and military bases. The Japanese attacked it, 1942.

Unamuno y Jugo, Miguel de, 1864-1936, Basque-Spanish philosopher. Professor and rector of the Univ. of Salamanca, he was a great literary representative of the Spanish spirit, torn between faith and reason. He may be counted among the modern intuitionists and anti-intellectuals. Fundamental to his philosophy is the concept of the concrete individual living man as against the mere abstraction of humanity and society. Among his many works, which include poetry and belles-lettres, are *Vida de Don Quijote y Sancho Panza* (1927) and *Del Sentimiento Trágico de la Vida en los Hombres y los Pueblos* (1913). Unamuno was a republican and enemy of the dictatorship of Primo de Rivera, who drove him into exile to France. Unamuno sided with Franco, however, at the outset of the Spanish Civil War.

Uncle Sam, name used to personify the U.S. government. It perhaps originated during the War of 1812 in the initials "U.S." marked on cases of government supplies by an inspector, Samuel Wilson, locally known in Troy, N.Y., as Uncle Sam. In time cartoonists came to personify the U.S. as a lanky man with a goatee and white

The legendary adventures of *Ulysses* (Greek: Odysseus) are related in the Homeric epic *The Odyssey.* Above, Ulysses accepts a boxing challenge from a Phaeacian shortly before his return to his kingdom of Ithaca. Below, Ulysses slays the suitors to his wife Penelope who have been living at his palace; thus he reclaims his place as the King of Ithaca.

UNCOMFORMITY

The image of *Uncle Sam*, the personification of the U.S., varies from country to country. These versions are from the mid-1930s.

hair, wearing a coat and trousers of red and white stripes, and a tall, blue hat marked with stars.

unconformity, in geology, a buried erosion (*q.v.*) surface (see *peneplain*) whose significance lies in the lapse of geologic time represented. Especially in arid sections of the western U.S., where vegetation is scarce, an unconformity may show up clearly on a hill as a dark line between groups of rocks which appear dissimilar. Looking deep into the inner gorge of the Grand Canyon (*q.v.*), Upper Cambrian (see *Paleozoic Era*) sandstone can be seen lying unconformably upon Pre-Cambrian (see *geology*) granite (*q.v.*). The sandstone at its contact with the granite does not show any metamorphism (*q.v.*) which would be expected if the granite had been intruded into the sandstone. Instead, the relatively flat surface of the granite and unaltered sandstone suggests that the granite was first worn down over a long period of time, and then the sandstone was deposited upon it after the land had sunk beneath the sea. An unconformity is evidence of a long period of time in geologic history; it is a record of erosion just as sediments are a record of deposition (*q.v.*). A buried erosion surface is helpful in determining the ages of the rocks as well as earth movements that influenced a particular region. Sometimes these earth movements are very important in the formation or accumulation of petroleum and mineral deposits. See *mineral; ores.*

unconscious or **subconscious,** in psychoanalysis, that part of the mind which directs much human behavior without the person being fully aware or conscious of the motivations of his behavior. Slips of the tongue, dreams, and mistakes, as well as more comprehensive actions, are considered manifestations of the unconscious. The concept of unconscious mental processes was common to the psychologist Herbart (*q.v.*) and the German philosopher Hartmann, whose book *Die Philosophie des Unbewussein* was widely read in the 19th cent. According to Freud, the unconscious is the residue of repressed memories, wishes, emotions, and instincts not subject to recall at will. The neurotic (see *neurosis*), unaware of these thoughts, is dominated by them. In the course of psychoanalysis, an effort is made to bring these thoughts to light and to interpret the behavior of the neurotic in terms of them. Psychoanalysts believe that when the unconscious is made conscious, the patient is better able to deal with his problems.

unconsciousness—see *first aid*.

underwater demolition team (UDT), specially trained naval units consisting of underwater swimmers, or "frogmen," whose mission is to destroy or remove all man-made or natural obstacles that interfere with the beaching of landing craft. These teams also reconnoiter landing beaches prior to attack. U.S. UDT's were first employed in World War II in the amphibious campaign at Tarawa in the Pacific. In the Normandy landings (June 1944), they cleared wide passages for the assault forces at Utah beach. At Omaha beach, the most heavily defended landing area in the entire war, they lost 50% of their forces in a maze of underwater snares, mines, and booby-traps. Frogmen of other navies fought notably in the Mediterranean. British divers attached mines to Italian ships at La Spezia.

underground—see *resistance*.

Underground Railroad, in the U.S., a semi-secret organization which illegally helped Negroes to escape from slavery in the South before and during the Civil War. It began operating *c*.1804. Fugitive slaves were taken, mostly at night, by "conductors" from station to station until they reached safety in the North or in Canada. Stations were the homes of abolitionists, including

The *underground railroads* helped thousands of slaves escape to the U.S. northwest and Canada. This sculptured relief by Edmond Amateis depicts the escape of two slaves from the South.

many Quakers. Levi Coffin (1789-1877), whose home at Newport, Ind., was an important station, was known as "president" of the Underground

Railroad; other leaders were William Lloyd Garrison, Wendell Phillips, Thomas Garrett, and the Negro Harriet Tubman. The "U.G." had stations in every Northern state, sometimes run by Negroes themselves. Probably more than 50,000 slaves in all were freed. After passage of the Fugitive Slave Law, 1850, operations became more difficult.

underground water—see *ground water*.

Underwood, Oscar Wilder, 1862-1929, U.S. political leader, b. Louisville, Ky. U.S. Representative from Alabama, 1895-1915, and Senator, 1915-27, he sponsored the Underwood Tariff Act of 1913, which sharply reduced customs rates. A Democratic Party leader in both House and Senate, he gave strong backing to Pres. Woodrow Wilson's foreign and domestic policies. He was delegate to the Washington Disarmament Conference, 1921-2.

Undset, Sigrid, 1882-1949, Norwegian novelist, b. Denmark. In 1911 she wrote her first successful novel, *Jenny*. It was followed by many other works, particularly historical novels, the best of which was *Kristin Lavransdatter* (1920-2), a trilogy. She was converted to Roman Catholicism 1924, and in 1928 was awarded the Nobel Prize in Literature. She lived in the U.S. during the Nazi occupation of Norway.

undulant fever—see *brucellosis*.

unearned increment, any increase in the value of land (or any other property) that is not due to its owner's efforts. Such value may be added through unexpected advantages in location, *e.g.*, those arising from urban developments or the building of new railroads. The single tax (*q.v.*) of Henry George was intended to make unearned increment a source of revenue.

unemployment, state of not being employed in a gainful occupation (particularly referring to persons who must earn their livelihood). Some are unemployed because of physical or mental disability (an estimated several million in the U.S.); their problem is one of rehabilitation, medical or institutional care, or dependency. Unemployment as a major national and worldwide problem refers more to persons able and willing to work but unable to find work. It is a particular problem of an industrial society, in which mass production, changes in fashion, introduction of new machinery, seasonal fluctuations in business, and similar factors share responsibility for varying amounts of unemployment. It becomes most acute in times of business depression. Some unemployment, perhaps 5% of employable persons, is considered normal in a free enterprise system, being the result of such factors as business relocations, shifts of workers from job to job, and temporary technological displacements. Since a perfect equilibrium between production and consumption can never be reached, unemployment is not likely to disappear unless the overflow is absorbed by public works and compulsory labor services. The latter, with their low level of wages, are contrary to democratic principles but account largely for the U.S.S.R.'s claim that it has banished unemployment. Dislocations and the spread of technology after World War I increased the number of unemployed in Western nations. In 1929, 4.25 million persons were out of work in the U.S., and in 1932, at the low point of the depression, 10 to 15 million. In the same year there were 3 million unemployed in England, 6 million in Germany, and similar large numbers elsewhere. To meet the problem, large sums were appropriated by governments, and bold relief, public-works, and social-security programs were introduced, particularly in the U.S. by F. D. Roosevelt, 1933. Attempts to meet the problem with unemployment insurance (*q.v.*) have been partly successful. During the 1940s and early '50s, employment was much stimulated by growth of

Unemployment occurs even during times of prosperity; the problem increases, however, during business recessions and slumps.

war industries, postwar reconstruction, and national defense programs, and in many countries manpower shortages occurred. Mild recessions since World War II have focused federal and state attention on techniques to mitigate the disrupting effects of unemployment on individual and family, and hence community, stability. For example, during the 1957-8 recession, many states raised the weekly unemployment insurance benefits, and the federal government furnished financial assistance. It also made possible extension of the number of compensated weeks in a given benefit year. By 1960, however, chronic unemployment was clearly traceable in large part to automation and consequent technological unemployment and to an increasing number of "dropouts" (students who failed to complete high school) as well as other unskilled laborers who were increasingly more difficult to employ. Programs were set up to train unemployed in new skills. See *National Recovery Administration;*

UNEMPLOYMENT

Public Works Administration; Social Security Act; Works Progress Administration.

unemployment insurance, a method of protecting employees against the hardships of unemployment. Such a system was adopted by the U.S. (1935) through the Social Security Act (q.v.), making it compulsory for most classes of employees, except domestic help, agricultural workers, civil servants, self-employed, etc. Legislation in 1950 widened the coverage to include most such employees. Federal and state authorities share in the administration of the plan. It works by the establishment of a fund from which regular maintenance payment may be made to those temporarily unemployed. The fund is built up by contributions from employers. Since 1911 unemployment insurance has been in effect in Great Britain. Even earlier legislation was introduced in Germany, Italy, and Switzerland. See *unemployment*.

Unesco—see *United Nations Educational, Scientific, and Cultural Organization.*

Ungava Crater—see *meteor.*

Uniat, Christian who follows one of the five so-called Eastern rites but accepts the authority of the pope and Roman Catholic Church. The Uniat churches include some Eastern creeds that remained with the Western church in the schism of 1054, and others that have returned since. They are organized among the Greeks, Armenians, Copts, most Balkan nations, Syrians, Egyptians, and Abyssinians; they use distinctive liturgies and their own language, permit marriage of priests, and often choose their own patriarchs, while remaining in communion with the Roman Catholic Church.

union, association or organization of workers, employees, or craftsmen, usually in the same or related lines of work. Membership is voluntary, though sometimes essential for the practice of certain trades. The main purposes are summed up in the phrase "collective bargaining." By banding together, workers may be better able to secure higher wages, shorter hours, and improved working conditions. Some unions, called vertical, include all those engaged in one industry, whatever their special trades—as all workers in the mining industry; others, called horizontal, include all workers in a given trade or craft, regardless of the industries to which they may be related, as all plumbers or carpenters. The former pattern was followed by the Congress of Industrial Organization (C.I.O.), the latter by the American Federation of Labor (A.F. of L.), prior to their merger in December, 1955. Early in the 19th cent., unions were formed in the U.S., but not until 1859 was there any national organization. In the early 1950s, union membership in the U.S. was 14,000,000 to 16,800,000—some 8,000,000 in the A.F. of L., 5,000,000-6,000,000 in the C.I.O.; and 2,400,000-2,800,000 in independent unions, of which the United Mine Workers of America (q.v.) was the largest. By the 1960s, more than 17,000,000 workers were in unions, of which more than 14,000,000 belonged to A.F.L.-C.I.O. unions. The million-member Teamsters Union was the largest union. U.S. unions have not joined international labor organizations to any great extent; those termed "international," e.g., International Ladies' Garment Workers' Union, have locals in Canada. See *American Federation of Labor–Congress of Industrial Organizations; open shop and closed shop; collective bargaining; Fair Labor Standards Act; labor; strike; Taft-Hartley Labor Act.*

Union City, city, NE New Jersey, adjacent to Hoboken and near the Hudson; pop. 52,180. It has numerous, varied industries.

Union Islands—see *Tokelau.*

Union League Clubs, Republican political clubs in various parts of the U.S., 1862-3, organized to promote the Union cause and Republican Party aims generally. After the war they worked for a severe Reconstruction policy and for a time had great influence on the Negro vote. The few remaining clubs today are social, with mostly conservative membership.

Union of South Africa—see *South Africa, Republic of.*

Union of Soviet Socialist Republics (U.S.S.R.), E European and central Asian state; 1950 area 8,650,069 sq. mi.; pop. 208,826,000; capital

The flag of the U.S.S.R.

Moscow. Largest nation in the world, covering about a sixth of the world's surface, in population it is inferior only to China and India. It extends from the Baltic on the NW to the Pacific on the NE, and from the Arctic on the N to the Black and Caspian Seas on the S. NW and SW it borders on Norway, Finland, Poland, Czechoslovakia, Hungary, and Rumania, some of whose territories it acquired during and after World War II. On the S it borders on Turkey, Iran, Afghanistan, China, Mongolia, and Manchuria. Topography and climate vary widely. European Russia is mostly a vast plain bordered by the Ural Mts., E, and by the Crimean and Caucasus Mts., S and SE. This plain extends into Asiatic Russia, where it reaches to the Pacific Ocean and leads to the Kolyma and Kamchatka Mts., NE,

Graphic House
The tall domes of the Uspensky Cathedral of the Kremlin in Moscow mark the spot where tsars were crowned since the late 15th century.

Saint Basil's church, left, graces Moscow's Red Sqare. At center, a Georgian goat herder tends his flock. At right is Moscow's huge G.U.M. state-owned department store.

and the high Pamirs in the SW. On both continents the northern plains are arctic tundra, below which is a forested section, then the fertile steppes and (in Asia) barren deserts. Among the great rivers are the Volga, Dnieper, Don, and Dvina (Europe), and the Ob, Yenisei, Lena, and Amur (Asia). There are 68,000 mi. of navigable rivers, besides thousands of miles of canals (Baltic and White Sea, Moscow-Volga, Volga-Don, etc.). There are 66,000 mi. of railways, and air service, the only means of travel across some desert areas, is well developed. Principal ports are Leningrad (Gulf of Finland), Murmansk (Arctic Ocean), Archangel (White Sea), Vladivostok (Sea of Japan), and Odessa, Sevastopol, Novorossisk, and Batum (Black Sea). Besides these and Moscow, the chief cities are Kiev, Kharkov, Baku, Gorki, and Tashkent. Soviet Russia's enormous natural resources make it, next to the U.S., the most self-sufficient nation in the world, especially in food crops, livestock, fisheries, lumber, and minerals, which include great quantities of oil, coal, metals, precious stones, salt, sulphur, and phosphorus. In recent years it has become a huge industrial state as well as an agricultural nation. The people are predominantly of Slavic origin (more than 75%), but there is an admixture of many Asiatic and other strains. About 130 languages are spoken. Though the government disestablished the Russian Orthodox Church, 1918, this still has more than 20,000 congregations. Islam is the 2nd-largest religion.

The U.S.S.R. consists of 15 constituent republics: the Russian Soviet Federated Socialist Republic, and the Ukrainian, Byelorussian, Azerbaijan, Georgian, Armenian, Turkmen, Uzbek, Tadzhik, Kazakh, Kirghiz, Moldavian, Estonian, Latvian, and Lithuanian Soviet Socialist Republics. Within these are autonomous republics, autonomous regions, and national districts. ("Autonomous" here refers to culture, not politics.) The Supreme Soviet of the U.S.S.R. is the highest legislature. It has two chambers, whose members are elected for 4-year terms: the Council of the Union and the Council of Nationalities. Council of the Union members are elected by citizens on the basis of one deputy for every 300,000 of population. Council of Nationalities members are elected by citizens, with 25 deputies from each constituent republic, 11 from each autonomous republic, 5 from each autonomous region, and 1 from each national district. The Council of Ministers of the U.S.S.R., until 1946 called Council of People's Commissars, is the nation's formal executive and administrative organ. The Presidium acts as a directive authority when the Supreme Soviet is not in session. The chairman of the Presidium is nominally the head of the state. Each constituent republic has a Supreme Soviet and Council of Ministers. The constituent republics have the formal right to conduct their own foreign affairs and maintain their own defense commissariats. The only political party in the U.S.S.R. is the Communist party (*q.v.*), whose directive body is the Central Committee, elected at party congresses. The party pervades all aspects of Soviet economic, political, and social life. Communist Party members actually control all aspects of governmental activity and secret police ensure discipline. The Communist Information Bureau (Cominform), set up 1947, coordinated activities of foreign Communist Parties with that of the U.S.S.R.; it was dissolved in 1956.

When the Revolution of 1917 (see *Russian Revolution*) overthrew the old Russian empire (see *Russia*), the provisional government of Prince Lvov and then of Alexander Kerensky attempted to function. On Nov. 7, 1917, the Petrograd Soviet seized power and turned it over next day to the All-Russian Congress of Soviets. Organization of a workers' and peasants' state with the above organs of legislative and executive power began. Lenin became chairman of the Council of People's Commissars, with Trotsky

U.S.S.R.

U.S.S.R.

Inset: Ukrainian S.S.R. area
Krasnyy Liman, Kremennaya, Rubezhnoye, Proletarsk, Lisichansk, Novo Aydar, Verkhne, Borovskoy, Yama, Slavyanoserbsk, Stakhanov, Luhansk, Kadiyevka (Voroshilovgrad), Kramatorsk, Popasnaya, Pervomaysk, Ivanovka, Rodakovo, Novo, Teploye, Artemovsk, Nikitovka, Gorlovka, Debal'tsevo, Gorodishche, Kamenka, Uspenska, Yenakiyevo, Krasnyy Luch, Roven'ki, Yasinovataya, Khartsyzsk, Snezhnoye, Donetsk (Stalino), Ilovaysk, Antratsit, Khanzhenkovo, Chistyakovo, D'yakovo, Mospino, R.S.F.S.R., Amvrosiyevka, Kuybyshevo, Lysogorka, Beshevo

UKRAINIAN S.S.R.

Inset: Kazakh/Kirghiz/Uzbek area
KAZAKH S.S.R., Chimkent, Sayram, Georgiyevka, KIRGHIZ S.S.R., Sharapkhana, Keles, Pskem, Yangi-Bazar, Muztag, Uchterek, Lenínskoye, Iskander, Chirchiq, Khodzhent, Aksabak, Urgench, Karavan, Saryagach, Ordzhonikidze, Gazalkent, Yangi, Kurgan, Kassansay, Oktyabr, Kok-Yangak, Tashkent, Beshkuduk, Yangi-Yul', Parkent, Shaydan, Namangan, Andzhizhan, Alay Range, Pskent, Chust, Pap, Kyzyl, Kigash, Aravan, UZBEK S.S.R., Charkas, Kokand, Naryn, Karasuu, Uzgen, Kara-Bazar, Kirovo, Shorsu, Margelan, Osh, Leninsko, Mirzachul, Kanibadam, Aim, Frunze, Ispan, Kizil-Kiya, Fergana, Ura, Sokh, Shaydaryn, Chauvay, Uch-Kurgan, Naukat, Neftabad, Lyalyuk, Shuryab, TADZHIK S.S.R., Ayni, KIRGHIZ S.S.R., Shakhristan, Isfara, Aley Range

Main map
UNITED STATES — ALASKA, Kotzebue, Point Hope, Norton Sound, Nome, Hooper Bay, Wales, Bering Strait, Diomede I., Gambell I., St. Lawrence I.

CHUKCHI SEA, Herald I., Wrangel I., De Long Is., Providence Bay, Chukchi Peninsula, Gulf of Anadyr', Anadyr' Range, BERING SEA, Koryak Range, Kamchatka Peninsula, Komandorskiye Is.

LAPTEV SEA, SEVERNAYA ZEMLYA, Komsomolets I., Oktyabr' Revolution I., Bol'shevik I., Shokal'skiy Str., C. Neupokoyev, Vil'kitskiy Str., Nordenskjold Arch., Cape Chelyuskin, Bolshoi Begichev I., Pronchishchev Bay, Khatanga, Taymyr Peninsula, Lake Taymyr

NEW SIBERIAN ISLANDS, Bennett I., Zhokhov I., Kotel'nyy I., Faddeyevskiy I., Lyakhov I., Bunge Land, EAST SIBERIAN SEA, Stolbovoy I., Peter I.

Norilsk, Dudinka, Igarka, Yenisey, Khatanga, Ust'-Olenek, Saskylakh, Udzha, Anabar, Olenek, Bulun, Tiksi, Kazachye, Ust'-Yansk, Khayagastakh, Svyatoy Nos, Ust'-Kuyga, Druzhina, Srednekolymsk, Nizhnekolymsk, Ambarchik, Pevek, Chaun Gulf, Chaun Bay

ARCTIC CIRCLE, Vilyuy Range, Verkhoyansk Range, Cherskiy Range, Kolyma Range, Gydan Range

Kyusyur, Sangar, Suntar-Khayata Range, Verkhoyansk, Tompok, Moma, Aldan, Yakutsk, Vilyuysk, Nyurba, Mirnyy, Lensk, Olekminsk, Ust'-Maya, Ayan, Okhotsk, SEA OF OKHOTSK, Magadan, Nagayevo, Yamsk, Penzhinskaya Guba, Gizhiga, Palana, Klyuchi, Ust'-Kamchatsk, Petropavlovsk-Kamchatskiy, Yelizovo

U.S.S.R. (UNION OF SOVIET SOCIALIST REPUBLICS)

Tunguska, Vanavara, Yerbogachen, Kirensk, Bodaybo, Mama, Nizhneangarsk, Severobaykalsk, Baunt, Chita, Nerchinsk, Shilka, Sretensk, Mogocha, Skovorodino, Tynda, Zeya, Blagoveshchensk, Svobodnyy, Belogorsk, Bureya, Komsomol'sk, Amursk, Khabarovsk, Birobidzhan, Nikolayevsk, SAKHALIN, Yuzhno-Sakhalinsk, Aleksandrovsk-Sakhalinskiy, Okha, Poronaysk, Korsakov, Holmsk, KURIL ISLANDS, Kunashir, Iturup, Paramushir, La Perouse Strait, Wakkanai, JAPAN, Hokkaido

MONGOLIA, Kyakhta, Ulan-Ude, Irkutsk, Cheremkhovo, Angarsk, Tulun, Tayshet, Nizhneudinsk, Kansk, Krasnoyarsk, Achinsk, Abakan, Minusinsk, Tuva, Kyzyl, Tora-Khem

CHINA, Manzhouli, Harbin, Mudanjiang, Jilin, Changchun, Vladivostok, Nakhodka, Ussuriysk, Voroshilov, Sea of Japan, Wonsan, Seoul, Taegu, KOREA

Inset: Kemerovo Oblast
Tomsk, Yaya, Izhmorskoye, Mariinsk, Anzhero-Sudzhensk, Tayga, Troitskoye, Chebula, Yurga, Yashkino, Barzas, Chumay, Berikul'skiy, KEMEROVO OBLAST, Kemerovo, Topki, Pioner, Strotel', Pervomayskiy, Leninsk-Kuznetskiy, Belovo, Plotnikovo, Krapivino, Tsentralnyy, Promyshlennaya, Panfilovskiy, Titovo, Vaganovo, Salair, Bachaty, Gur'yevsk, Artyshta, Kiselevsk, Usyaty, Prokop'yevsk, Novokuznetsk (Stalinsk), Myski, Mundybash, Kondoma, Tashtagol, ALTAY KRAY, Sorokino, Zalesovo

Inset: Sverdlovsk / Ural area
PERM OBLAST, Krasnotur'insk, Karpinsk, Kytlym, Rudnichnyy, Serov, Pavda, Lobva, Sos'va, Novaya Lyalya, Tepiyak, Artel'nyy, Nizhnyaya Tura, Verkhotur'ye, SVERDLOVSK OBLAST, Kos'ya, Verkhnyaya Tura, Makhnevo, Kushva, Baranchinskiy, Krasnoural'sk, Nizhnyaya Salda, Nizhniy Tagil, Salda, Sinyachikha, Visimo-Utkinsk, Nevyansk, Alapayevsk, Visim, Neyvo-Rudyanka, Kirovgrad, Verkhne-Neyvinskiy, Yegorshino, Sylva, Staroutkinsk, Sredne-Ural'sk, Asbest, Kuzino, Bilimbay, Pyshma, Karachel', Pervoural'sk, Berezovskiy, CHELYABINSK OBLAST, Biser, Revda, Sverdlovsk

Legend: Administrative Divisions of Union Republics

Division	Capital	Ref.	Division	Capital	Ref.
Abkhaz A.S.S.R.	Sukhumi	F5	Kashka-Dar'ya Oblast	Karshi	H6
Adygey Aut. Oblast	Maykop	F5	Khakass Aut. Oblast	Abakan	L4
Adzhar A.S.S.R.	Batumi	F5	Khorezm Oblast	Urgench	H5
Aginsk Nat'l Okrug	Aginskoye	N4	Komi A.S.S.R.	Syktyvkar	G3
Altay Kray	Barnaul	K4	Komi-Permyak Nat'l Okrug	Kudymkar	G3
Amur Oblast	Blagoveshchensk	O4	Koryak Nat'l Okrug	Palana	T4
Bashkir A.S.S.R.	Ufa	G4	Mari A.S.S.R.	Yoshkar-Ola	F4
Buryat A.S.S.R.	Ulan-Ude	M4	Maritime Kray	Vladivostok	P5
Chechen-Ingush A.S.S.R.	Groznyy	F5	Mordvinian A.S.S.R.	Saransk	F4
Chukchi Nat'l Okrug	Anadyr'	U3	Nagorno-Karabakh Aut. Oblast	Stepanakert	F6
Chuvash A.S.S.R.	Cheboksary	F4	Nenets Nat'l Okrug	Nar'yan-Mar	G3
Crimean Oblast	Simferopol'	E5	North Ossetian A.S.S.R.	Ordzhonikidze	F5
Dagestan A.S.S.R.	Makhachkala	F5	Sakhalin Oblast	Yuzhno-Sakhalinsk	R5
East Kazakhstan Oblast	Ust'-Kamenogorsk	K5	South Kazakhstan Oblast	Chimkent	J5
Evenki Nat'l Okrug	Tura	L3	South Ossetian Aut. Oblast	Tskhinvali	F5
Gorno-Altay Aut. Oblast	Gorno-Altaysk	K4	Surkhan-Dar'ya Oblast	Termez	H6
Gorno-Badakhshan Aut. Oblast	Khorog	J6	Tatar A.S.S.R.	Kazan'	F4
Issyk-Kul' Oblast	Przheval'sk	J5	Taymyr (Dolgano-Nenets) Nat'l Okr.	Dudinka	K3
Jewish Aut. Oblast	Birobidzhan	P5	Trans-Carpathian Oblast	Uzhgorod	D5
Kabardin-Balkar A.S.S.R.	Nal'chik	F5	Tuvinian Aut. Oblast	Kyzyl	L4
Kalmuck A.S.S.R.	Elista	F5	Tyan'-Shan' Oblast	Naryn	J5
Kamchatka Oblast	Petropavlovsk-Kam.	T4	Udmurt A.S.S.R.	Izhevsk	G4
Karachi-Cherkess Aut. Oblast	Cherkessk	F5	Volyn Oblast	Lutsk	D4
Kara-Kalpak A.S.S.R.	Nukus	G5	West Kazakhstan Oblast	Ural'sk	G4
Karelian A.S.S.R.	Petrozavodsk	E3	Yakut A.S.S.R.	Yakutsk	O3
			Yamal-Nenets Nat'l Okrug	Salekhard	H3

U.S.S.R.

Above: Russian peasants haul onions by ox-cart.
Below: Russian farmers return from the fields.
Graphic House

Graphic House
The city of Moscow as seen from the 24th floor of the University of Moscow on Lenin Hills.

Above: greenhouses on a collective farm
Below: private peasant home in Russia
Graphic House

and Stalin as other members. The Soviet government made peace with Germany at Brest-Litvosk, Mar. 1918, and began converting the nation to socialism. Opposition was undermined by secret police, and counterrevolution was put down by the Red Army after fierce struggles during 1918-20. The Communist International (Comintern) was formed, 1919, to promote world revolution. Instant transformation of the country being impossible, the New Economic Policy was adopted under Lenin's leadership, 1921, to stabilize the nation's economy by means of compromise while the work of socialist organization went forward. The greater famine of 1921-2, caused partly by rural resistance to the Bolsheviks, was a severe blow to the new regime. On Lenin's death, 1924, the government was torn by the struggle between Stalin and Trotsky over the issue of whether to concentrate on building socialism in Russia or to hold to the immediate, larger aim of world revolution. Stalin was the victor, Trotsky being forced into exile, and an aggressive program of modified Marxism was then launched. The first Five Year Plan, adopted 1928, called for rapid development of industrial facilities and collectivization of agriculture. Meanwhile, throughout Russia, religion was being discouraged; the schools and universities were reorganized to train the young according to Bolshevik principles; the press was taken over by Communists or Communist-approved staffs; and art, scientific research, entertainment, and other

The "Statue of Labor" in Moscow is dedicated to the honor of the common working man.
Graphic House

Russian citizens relax in the gardens at the eastern wall of the Kremlin in Moscow.

Above: the city of Yalta on the Black Sea
Below: modern subway train in Leningrad

forms of intellectual and cultural activity came under state control. Purges of suspected dissidents were violent, and in 1934, many old Bolsheviks and alleged members of Trotskyite and other opposition groups were imprisoned or executed. In the same year the U.S.S.R. became a member of the League of Nations and made gestures of cooperation with W Europe. After the Munich appeasement, 1938, of Hitler, however, the U.S.S.R. oriented its policy toward Germany, and the Nazi-Soviet nonaggression pact of Aug. 23, 1939, resulted. Hitler then invaded Poland, Sept. 1, and the Soviet army made a prompt counter-advance into E Poland. Finland's refusal of Soviet demands for military bases led to the Russo-Finnish War, 1939-40, by which the U.S.S.R. gained the Karelian Isthmus and other Finnish territory, which was incorporated into the Karelo-Finnish Soviet Socialist Republic. In 1946, the southern part, including the seacoast and Vyborg was attached to the R.S.F.R.; in 1956 it was reduced from a constituent to an autonomous republic. In 1940, Estonia, Latvia, and Lithuania were seized and made into Soviet Republics. Bessarabia and N Bukovina were ceded to the Soviet Union by Rumania. Then, June 22, 1941, the Nazi armies invaded the U.S.S.R., with Italy, Finland, Hungary, and Rumania as Germany's allies. The Germans overran the Ukraine and Byelorussia and besieged Leningrad, 1941. Their drive to the Caucasus was stopped at Stalingrad, Feb. 1943.

The pedestrian underpass on Moscow's Gorki Street leads to the city's subway system.

Above: woman ice-cream vendor in Moscow
Below: Russian gymnasts train for the Olympics

Modern Russian art is based on the doctrine of "socialist realism," which emphasizes contemporary subjects and naturalistic techniques, generally pointing to a moral of social or political significance. Some examples: Top left, T. Salakhov (Azerbaijan), "Composer Kara-Karayev." Top right, T. Ivanov (Uzbekistan). "Girl's Head." Left, A. Deineka (Russia), "Conquerors of Space," a design for a mosaic. Below, Popkov (Russia), "To Work."

German offensives and Russian counteroffensives, with fierce ground fighting and heavy air attacks, continued until 1944. By then the Germans had been expelled, but the Russian land had been devastated by the scorched-earth practices of both sides. Germany was entered by Red forces, 1944, and the drive on Berlin, matched by the Allied drive from the west, ended with German surrender, May 2, 1945.

During the war the Allies and Russia, fighting

in a common cause, cooperated. Allied military pressure supplemented by U.S. Lend Lease made possible the heroic Red resistance of 1942-3 and the great counteroffensives that followed. Conferences on grand strategy between Stalin and Roosevelt, Churchill, Truman, and other Allied leaders bred hopes of continued cooperation after the war. As hostilities neared an end, however, the prospects changed. With Japan tottering, Aug. 1945, Russia hastily plunged into the war against her and seized Manchuria. The W Allies in Europe accused Russia of sacking E Europe and setting up puppet Communist regimes there contrary to her previous promises. But Russia, now a world power, with much-expanded territories, energetically labored not only at her internal reconstruction but at building Communist power all over the globe. Acute disagreement between Russia and her erstwhile Allies over policies in Germany and Austria,

Vacationing citizens of the *U.S.S.R.* bathe at Sochi, South Krasnodar, on the Black Sea.

over Soviet seizure of Czechoslovakia, and over renewed Communist expansion, especially in the Far East, developed into the "cold war." Within the United Nations, of which the U.S.S.R. was a charter member, division between East and West widened, with constant tension, accusation, and recrimination, accentuated after the communization of China, 1949, and the Korean conflict, 1950-3. Internal tensions also appeared after Stalin's death, Mar. 5, 1953, when G. M. Malenkov, V. M. Molotov, and L. P. Beria emerged as the outstanding figures in the government. By Dec., Beria, powerful head of the secret police, was executed on charges of treason, and other changes suggested the struggles for power that had followed Stalin's accession to the dictatorship. In 1954-5, Nikita Khrushchev emerged as the real leader who finally consolidated control in 1958. While denouncing Stalin as head of a "cult of personality," he allowed himself to be similarly glorified. While advocating peaceful coexistence with the West, Khrushchev prepared for possible war, devoting Soviet science especially to missile development. A new 20-year plan in 1961 promised pure communism by 1980.

union shop—see *open shop* and *closed shop*.

Unitarianism, doctrine of the single person of God, as opposed to the three persons of the Trinity. It arose independently in various places during the Protestant Reformation, but was most successful in Poland, Transylvania (now in Rumania), England, and the American colonies. The Polish form resulted from the teachings of Laelius Socinus (1525-62), and his nephew, Faustus Socinus (1539-1604), both born in Italy with the name Sozzini. Persecuted for their beliefs, they found refuge in Poland, where their followers flourished. Simultaneously a sect of the Reformed Church of Transylvania adopted Unitarian principles, 1568. Both groups soon suffered persecution; the Socinians were almost wiped out, but some migrated to the Netherlands and there influenced English Dissenters, who introduced Socinian Unitarianism into England. The Transylvanian group survived and still exists. In England Unitarian doctrine permeated many presbyterian congregations and influenced some Anglicans. The first Unitarian chapel was organized, 1774, and a movement appeared, 1825. English Unitarianism was carried to America by Joseph Priestley, but was less successful than an indigenous form already accepted by a large minority of the Congregational churches of New England before 1800. Its most noted exponent was William Ellery Channing, whose sermon at Baltimore, 1819, gave impetus to the formation, 1825, of the American Unitarian Association. This group joined (1961) with the Universalists (*q.v.*) in the U.S. to form the Unitarian Universalist Association with a total of *c.*175,000 members. The Unitarian churches reject the Calvinist doctrines, observe the Lord's Supper symbolically, and stress the human character of Jesus; they discourage theological formalism; their polity is usually congregational.

United Arab Republic—see *Egypt; Syria*.

United Garment Workers Union—see *clothing manufacture*.

United Kingdom, short form of **United Kingdom of Great Britain and Northern Ireland,** a title

Union Jack—flag of the *United Kingdom*

officially adopted 1927; area 93,895 sq. mi.; pop. 55,706,133; capital London. It includes England, Wales, Scotland, Northern Ireland, the Isle of Man, and the Channel Islands. Originally it

UNITED

was the United Kingdom of Great Britain and Ireland, created 1800 when the Act of Union joined Great Britain (England and Scotland) and Ireland. With the birth of the Irish Free State, 1922, the designation ceased to apply to S Ireland. The United Kingdom is the principal constituent of the British Commonwealth of

Graphic House
Autumn in Glen Affric, Scotland

Nations. It is a constitutional monarchy with the succession passing through the eldest son or, if he has no son, through his daughter. Supreme legislative power is vested in Parliament (*q.v.*).

Scotland is represented in Commons by 71 members. Northern Ireland has its own semi-autonomous Parliament. The Isle of Man has a crown-appointed lieutenant governor, a legislative council, and a House of Keys. It has its own laws and is not affected by acts of Parliament unless it is specifically named. This is true also of the Channel Islands, whose local governments are headed by crown-appointed lieutenant governors. See *Great Britain*.

One of the high-points of the Highland Games is the Highland Fling. Amid the swirl of plaids and the skirl of bagpipes, these lassies perform the ancient traditional dance.

United Mine Workers of America (U.M.W.), labor union set up, 1890, at Columbus, Ohio, by the merger of earlier groups. It joined the American Federation of Labor and is principally made up of coal miners. The union became powerful under the leadership of John L. Lewis, who became its president, 1920, and through militant policy secured many advantages for the miners. In 1935, the U.M.W. helped organize and joined the Committee for Industrial Organization (C.I.O.) and was, with the latter, expelled, 1937, from the A.F. of L. In 1942, the U.M.W. withdrew from the C.I.O. Readmitted, 1946, to the A.F. of L., it seceded again a year later and remained independent after the A.F. of L.-C.I.O. merger. Because of a wartime strike, 1943, the government seized and held the mines until 1947. Attempted strikes during this period resulted in major fines for Lewis and the union. Lewis retired in 1960, and was succeeded by Thomas Kennedy.

A young couple honeymoon in romantic Northern Island. At this picturesque spot, the Mountains of Mourne sweep down to the sea.

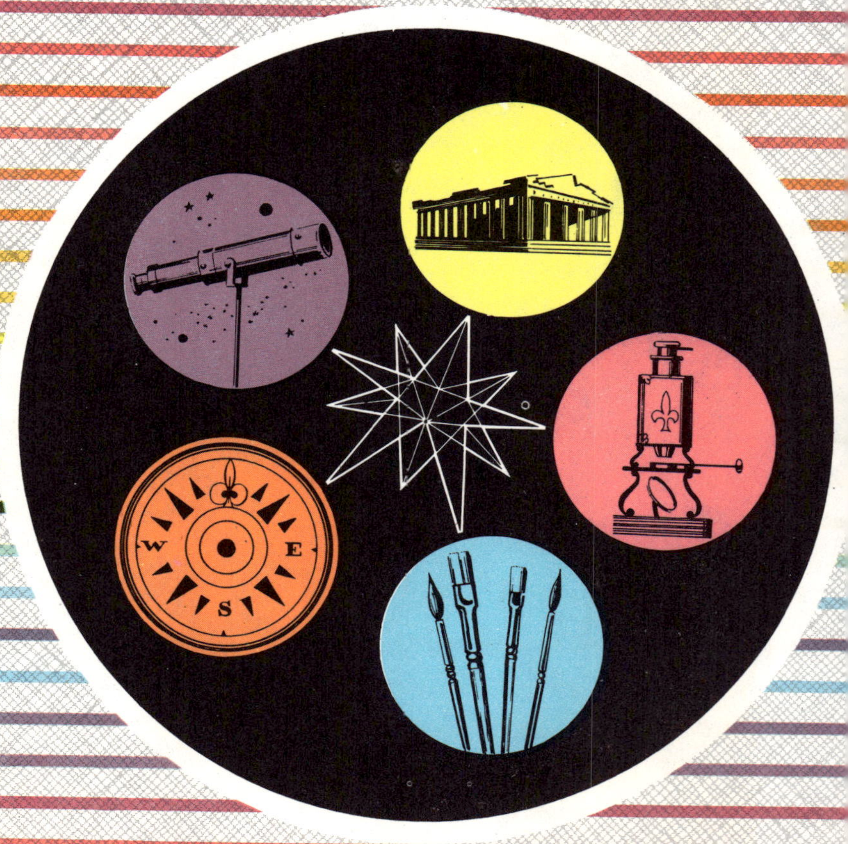
W
E
S

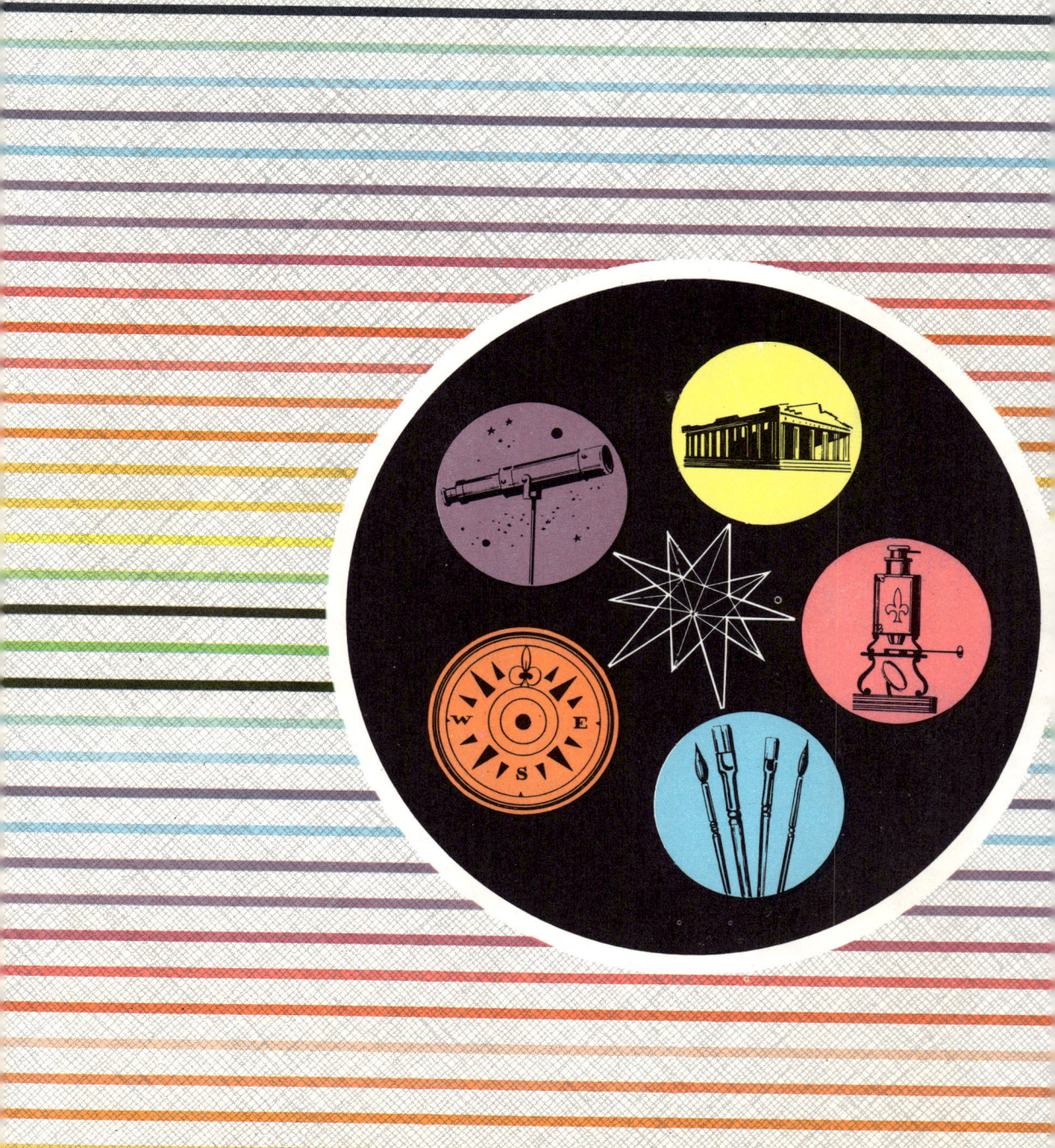